Luther: Gospel, Law, and Reformation
Part I

Professor Phillip Cary

we view life thru his life...

THE TEACHING COMPANY ®

PUBLISHED BY:

THE TEACHING COMPANY
4151 Lafayette Center Drive, Suite 100
Chantilly, Virginia 20151-1232
1-800-TEACH-12
Fax—703-378-3819
www.teach12.com

ISBN 1-56585-959-6

Phillip Cary, Ph.D.

Director of Philosophy Program, Eastern University

Phillip Cary is Associate Professor of Philosophy at Eastern University in St. Davids, Pennsylvania, where he is also Scholar in Residence at the Templeton Honors College. He received his undergraduate training in English Literature and Philosophy at Washington University (MO), then earned an M.A. in Philosophy and a Ph.D. in both Philosophy and Religious Studies at Yale University. Professor Cary has taught at Yale, the University of Hartford, the University of Connecticut, and Villanova University. He was an Ennis Post-Doctoral Fellow at Villanova University, where he taught in Villanova's nationally acclaimed Core Humanities program. At Eastern University, he is a recent winner of the Lindback Award for excellence in undergraduate teaching. Professor Cary has published scholarly articles on Augustine, Luther, the doctrine of the Trinity, and interpersonal knowledge. His book, *Augustine's Invention of the Inner Self*, was published by Oxford University Press in 2000. Professor Cary produced the popular Teaching Company courses *Augustine: Philosopher and Saint* and *Philosophy and Religion in the West*, as well as contributing to the third edition of the course entitled *Great Minds of the Western Intellectual Tradition*.

Table of Contents

Luther: Gospel, Law, and Reformation
Part I

Luther: Gospel, Law, and Reformation

Scope:

Martin Luther (1483–1546) is the founding figure of the Protestant Reformation, the decisive break from the medieval Catholic church, which in many ways, marks the beginning of modern Europe. An eloquent preacher and voluminous writer, Luther attacked many abuses of the medieval church, especially the papacy. However, the source of his religious vision was not political or institutional but a deep inner struggle of conscience. Like many people of his time, Luther was terrified that God would ultimately reject him for his sins. He found in the Bible a word of God that he called "Law," which increased this terror, but he also found another word that he called "Gospel," the good news and promise of mercy in Christ, which banished all his fears. His famous doctrine of justification by faith alone meant that simply believing the Gospel was enough to make one stand justified before God. This doctrine was meant to free people from anxious attempts to justify themselves by doing the works of the Law or seeking grace from the hierarchical machinery of the church. The Reformation resulted from Luther's efforts to make sure everybody had an opportunity to hear this good news.

Lectures One through Seven trace Luther's discovery of the Gospel and set it in medieval context. The medieval church at its worst was an institution that funded itself by playing on people's fears of purgatory and hell, while at its best, it taught an Augustinian spirituality of grace, in which life is a journey toward God motivated by love. Young Luther became a monk in order to seek grace for this journey by means of penance, confession of sins, self-accusation, and even self-hatred. The discovery of the Gospel meant that such efforts were worthless, because grace becomes ours only when God gives us his own son, whom we receive simply by believing the good news. From this gift follow all our good works, which are works of love for our neighbors, not attempts to earn grace or justify ourselves. Strikingly, Luther finds this gracious word of the Gospel by turning to the heart of Catholic sacramental theology in baptism, penance, and the Eucharist.

Lectures Eight through Sixteen trace the course of the Reformation. While still a monk, Luther initiates a controversy over indulgences, attacking some flagrant efforts of the church to sell grace. What began as an academic disputation in 1517 becomes, by 1520, a rallying cry for Germans to throw off the yoke of the papacy, affecting everyone in Europe because of the recent invention of the printing press. Luther attacks the papacy's attempt to take the sacraments captive for purposes of money-making and power, preventing them from being the vehicle of the Gospel that God intended. At the head of a growing movement for reform, he takes practical steps to form a new kind of church, one in which people can hear, read, and even sing the Gospel in their own language, thanks to Luther's translation of the Bible, his sermons and catechisms, and his hymn-writing (including the famous "A Mighty Fortress is Our God"). Soon, however, he must deal with Protestant critics who want the Reformation to move faster or even become revolutionary. Some of them support the peasant rebellion, which Luther deplores; others reject infant baptism, which Luther defends; and many think his insistence on finding Christ's body literally present in the bread of the Eucharist is a leftover from Catholicism.

Lectures Seventeen through Twenty-Four examine Luther's views on several important topics ("Luther and…."). Most fundamental is Luther's turn to the Bible as the source of the transforming certainty of God's promises. In contrast to the humanist Erasmus, who found in the Bible a resource for moral self-development, Luther insists that God's Word changes us without our good works and despite the bondage of our will. He does not hesitate to affirm a robust doctrine of predestination, though he tends to warn individuals not to pry into the question of whether or not God has predestined them to be saved—in contrast to John Calvin, who initiates the Protestant insistence that Christians should know they are eternally saved. In his politics, Luther is authoritarian, supporting the duty of secular rulers to suppress rebellion and even reform the church. In his polemical writings, Luther is often fierce and abusive, attacking his opponents as if they were spokesmen for the devil—a tendency that reaches depths of vileness in his writings against the Jews. By any measure, the legacy of Luther is mixed: There is much here for even Catholics to learn from and even Protestants to be ashamed of.

Lecture One
Luther's Gospel

Scope:

How are we to come to grips with so controversial a figure as Martin Luther? We can focus on the central concept of *Gospel*, noting that the essential content of Luther's Gospel is something all orthodox Christians believe: the story of Christ dying for us sinners. What's new and controversial is Luther's doctrine *about* the Gospel—about exactly how we are changed by hearing this story. This is Luther's doctrine of justification by faith alone. To see how this common story is related to the controversial doctrine, I tell a kind of parable to illustrate the experience of faith in the Gospel as Luther understands it. In future lectures, we will get further into Luther's experience, his doctrine about the Gospel, and how it sparked a Reformation that changed the course of history.

Outline

I. Luther is a man of controversy.

    A. Not only was Luther involved in a great many controversies in his lifetime, but he has been the object of controversy ever since—especially, of course, between Protestants and Catholics.

    B. Yet the current ecumenical situation, where Catholics and Protestants talk about restoring the unity of the church, has changed the tenor of these controversies.

        1. Ecumenically-minded Protestants often regret the splitting of the church in the 16th century.

        2. Ecumenically-minded Catholics often wish their church had the flexibility to change and reform itself as the Protestants have done.

II. At the heart of Luther's thought and life is his doctrine about what he calls the Gospel.

    A. Problem: Luther insists that the content of his Gospel is simply the creed that every good Christian believes; yet

Luther's doctrine about the Gospel stirs up controversy as if it were something unheard of. How can this be?

B. Luther's concept of Gospel can be summarized as follows:

   1. Definition: The Gospel is the good news about Christ, a story containing his promises. The four Gospels in the New Testament are different ways of telling this one story.

   2. Content: What the Gospel says is what is summarized in the creed. You can find the content of the Gospel not only in the New Testament Gospels but everywhere in the Bible, including the Old Testament, which prophesies and promises Christ's coming.

   3. Doctrines *in* the Gospel: The Gospel contains doctrines (that is, teachings), such as "Christ died for our sins." This is not the controversial part of Luther's theology.

   4. Doctrines *about* the Gospel: Luther has a great deal to say about how the Gospel of Christ saves us, such as his teaching that we are justified by faith alone; these doctrines are *about* the Gospel but are not the Gospel itself (that is, not part of the Gospel's content). This is where Luther's theology becomes controversial.

   5. Gospel as promise: According to Luther's doctrine about the Gospel, it is not only a story, but also a promise contained in the story, by which God gives Christ to those who believe.

   6. *Pro me*: Faith in the Gospel means not just believing that the story is true (*fides historica*, "faith in the story") but also believing that what Christ did, he did for me. This *pro me* ("for me") aspect of the Gospel does not mean the story is all about me, but that I am included in Christ's story—because he died *for me*.

C. What Luther is afraid of is not punishment and hellfire but God himself and his judgment. Thus, the experience of believing the Gospel can be compared with the following parable:

   1. Imagine that you push your little brother down the stairs, he breaks his neck, and you must face your father. What is it you are afraid of—a spanking?

2. Luther, likewise, in facing the judgment of God is not afraid of fire and brimstone but of God—of hearing something like: "Get out. You are not my son."
3. The Gospel is like coming to face your father in the presence of your brother, who loves you and insists on your father forgiving you.
4. Imagine the first thing you hear is your brother saying, "My sister!" and your father saying, "My daughter!"
5. Then imagine also that it turns out your brother will be all right (like Christ risen from the dead).

III. The approach taken in this course to the controversial figure of Martin Luther will not be neutral, but both sympathetic and critical.

A. There are historical figures who call not for neutrality but condemnation (for example, Hitler), or admiration (for example, Gandhi), or sometimes a fair amount of both (Luther).

B. Yet we cannot understand these figures well enough to judge them without entering with imaginative sympathy into their minds and their worlds, which may require us to think critically about some of our own assumptions.

C. Protestants, Catholics, and anyone interested in the history of the modern world all have much to gain from a sympathetic and critical understanding of Luther.

IV. This course is structured as follows:

A. Section 1 ("Discovering the Gospel") focuses on what the Gospel meant in Luther's personal experience and his doctrine about it.

B. Section 2 ("The Course of the Lutheran Reformation") examines the Reformation that resulted when Luther's doctrine about the Gospel went public.

C. Section 3 ("Luther and….") tackles Luther's stand on key issues

D. In the next lecture, we begin to get at Luther's personal experience by examining his historical and social context, the church of the Middle Ages.

Essential Reading:

Luther, "A Brief Instruction on What to Look for and Expect in the Gospels," in *Luther's Works*, vol. 35, and Lull, chapter 8.

Luther, "Preface to the New Testament," in *Luther's Works*, vol. 35, and Lull, chapter 7.

Supplemental Reading:

Braaten and Jenson, *The Catholicity of the Reformation* (for Lutheran perspectives on ecumenical dialogue).

Nestington, "Approaching Luther," in McKim, chapter 14.

Questions to Consider:

1. Before you began this course, what was your impression of Martin Luther: hero, heretic, rebel, troublemaker, sick, obsessed, magnificent, or something else?

2. Do you suppose we could be such sinners as Martin Luther imagines we are, deserving to be rejected forever by God?

Lecture One—Transcript
Luther's Gospel

Martin Luther is familiar as the founding figure of Protestantism. Born in 1483, he died 63 years later in 1546, living most of his adult life in the sixteenth century, the century of the Protestant Reformation where he was the central figure, that huge upheaval called the Reformation, an upheaval in Western culture, society, religion. He changed the world, but he is someone who changed the world in ways that are very controversial. He himself participated in many controversies. He fought by writing, verbally in his writings and his preachings against Catholicism, against other Protestants. He was in the middle of controversy in his own day; he is still controversial today.

There have been lots and lots of Protestants who idealize him, make him a hero. There have been plenty of Catholics who of course have despised him, even vilified him. But that's not actually the situation nowadays, and that's one of the first things to think about as we approach this huge figure of Martin Luther, this huge figure in Western civilization.

Protestants and Catholics are now talking to each other in a different way than they used to. They're part of what's called an ecumenical discussion, a discussion about the unity of the church, of how everyone both Protestant and Catholic are still Christians and maybe they belong together in one church, not in a divided church. From that standpoint, now there are many Catholics who look at Luther and see something that their own church is missing, and there are many Protestants, call them ecumenically minded Protestants, who regret some of the things that Luther did and said, some of the really nasty things he said about Catholics, and who regret in particular the splitting of the church that happens at the Reformation, the split between Protestants and Catholics.

If you think that the church ought to be one, as many ecumenical minded Protestants like myself do believe, then there are things to regret in Luther, so if you are an ecumenically minded Protestant as I am, you're going to find something to admire in Luther, you're going to find something to regret in Luther. The situation is complex. It's not just Protestants, "Yeah, Luther!" and Catholics, "Boo, Luther." It's much more like here is this hugely important figure, everyone agrees that there are some things that went wrong with Luther and some things that went right. We need, in order to understand Luther, to be both sympathetic to some of the things he said and critical to others. That's true of both Catholics and Protestants.

I want to focus on what makes Luther controversial, but first, even more fundamentally I want to focus on what I will call the central core belief of Martin Luther. I think we can give a one-word label for that central core belief, that central concept in Luther's theology and thought. I will call it simply Gospel. Luther talks about the Gospel all the time. That raises an interesting question right away.

Luther's very controversial, but the Gospel that Luther points to is not particularly controversial. When you ask Luther "What do you mean by the Gospel?" he will typically respond by summarizing or even reciting a part of the Christian creed. He'll say things like this, "The Gospel means that Jesus Christ is the eternal Son of God, he is God in the flesh, he was born of the Virgin Mary, he suffered under Pontius Pilate. He was crucified, he died, he was buried, and on the third day he rose from the dead, he ascended into Heaven, he sits at the right hand of God, the Father Almighty."

That is a very familiar thing to say for most Christians. This is something that most Christians—eastern Orthodox, Roman Catholic, Lutheran, Episcopalian, many Protestants—recite every Sunday in their worship. It is called the creed, that fundamental formulation of Christian belief. In other words, Luther thinks that the Gospel, which is at the center of his life and work, is the same Gospel that all Christians believe. It is not something unique to Luther. It is not a Lutheran Gospel; it is a Christian Gospel.

Luther himself will say, "I ask people not to make reference to my name. Let them call themselves Christians, not Lutherans. What is Luther? After all, his teaching is not mine, nor was I crucified for anyone. How should I, poor bag of worms that I am, come to have men call the children of Christ by my wretched name?" The Gospel is not Luther; the Gospel is Christian, Luther thinks. Another remark he makes, "I hold together with the universal church the one universal teaching of Christ, who is the supreme teacher." The Gospel that Luther says is the Gospel of Christ, not the Gospel of Luther. It's all about this good news about who Jesus is, so why would that be controversial? We need to think about what makes

Luther's relationship to the Gospel so controversial, what makes it split the church.

Let's think about this notion of Gospel. What does Luther mean by Gospel? When he has to explain this term, the first thing he'll do is talk about the Greek term *evangelium*, which is a Greek term in the New Testament that gets translated as Gospel. The term means good news; this is a familiar point. When Luther speaks of the good news, the Gospel of Christ, he's thinking there's only one Gospel. He always talks about the Gospel, so he's not talking about one of those four books called the Gospels in the New Testament. There's the Gospel of Matthew, the Gospel according to Mark, the Gospel according to Luke, the Gospel according to John. Those are four different ways of telling the one Gospel story. For Luther, there's one story about Christ, many different ways of telling it, so there's four different Gospels in the New Testament.

But that's not the only place that you run into the Gospel, Luther thinks. The letters of Paul in the New Testament are frequently telling the story of Christ, and also the Hebrew part of the Bible, which for Luther as for other Christians is called the Old Testament. It is called the Old Testament because it is the ancient witness to Jesus Christ, and therefore the Old Testament contains lots of the Gospel. That's what the prophets are doing, predicting Jesus Christ and therefore they're telling the Gospel in advance. So there's one Gospel, many ways of telling it, and Luther's always fundamentally focused on this one Gospel, this good news about Jesus Christ, which is a story about Christ.

That's the crucial content of the Gospel. The content of the Gospel as a matter of genre is a story. It's a narrative genre; it's a story about Jesus. Surprise, surprise; this is so far nothing controversial here. The story about Jesus is a story about what he does to save us. He dies for our sins; all that is absolutely familiar Christian stuff. The Gospel is a story also that contains what we can call doctrines, teachings, "Christ died for our sins, he was raised from the dead," that's all familiar stuff too. But then there's something else, and here's where we get to the controversy.

Luther has things to say about the Gospel. I think this difference is rather technical, but I'm going to try to work through this to clarify what the Gospel is for Luther. There's the Gospel and its content on the one hand, and then there's doctrines about the Gospel, the Gospel and what it contains, this story of Christ, and then doctrines about the Gospel. Luther has a very distinctive and controversial doctrine about the Gospel, and that's his famous doctrine that we are justified by faith alone and apart from works of law. What that means is you become saved, justified, your relationship with God is set right simply by believing the Gospel, simply by believing the story about Jesus. Faith alone, just by believing; that's what he means.

Apart from works, which are the second half of the formula of this doctrine, it means you don't have to do anything about it. You don't have to do something about the Gospel—that would be works—you simply have to believe it's true. That saves you, that changes you, that makes you God's child and all that. That's the doctrine of justification by faith alone; that's the doctrine that all the fighting was about in the Reformation, or at least it's the central point of all the fighting in the Reformation between Protestants and Catholics, as we'll see. We'll spend a lot of time on that point in these lectures.

Let's think through this as we introduce ourselves to Luther's key concepts now in this first lecture. Why would Luther think that just believing something makes all the difference? Just believing that it's true, that's all there is to it. Why would that save you, justify you, make you a child of God and all that? There's one more feature of the Gospel as a genre of discourse that we should look at that will help explain this – the Gospel is a story, but it contains promises. Luther will often speak of the Gospel as the promise of Christ or the promise of God. Think about how a promise works, and we'll talk specifically about the promise of Christ.

I can put a ring in your hand and say "Look at this, look at this ring. Isn't that interesting?" That's mere words. I'm just describing something real, and the reality is a ring and the words are just mere words. But there are some words that do what they say. I can put a ring in your hand and say "I give you this ring," and then my words are not mere words; they are an act of giving you the ring. A promise often works like that. A promise is not mere words; a promise gives you what is promised if you're willing to receive it. You could of course say "I don't want this ring, don't give it to me," but if you acquiesce, if you open your hand and let the ring fall into your hand and you don't even say no, that's what faith amounts to for Luther.

What faith amounts to is saying, "God's promise is true. What God promises to give, he actually has given."

Let me illustrate what Luther's thinking about here by actually giving you a crucial example of a Gospel promise, probably the central example of the Gospel promise for Luther. You all know the story of Jesus at the Last Supper, with the bread and the wine. He takes the bread and he breaks it and he blesses it and he says to his disciples "This is my body given for you." Luther loves those words; they are at the center of his life because he interprets them of course as a promise in which Jesus Christ is giving you what? Himself, not just a ring, but rather he gives us his own body, saying "This is for you."

Think of how that works. It's rather like a wedding vow, where one person promises not just a ring, but him or herself to the other. By making this promise, they do what they promise if the other person is willing to receive it. That willingness to receive it, that's faith, just saying "You're giving me this ring, you're giving me yourself. That's wonderful, I believe you." The promise is true. Luther will say if you believe it, you have it. What that means is God keeps his promises. He makes his promise, you believe it, then you will receive what he's promised because he will keep his word. God is true to his word. Luther will emphasize this over and over; if you read a lot of Luther, keep your ears perked for the places where he says "God is true, let God be true in every man alive."

The truth of God means above all the truth of God's promise. He keeps his word, and that's why the Gospel has the power to save you for Luther, because it's a promise, God keeps his promise, by believing you receive the power of God. Indeed, you receive God himself in the flesh because that's what Jesus is doing when he says "This is my body given for you." That's God in the flesh giving you nothing less than himself, sort of like a bridegroom giving himself to his bride by a wedding vow.

Let me mention one more feature of the Gospel. It's a story that contains a promise, but the story is for us. This is one of the most complicated features of Luther's thinking about the Gospel, and I want to set this clear so that we can distinguish it from lots of other ways of talking about the Gospel that are present in later forms of Protestantism. Luther said the Gospel is for me, that to believe the

Gospel is to believe that it is for me. Think about how it is again to receive a ring. "I give you this ring." To receive that ring is to believe that I gave the ring to you, that belief that it's for me, for you. That's essential to the belief, to the faith and the promise.

Likewise, Luther loves this moment where Jesus says, "This is my body given for you." He says "Yes, that means for me. Jesus is giving himself for me." Notice how *I* appear in the story. This is the story about Jesus Christ, not about me. Jesus does all this stuff; he dies, he's risen from the dead, he sits at the right hand of God the Father Almighty, he saves us from our sins. That's all Jesus being the subject of the verb. This is the story about Jesus, so the grammatical form of the Gospel is Jesus as the subject of a bunch of active verbs. He died, he arose, he ascended, he loves, he saves etc.

But we appear in the story, Luther thinks, I appear in the story because he did it for me. But I appear not as *I*, the subject of the sentence, but as me, the object, grammatically speaking. Jesus Christ died for me. I am the object of that preposition; Jesus loves me and died for me. I am the object, not the subject. I am not the one doing something in this story. Jesus Christ is the one doing something. If I were the one doing something, then it would be a story about me and my works.

Remember, the formula is you're justified by faith alone apart from works. Works means things that we do, so if the story was about what I do, how I believe or how I take Christ to my heart or how I give my thoughts to Christ, that would not be about Gospel. That would be about us; that would be about our works. The Gospel is received by faith alone because it is a story about what someone else does, but we're included in the story because it's a story about what someone else does for me. Luther will emphasize this over and over again, and you will see this in writings about Luther. Typically in Latin, they'll say Luther emphasizes the *pro me* aspect of the Gospel, *pro me* being Latin for *for me*.

But I want to emphasize also that because the Gospel is a story about someone else, about Jesus and not about me, Luther will over and over again emphasize the point that the Gospel directs our attention away from ourselves. It's for me, but it's not about me. But it's not my story, it's Jesus' story, so Luther's always saying pay attention to Christ, not to yourself. Don't look at what's in your own heart; don't even look at your faith. Look at Christ. Faith does not say, "I believe"; faith says "Christ died for me." Faith tells the Gospel story and we believe the Gospel story. Faith is all focused on the truth of this Gospel story and its promise. Christ died for me, is what faith says. That's true is what faith says. I believe is about me; that's a different story. That's the doctrine of justification by faith.

The Gospel and its content is about Christ and his dying for us. You see that difference, that difference of where you direct your attention, which is very important for Luther. The Gospel directs our attention away from ourselves and to Christ. It even directs our attention away from our own belief. The Gospel is not about my belief. The Gospel is about Christ died for me. I appear in that story as the object of God's love and concern, not as the subject. But it is a story that includes me; it includes all of us. That will do, I suppose, as a preliminary introduction to this key notion of Gospel. We're going to be seeing more and more about this from many different angles as these lectures go, but I want to get a preliminary sense of what Luther is doing when he talks about Gospel.

I'm thinking we want to get a sympathetic understanding of what Luther is talking about here, and there might be some worries already arising in your mind as you hear this. In fact, I have two opposite worries, which I'd like to address. Worry number one, all this stuff about the Gospel for me, doesn't it sound kind of egocentric? All about me, as if everything in the universe is about me, as if God is all concerned about me. Why be so egocentric about this? For Luther, the answer is if God gives you something and says "This is for you," then who are you to say no? If God wants to give you something and says it's for you, you might as well just agree and say "God wants to give me something."

You see what's going on here; you see the power of the notion of a word. The Gospel is a word; it's God speaking, and he speaks to me. He's speaking to me. It's not my job to decide that God has no right to speak to me. If he's speaking to me I'd better listen and maybe believe it. Of course, this is all assuming that this actually is God's word. Luther's usually speaking to Christians and assuming that you're right, this is the Gospel, it's for you. If God's speaking to me, I have to believe it.

Suppose we have an opposite worry? Suppose the worry is like this: why do we need to hear this? After all, everyone knows that God loves everyone. God is all-loving. I don't need to hear that God loves me; God loves everyone. Don't we all know this about God? We don't believe in this angry God who's going to smite you with thunderbolts anymore. God is all-loving. God doesn't want to hurt any of us; God wants the best for everybody.

Here Luther gets off the boat. Luther believes in sin and judgment, and how does Luther believe in sin and judgment. He's a big-time believer in sin and judgment; we are sinners who deserve from God nothing but hell and damnation and rejection, and we can expect from God nothing but hell and damnation and rejection, apart from this kind and gracious promise in the Gospel of Christ, a promise of mercy, so apart from Christ, apart from that promise of mercy, we can't expect anything good from God, Luther thinks. That is a view of God and of our sin and so on, sin and judgment, wrath of God and so on, which is very foreign to the way most of us think nowadays, so it's going to take some sympathetic imagination to understand why any decent, sane human being could believe in this.

Let me contrast Luther's focus on sin and judgment, which is very severe, with certain kinds of vivid stereotypes. Luther never worries about hellfire and brimstone and devils with pitchforks. That plays no role in his theology or in his imagination. Hell plays a huge role, but not that fiery pit with demons cackling as they torture people. Luther is not so much afraid of hellfire—indeed, he's not afraid of hellfire—he's afraid of God. The terrifying thing is not hell, but God. It's all about us and God; that's what it's really about. Just as the Gospel is about God giving to you nothing less than himself in the flesh, so also hell, or what Luther would call the law, is about God accusing us, rejecting us, saying "No, I want nothing to do with you. Get out of here."

Those are the two fundamental ways that God talks to us, Luther thinks. There's Gospel, this beautiful story with this promise in which God gives himself to us, and then there's law, which not only commands us to do stuff, which we are not able to do because we're sinners, but also accuses us, condemns us because we are not able to keep the commandment. So when we're dealing with God, it's either accusation and condemnation under the law, or promise and comfort under the Gospel.

Let's talk about what goes on in the notion of law and condemnation in Luther. What is Luther afraid of if it's not hellfire? In fact, Luther will define hell as terror. What hell is, is terror that goes down to your toes. What are you afraid of, Mr. Luther, you might ask. Let me tell a story which I made up, it's a parable, designed to get you some sense of what Luther's afraid of and why it's not some superstitious notion about hellfire and brimstone and some picture of eternal torture. It's something much worse than that. Let's see if you can imagine this.

Here's how I'd like to imagine it. Imagine that you are a little girl and you have a brother that you don't like very much, so you sneak up behind him and you push him down the stairs and he breaks his neck. The ambulance drivers comment, they're talking about a broken neck, and you know your brother has broken his neck. There's tumult in the family, and when the dust settles the very next day, you have to walk up to your father and talk to him about this. Imagine it's a rather old-fashioned household; your father goes into his study, closes the door, and now you must come up to the study door, open the door and go in and face your father, like facing the judgment of God the father. That's the analogy that I'm setting up here.

As you open that door and go to face your father, I take it you're terrified. What are you afraid of? A spanking? That would be too easy. Wouldn't that be nice, just getting a spanking? If that was the only punishment for this deed, then you would be having an easy time of it, but it's much worse than that. You're afraid of something much, much worse than punishment. Isn't what you're afraid of something like this: your father's going to look at you and say, "You are not my daughter. You are not my child. I never knew you, I thought I knew you, but I don't know who you are. I don't want you, I don't want you in this house. I want you to go away, you do not belong here. Get out. I have nothing to do with you from now on."

Imagine God saying that. God your father, the one who created you and the whole universe, the very source of all being is saying "Get out, I want nothing to do with you. Be gone, I hate you." That's what Luther is afraid of, I think, of this word of ultimate utter rejection. That's the word of the law, the word of terror. You can now see how the Gospel would be wonderful news. Let's continue the story. Suppose you open that study door, and there, sitting on your father's lap is your brother, the one you pushed down the stairs.

The first thing that happens is he smiles, and the second thing that happens is he says "My sister, my sister," and the third thing that happens is of course your father has to follow suit and say "Yes, my daughter, my child." Then you know that everything is going to be all right. Maybe you'll get a spanking. Who cares? Everything is going to be fundamentally all right, and your brother continues saying something like "I want you to be my sister, I want to be your brother, I want us to be brother and sister again. You're my sister. Will you believe that?

"Don't think of yourself as someone who's hurt me; that doesn't matter to me. You're my sister; that's who you are. Will you believe that?" That's the Gospel; that's the good news that restores you, that comforts you. You will always have that comfort and consolation of the Gospel. Someone who has every right to hate you says to you, "I want to be your brother. I want to give myself to you. We want to be happy together, don't we, for eternity." Of course, the brother here now represents Christ.

The story gets even better; the Christian Gospel story is a very happy story. Imagine that your brother in fact is going to get better. His neck is not going to be broken, he's injured but he's going to be OK. That's like the resurrection; Jesus Christ is the one that we crucified, but he's raised from the dead because he defeats death. He defeats all the evil that we can do to him. That's the Christian story. It is really good news, and Luther thinks that just by believing it, you become an entirely different person, and that's what he wants to preach and teach, and that's what changes the world, just by believing it, by faith alone, everything changes. We'll have to talk about why people found that controversial and what that did to change the world in this immense event called the Reformation.

But let me say just a little bit about how to deal with controversial figures and my thoughts about what we should think about this difficult man Martin Luther. I've been emphasizing things that I think we can be sympathetic with. I've been trying to promote a sympathetic understanding of Luther because I think you can't understand someone like Luther without a little sympathy. It takes a little sympathy and understanding to cross a huge historical divide of about 450 years that separate us from Luther. We can't just think about him the way we think about ourselves because he's different, and crossing that historical divide requires some sympathy.

But we should also be thinking critically about Luther, as I've suggested, and the critical thinking will have to deal with moral issues. By the end of these lectures, I'm going to be talking about really awful things that Luther says about people he disagrees with, especially the Jews. What Luther says about the Jews is wicked, inexcusable and wrong; we have to make moral critical judgments about Luther. You have to do that when dealing with certain historical figures. If you don't make a moral judgment about Adolf Hitler, then you don't understand him. If you don't make a positive moral judgment about Mahatma Gandhi, I think you don't understand him, so we make some positive and negative moral judgments about Martin Luther, both sympathy and criticism.

The aim here I think should not be a kind of neutral objectivity, as if there was some kind of scientific method for achieving a neutral judgment about such a controversial figure. What we need is rather what I call good judgment, a good judgment like the good judgment you exercise in deciding whether someone is trustworthy or whether you can trust them in one regard or another, this is a moral issue. It's a matter of judgment; it's not a matter of scientific objectivity. The judgment should aim at truth and also justice, at being fair to this very complex and somewhat tormented figure Martin Luther. That's what I'll aim at in this lecture.

Let me say in conclusion a little bit about what we're heading for in the set of lectures that's coming up, 24 lectures on Martin Luther. We'll begin in Part I of these lectures by talking about this central concept of Gospel. There's a whole lot to say about how it works, how Luther ended up formulating this concept, how it fit into his experience, his experience of terror on the one hand and consolation on the other, this dialectic or back and forth between Gospel and the law that is at the center of his theology and his life. Then in Part II, we'll talk about the public event called the Reformation. Part I is about what happens in Luther's heart, his experience of law and Gospel.

Part II is about the Lutheran Reformation, the course it takes in the early sixteenth century, how it changes the world, how it creates this enormous split between Catholic and Protestant, how it creates in fact a split between Lutheran Protestants and other kinds of Protestants, especially the Swiss reformers, the Reformed tradition, as it's called. Then in Part III, we'll deal with a series if related topics, Luther and X: Luther and the Bible, Luther and Protestantism, Luther and predestination (lots of fun) and also Luther and his enemies, Luther and the Jews, where we say some very critical things about Luther and make some moral judgments.

Next time, we'll be launching ourselves into Part I, and we'll start with some context for Luther. Part I is about Luther's experience with the Gospel, but to begin with, we have to start not with Luther's experience, but its historical context. We'll talk about the medieval church; we'll talk about the medieval papacy and its history. Then in Lecture 3, we'll talk about medieval piety, medieval religion, the spirituality in which Luther was raised, then we'll be ready to talk about why this notion of Gospel drops into the middle of this medieval piety of Luther's and changes everything in his heart and then everything in European history in the Reformation.

Lecture Two

The Medieval Church—Abuses and Reform

Scope:

This is the first of two lectures examining the context of Luther's experience of the Gospel. Here, we begin with the external context, the history of the medieval church, which was the most powerful institution in the Western world for many centuries. We briefly examine the history of the papacy, as well as the varieties of Catholic clergy. We look in particular at clerical abuses that were prevalent in Luther's time, most of which have to do with money. The late medieval church funded itself and maintained its cultural position in large part by virtue of its claim to authority over individuals' consciences, playing on their anxiety about their status in the next life. Luther's doctrine of justification by faith alone freed people from this kind of authority and its anxieties, which explains much of the popularity of the Reformation among the laity.

Outline

I. In the medieval church—and, therefore, in medieval society—the clergy was a distinct class of people, its members different from the laity in both their spiritual and social status.

   A. Priests had special spiritual powers, as well as distinctive social functions.

      1. Priests had the spiritual power of saying Mass, in which bread and wine were changed into the body and blood of Christ.

      2. The Mass was of spiritual benefit both to those who heard it and to those for whom it was said.

      3. For pay, Masses could be said for souls in purgatory, easing punishments there. Purgatory is the place for Christian souls who will get to heaven but are temporarily suffering punishment until their souls are purified (purged of sin, hence, *purgatory*).

      4. Masses were often funded for this purpose, so that a major portion of the medieval economy centered on

paying for Masses for the dead, a spiritual service that could be provided only by a priest.

5. Side altars in churches were devoted to private Masses, often attended by no one but the priest who was being paid to say them.

B. Monks and friars (not all of whom were priests) took special vows of poverty, obedience, and chastity.

1. In contrast to parish priests, who were called *secular clergy* because they lived in the world (not separated from other people), monks and friars were *regular clergy*, living under a special rule (Latin *regula*) that separated them from the world.

2. Different orders of monks and friars lived under different rules (for example, Benedictine monks, Franciscan friars, and Augustinians, who could be called both monks and friars). Young Martin Luther was an Augustinian monk or friar (he was called both), as well as a priest.

3. The monks' and friars' vows of poverty, obedience, and chastity separated them from ordinary economic, political, and domestic life, respectively. They did not own land or feudal property; they owed allegiance to their spiritual superior before any secular ruler; and they were not married.

4. Though individual monks were not property owners, monasteries were often very wealthy and powerful institutions.

II. Medieval clergy often had temporal, as well as spiritual power.

A. The spiritual power of the clergy, which was ordained to help people toward eternal life, was contrasted with the temporal (that is, political) power of the laity, which was concerned with governing things in this transitory mortal life.

B. Bishops (including the pope, the bishop of Rome) often had great temporal power.

1. The feudal church was funded by a system of benefices, which were, in effect, ecclesiastical fiefs, giving clergy a right to tithes (church taxes) and often meaning that the

clergy controlled a great deal of land and wealth in return for spiritual services.

2. This meant that bishops, whose benefices could be quite large, were often feudal lords involved in power politics with other feudal lords. Therefore, in the medieval church, political and economic power was tied up with spiritual power.

3. Because benefices were not private or family property (bishops were not supposed to have children to pass them on to), they were one of the most important sources of wealth and power. They were often fought over after the bishop died and the benefice became vacant.

4. Secular rulers typically wanted to control the benefice in order to collect its revenues; they did not want to have that wealth shipped off to a foreign prince (the pope).

5. Popes also competed for the wealth of benefices by insisting on the right of providing their own candidates for bishoprics and by imposing a hefty tax on the first year of income (called *annates*) when someone acquired a benefice.

C. The pope, both theoretically and practically, had temporal and spiritual power.

1. The pope's benefice was most of central Italy. He was a ruler of the Papal States, he derived income from them, and he was involved in wars in Italy.

2. The pope was the chief bishop of Rome, the successor of St. Peter, and the chief of the apostles of Christ.

3. Medieval popes made forceful claims for their role as the Vicar of Christ, that is, Christ's representative on earth, ruling over the body of Christ with the authority of its head.

4. Throughout the Middle Ages, the popes claimed that spiritual power was superior to temporal power, and that the latter should be exercised at the behest of the former (for example, in Pope Boniface VIII's bull, *Unam Sanctam,* in 1302).

5. Temporal rulers who rebelled against the spiritual power could be excommunicated, their lands put under interdict, and their subjects absolved from obedience. An

example was King John of England, who caved in and made England a fief of the pope.

6. Yet papal claims, which were often extravagant, should not make us accept the stereotype of a monolithic and all-powerful church. The papacy was constantly involved in feudal power politics and did not always win. An illustration of this is the lay investiture controversy between Pope Gregory VII and the emperor Henry IV.

7. The emperor was the Holy Roman Emperor, but in fact, he was the feudal overlord of Germany, to whom the various princes of Germany owed allegiance. This was the situation in Germany in Luther's time. In his view of medieval history, Luther was always on the side of the (German) emperor versus the (Italian) pope.

D. Precisely because the papacy was powerful, it often became a bone of contention in power politics.

1. For much of the 14th century, the papacy was located in Avignon, not Rome, conveniently under the control of the king of France (the *Babylonian Captivity* of the papacy), keeping the pope out of reach of other monarchs, such as the emperor of Germany.

2. In the last quarter of the century, the situation became even worse. Rival popes lived in both Avignon and Rome, each excommunicating the other's followers (the *Great Schism*).

3. These 14th-century events not only undermined people's confidence in the papacy but also made them anxious about their salvation (suppose I follow the wrong pope?) and prompted them to wonder whether their salvation really was dependent on such an institution.

4. At the beginning of the 15th century, the Council of Constance put an end to the Great Schism by deposing several rival popes.

E. The Renaissance papacy developed in the 15th century, rich in wealth, artistic splendor, and abuses.

1. The pope was the temporal ruler of most of central Italy and was frequently involved in Italian power politics, family intrigue, and warfare.

2. The Renaissance popes built Rome back up after it had fallen into decay during the Babylonian Captivity of the 14th century, including the new St. Peter's church and the paintings of Raphael and Michelangelo (such as the frescoes on the Sistine chapel) commissioned by Julius II.

3. All this took money, which was raised from the pope's lands in Italy, from annates and other taxes, and from some new means of fundraising, such as the aggressive selling of offices in the papal bureaucracy, as well as indulgences.

4. During Julius II's reign, an unknown young monk named Martin Luther visited Rome in 1510, found it disgustingly worldly and cynical, and wondered about its spiritual claims as a pilgrimage site.

5. A crisis was brewing: The Renaissance papacy depended on late-medieval piety for its funding (much of it from Germany), and late-medieval piety did not approve of the Renaissance papacy.

III. Lay piety in the late Middle Ages centered on getting supernatural help for the dead.

A. The overriding concern for late-medieval piety was about one's state in the life after death.

1. People were concerned that they be in a state of grace when they died, not in a state of mortal sin.

2. The living could help the dead by reducing their time in purgatory through prayers, Masses, pilgrimages, and indulgences.

3. Masses for the dead were a major part of the medieval economy.

4. Indulgences were an official declaration that you (or someone to whom you assigned the indulgence) would have your stay in purgatory reduced by a specific amount of time.

B. Luther's doctrine of justification by faith alone dropped into this culture like a bombshell.

1. It offered certainty (the promise of God!) for consciences anxious about their place in the afterlife.

2. It freed the consciences of the laity from the domination of the clergy, which was often motivated more by financial than pastoral considerations.
3. The doctrine undermined some of the most important money-making schemes available to fund the papacy, such as the sale of indulgences.
4. It spoke to anxious consciences: people worried about how to escape gruesome torture in the next life and uncertain about what would really work.
5. It addressed the faithful German laity, who had been paying for Masses, indulgences, and pilgrimages as ways of relieving spiritual anxiety, only to see their money sent to Italy, where it was used to fight wars and build huge churches.
6. Finally, the doctrine paved the way for pious German believers, beginning with Martin Luther, to say "Enough!" and to begin the Reformation.

Essential Reading:

Duffy, *Saints and Sinners*, chapters 2–3.

Supplemental Reading:

Bettenson and Maunder, *Documents of the Christian Church* (includes many of the documents used in this lecture).

Duffy, *The Stripping of the Altars*, chapters 9–10 (for medieval lay piety of dying).

Greenblatt, *Hamlet in Purgatory*, chapters 1–2 (for a history of purgatory).

Kelly, *The Oxford Dictionary of Popes* (wonderful for browsing in this era).

King, *Michelangelo and the Pope's Ceiling* (for a vivid portrayal of the Renaissance papacy).

Questions to Consider:

1. How is the church Luther confronted different from the church today?
2. How is your experience of the clergy different from that of medieval people?

Lecture Two—Transcript

The Medieval Church—Abuses and Reform

In our first lecture, I presented Luther as a man of controversy at the center of swirling controversies between Catholics and Protestants, and as central to Western history as a result. I presented a kind of parable to get at the heart of what Luther is talking about when he says this word, "Gospel," which is his designation for what's at the very center of his thought and his work. I think if we work outward from that center—"the Gospel of Christ" Luther calls it—we'll be able to understand where the controversy came from. But now, we need to get beyond my parables and get to the historical context in which Luther actually formulated the Gospel. No more of my parables now; let's talk about Luther's times, how Luther looked at these and try to see these in Luther's own terms. That means to begin with, that we need to think about the medieval context and, especially, of course, the medieval church. That's the historical context in which Luther grows up and his thinking takes shape.

Let's think about the medieval church; let's think first of all about a crucial social division, the division between clergy and laity. This is not just the familiar division between ministers and people in the congregation. That's how Protestants think about it, but in Catholicism, and especially in medieval Catholicism, the clergy have a special spiritual power. This is actually a technical term in medieval theology. Priests, in particular, are ordained so that they have this special power of saying Mass. When a priest says Mass, bread and wine are changed into the body and blood of Christ, Catholic theology teaches. That's a special spiritual power that laity, people who aren't clergy, do not have, and that spiritual power becomes really socially important, economically important it turns out, as we'll see.

The Mass is of great spiritual benefit. In addition to this miracle of transformation, the Mass can do spiritual good and not just for you who are attending it say, but also for people for whom you say Mass. What you can do in the Middle Ages can still be done today, but it's not economically as important as in the Middle Ages; you can pay for Masses to be said for the souls of people in purgatory, for instance. Purgatory is where Christian souls go when they're not quite ready for heaven; they're not going to go to hell, but they still have some purification to go through. That's their purgation in purgatory. It's painful, and we can help them by praying for them, and by having Masses said for them. Masses need to be paid for; there can be endowments for Masses—people will put money aside in their wills to pay for Masses for their souls after they die, and they will expect their family members to pay for Masses for their souls.

This becomes part of the medieval economy in a way that just doesn't happen today, even in Catholicism today. It's a different social world where the spiritual power of the Mass is something that becomes an actual commodity that is bought and sold and becomes an economically important one. To see the kind of importance of this, imagine walking into the church in Wittenberg in 1519. This is where Luther is teaching; he's already posted the famous 95 Theses, which we'll talk about; he's already set the ball rolling that will create the Reformation, but it hasn't happened yet. You're walking into the church in Wittenberg sometime in 1519, and you're walking down the main isle of the church called the nave, and you're heading toward the high altar, which is at the center of the church, and if you're familiar with the architecture of most churches, especially Catholic churches, on either side as you walk down the nave, there will be side altars, they're called.

In 1519 in Wittenberg, you will see dozens, at least a dozen or so priests saying Mass at these side altars. Why? They're paid for. Nine thousand Masses were paid for in 1519 in Wittenberg. That means the priests are busy most of the time. Most days, you can see half a dozen, a dozen of them, probably most of them alone. Nobody needs to be hearing this Mass; this Mass is said for somebody who's not even present, they're in purgatory. Although you occasionally will have onlookers, most people in fact, most of the time, do not take communion at the Mass except at Easter, when they were required to.

They hear Mass and, of course, many Masses at these side altars are not heard by anyone but the priest because the Mass is supposed to do good for people just because it's being performed. It doesn't matter who hears it; it doesn't matter if anyone takes the bread and wine and eats it. It just needs to be performed and it does someone good. That's why you pay for it. Luther will attack this whole practice. Two years after 1519, it gets abolished in Wittenberg. It looks for Luther like a kind of magic that you pay for, to pay for spiritual favors, and you get sort of a sense of the Reformation critique of Catholicism at this point, and we'll deepen that as we go.

Let me mention another kind of clergy—monks and friars, people in monasteries. They're not necessarily priests; lots of monks and friars are not priests. They're called "regular clergy" because they live under a monastic rule, an official rule that in Latin is called a *regula*, so regula means "ruled." They live under a regula, an official rule that governs their lives, that sets them apart from other people, just like priests in that regard. They're set apart; in fact, they're more set apart than regular priests. Parish priests are called "secular clergy" because they live in the world with other people. The regular clergy live separate lives bound by these separate and special rules that include always all the rules, whether they're Augustinian, or Franciscan, or Benedictine. This includes vows of poverty, obedience, and chastity—those three vows.

Then they'll be fleshed out in different ways by the Benedictines' monastic rules, the Franciscan rule for the friars of St. Francis of Assisi, the Augustinian rule for people who are called monks or friars. Luther, it turns out, is an Augustinian. We never know whether to call him a monk or a friar because Franciscans (you know) are friars, Benedictines (you know) are monks, but Augustinians can be monks or friars, and Luther called himself both. It doesn't matter too much.

The important thing to know about Luther is that he's also a priest, as well as a monk and a friar, and he's at the center of all this clergy business. He also, as a monk or friar, takes this vow of poverty, chastity, and obedience. That separates him from the world because poverty means he's not supposed to own any property; that separates him from the economic life of society. Chastity separates him, of course, from the domestic life, the family life of society, and obedience means his primary obedience belongs to his monastic superior, the abbot of his monastery or whoever is in charge of him, and there's always someone in charge of you if you're a monk or a friar, and that means that your primary obedience is not to the local political authorities. The political authorities sometimes don't like this, so there's this separation of the clergy from the laity that is profound in the Middle Ages, a massive and important thing.

One more thing about monks; individual monks are vowed to poverty, but monasteries themselves—the settings in which monks live—can be very, very wealthy and powerful institutions. When William the Conqueror took over England in 1066, the monasteries owned somewhere around a sixth of the land and wealth of England. That's a lot of power and wealth. There's this real mixture of spiritual power and political power in the Middle Ages. At the end of the Middle Ages, Henry VIII—King Henry VIII, who inaugurated the English Reformation—dissolved the monasteries. He got rid of them and he collected a large amount of wealth as a result, so the Reformation had economic consequences, and how.

That leads me to the next point. Medieval clergy, with the spiritual power, also had temporal power. Spiritual power and temporal power were intertwined. Temporal power means political power basically, but also economic power. Temporal contrasts with eternity; temporal has to do with time. Spiritual power has to do with eternity because it's about eternal life; temporal power has to do with life in this world, the earthly life, this transitory mortal life. That's why it's called temporal, but it's also political power. Clergy had political power, especially the bishops. Let me talk about bishops. All bishops are priests; they supervise other priests and other churches, and typically they hold a benefice. This is a really crucial social and economic notion in the Middle Ages.

A benefice is like an ecclesiastical fief, a church fief. You know how fiefs work in the feudal system, a king grants land to a nobleman who then owes the king military service in payment for this fief, which is landed wealth, which means that they own a bunch of serfs who are bound to the land, so a fief is both economic and political power in return for which the nobleman owes his lord military service. Likewise, a bishop gets a fief called a benefice, which means typically land, the peasants who belong on the land, the produce of the land, the wealth of the land, and in return they offer to the sovereign or the local lord spiritual services, like the saying of the Mass and the organizing of the sacramental life of the church, which is for the good of all these people in purgatory and for the salvation of the people in the church. In return for spiritual services, they get this benefice, this piece of land that is both political and economic power.

In the feudal system in the Middle Ages, political and economic power go together. You own land, you own the serfs on the land, and then in the medieval church, the political and economic power is tied up with spiritual power. Political, economic, and spiritual power are intertwined, inseparable, and that causes the whole dynamics of medieval church politics. That means, in fact, that bishops become involved in power politics. Power is a double-edged sort of thing. To have power is to enter into power politics—that is, to enter into competition with other people who have power, and you don't always win. To have power means that you've got powerful enemies. Power politics in the Middle Ages tied bishops up into competition with lords, kings, and rulers. There are several ways this happened.

First of all, be aware about benefices; they're a very unusual kind of fief because unlike your normal fief, they're not going to be passed on down to the family. Bishops may have children, they often do, but they're not supposed to have children. Their children are not legitimate heirs; they cannot pass the benefice down to their children, so every time a bishop dies, the benefice becomes vacant and it can be fought over. Who's going to occupy this benefice? Who's going to reap the wealth of this benefice? The king of the territory is going to want to have someone loyal to him. The pope is going to want to have someone loyal to him. The king doesn't want the bishop to be someone who is loyal to a foreign prince, like the pope. The pope really is a foreign prince.

The benefice is wealth from this country, the local royalty do not want wealth from the country to be shipped abroad to Rome and, of course, the pope doesn't want wealth from these benefices to be shipped abroad to Rome. He actually claims (as a right) a kind of tax on the first year's income of the benefices. This tax is called *annates*. It's a special tax that, when you acquire a benefice, you pay (this tax) to the pope. It's often a very hefty tax, so basically you're paying the pope for your benefice. You need a lot of money to pay the pope so that you can acquire this benefice, and what that essentially means is that wealth from this country is going off to Rome. The pope needs this wealth; the papacy is expensive, and the pope is always looking for ways of increasing fundraising. That's one of the things that is being fought over all the time in the Middle Ages.

The pope, in fact, is—himself—a temporal lord of no small stature. His benefice, in fact, is most of central Italy. He is the ruler of the

Papal States; he is a prince. Let me just say by "prince" in these lectures, what I mean is any territorial ruler, a duke, a margrave—these are all princes, not necessarily just a son of a king. The pope is a prince in this sense. He rules over a large territory in Italy—he gets the income from the territory—he's involved in wars in Italy throughout the Renaissance. But he's also, of course, someone who has spiritual power, and that's his real claim to power. He's the bishop of Rome; the pope is a bishop, but he's the chief bishop. He's a successor of St. Peter, who is by legend the first bishop of Rome, and that makes him the chief of all the bishops because Peter was the chief of the apostles, so the pope consulate calls himself by the name, Peter.

As Peter, the pope is the Vicar of Christ. Christ is in heaven, Christ is the head of the church in heaven, but the pope is the head of the church on earth, the head of the body of Christ, the body of Christendom. All these Christian believers are one body, and the pope is the head of that body on earth as representative of Christ, who's the head of that body in heaven. That means that the pope claims a very special and supreme spiritual power. He's always, in fact—throughout the Middle Ages—claiming that the pope's spiritual power is superior to any temporal power. Here's an example from 1302. Pope Boniface VIII publishes a document called *Unam Sanctam*, one holy church. Here's what he says about the power of the pope: "There's only one Church, with only one body and one head, which is Christ; but the Vicar of Christ is Peter, and Peter's successor," that is the successor of Peter, the pope, represents Christ on earth as head of the church. He continues:

> There are two swords, spiritual and temporal [the sword is a metaphor for power], and the temporal sword is in the power of Peter. [The temporal sword is in the power of the pope.]…Both are in the power of the Church—the spiritual sword and the temporal sword. The temporal sword is to be used *for* the church, the spiritual sword *by* the Church: the spiritual sword by the priest, the temporal sword by kings and commanders, but at the will and by the permission of the priest. The one sword then, should be under the other, and temporal power must be subject to spiritual power.

Bold and rather extravagant claims Boniface is making. As it turns out, the temporal powers in Europe were not very impressed. Kings did not have a habit of obeying popes. If you've got this stereotype of the all-powerful monolithic medieval church, then drop it. The church is not all-powerful; it's involved in power politics. It's a very powerful institution; therefore, it's always being contested. Power is always double-edged. Boniface VIII himself died shortly after a traumatic experience in which French soldiers nearly succeeded in kidnapping him and taking him to be the captive of the King of France. A few years later, the next pope—or rather the pope after the next pope—does, in fact, move to France and basically becomes captive to the king of France, and the papacy becomes a tool of the king of France for about 70 years. That's what power gets you; it's double-edged. You have power; you're part of a fight for power.

But the popes win a few as well. They have spiritual weapons that are of real social consequence. For instance, in one power struggle, the Pope Innocent III in the early 1300s excommunicates King John of England. Excommunication means that King John doesn't get to take communion—that is, he doesn't get to participate in Mass, which means that he cannot receive the kind of grace that he needs to get into a state of grace in his soul, which is what he needs to go to heaven. Without the sacrament, he is bound for hell. People took this very seriously; what it means is that the pope has a weapon that is more powerful than any sword made of steel. He can not only kill you, he can send you to hell. It's a very powerful weapon, and the pope went even further.

He didn't just excommunicate King John; he didn't just release all of King John's subjects from obedience to the King. He did that, but even more, he put the whole kingdom of England under *interdict*. *Interdict* means that nobody in the kingdom gets the sacraments. The Mass cannot be performed, Christian burial cannot be performed, confessions can't be heard, nobody gets the grace that they need to escape hell. Enormously powerful, this is a cruel weapon. People worry about whether they're going to hell because the king is having a fight with the pope. This was a fight that the king lost; he caved in and he made England an official fief of the pope and paid 1,000 marks a year to the pope. That didn't last real long, but it actually did get John some benefits.

The pope obliges John by declaring the Magna Carta null and void. Remember, this is King John who signed the Magna Carta, giving up some of his royal prerogatives to his barons. The pope said, "No, this was signed without my permission; therefore, it's null and void. King John gets his prerogatives back." This is power politics again. You cave in to the pope and things go OK, sometimes. You can't believe this picture of the monolithic medieval papacy. Let me tell you one brief story.

In the 11th century, we've got Pope Gregory VII lining up against Emperor Henry IV. The pope deposes Henry IV, or threatens to. Henry has to actually repent, walking in the snow outside the castle at Canossa, in Tuscany, in Italy, to show his repentance. The pope restores him after having threatened to release all of his subjects from obedience. Later on, Henry deposes the pope and, in fact, he invades Rome. The pope has to hole up in his Castel Sant' Angelo in the Vatican, that famous round castle that you can see in pictures of the Vatican, and he gets rescued by Robert Guiscard, down from Naples. It's a mess; the people in Rome hate the pope because these folks from Naples are trashing the place in order to rescue the pope from the emperor. What happens is there's this high point in the medieval papacy when the Emperor Henry IV is repenting in the snow in Canossa. A few years later, the pope is holed up like a rat in a castle, and everyone hates him and he dies a broken man. High point and low point within a few years of each other.

Let me say briefly something about emperors. The emperor is the emperor of Germany, it turns out; this is important because Luther is living under an emperor. He's officially the Holy Roman Emperor, but he lives in Germany. He's more or less the elected monarch of Germany, but the real powers in Germany are local princes. He's not really a king and therefore doesn't have the kind of power of a king. He has to work through these elected princes. That'll be an important feature of the politics of Luther's time. Luther himself is always on the emperor's side when he reads medieval history, which is full of these conflicts between the emperor in Germany and the pope down in Italy. The emperor invades Rome and all that sort of stuff. Luther is always on the side of the emperor.

Because the papacy is powerful, it becomes a bone of contention in power politics. As I mentioned before, in the early 14th century, right after Boniface VIII, the papacy gets moved to Avignon, which is in France, under the shadow of the king of France, very convenient for the king of France, inconvenient for the emperor of Germany. This is described by medieval writers as a "Babylonian Captivity," like the captivity of ancient Israel in the Bible, going off to Babylon, leaving their lands. The pope belongs in Rome, but he's off in Avignon, captive. That becomes an important theme. It gets worse though. Late in the 14th century, there's the Great Schism.

A pope comes back to Rome, and another pope stays in Avignon, and we've got two rival popes. Each excommunicates the followers of the other, puts their lands under interdict, this interdict where no one gets the sacraments, so if you're with one king, then you're with this one pope, and the other pope is saying that your sacraments are not valid and you're going to hell, and if you're with the other king, there's the other pope saying you're going to hell. Which side do you want to be on? Which side is safe? How can you gain salvation in a situation like that? It really undermined your confidence in the church, and it makes you terribly anxious about your own salvation. Very bad news. How do you solve a situation like that?

At one point, there were actually three popes, not just two, and at the beginning of the 15th century, there's a church council that's held called the Council of Constance, which deposes all three popes and then puts a new pope in its place and finally solves the issue. That became actually a basis for one version of the theology of the church, thinking that maybe the pope ought to be under the authority of the Council. The popes didn't like that and they won because the next feature of the history of the papacy is the Renaissance papacy. The popes got out from under the power of the councils, they built, they got wealthy, they fought wars.

One of them was the warrior pope Julius II, who is the same guy who commissioned the paintings of the Sistine Chapel by Michelangelo. He was wealthy, he was powerful, he was terrifying. They called him Il Terrible, the terrifying. His uncle, Sixtus IV, after whom the Sistine Chapel was named, was involved in a conspiracy to murder the Medicis, yes those Medicis, the Medicis in Florence. He got one of them killed, and the other one was Lorenzo the Magnificent, whose son Leo became pope when Luther was trying to reform the church. Very complex Italian family politics played a huge role, money being given to nephews and illegitimate sons like Caesar Borgia, the son of the Borgia pope, Alexander IV.

There's money; the Renaissance papacy is awash with money. They sell offices in the bureaucracy of Rome. You can buy a place as some kind of Roman official, you don't have any work to do, but you get the income from all sorts of benefices. Money is flowing into Rome, a lot of it is flowing into Rome from Germany; that's going to be a big issue for Luther. Luther, in fact, visits Rome in 1510 under Julius II, the warrior pope, the one who is commissioning the Sistine Chapel for Michelangelo. He's only an unknown priest at this point; in 1510, it's long before the 95 Theses. Nobody knows who Luther is; he's just an unknown monk from Germany visiting Italy, and he finds it worldly, cynical, atheistic. Italian priests don't believe the Gospel; they don't believe anything, they're just in it for the money, and their word for a fool is a good "Christian," Luther remembers.

He is shocked by these people. They keep the prostitutes in the red light district very busy. They all have mistresses, or prostitutes, or both—many of them have children, of course, and in this environment Luther makes a special pilgrimage to seek the grace of God for his relatives in purgatory. For his grandfather, whom he assumes is in purgatory, he climbs the sacred steps on his knees one step at a time. These are the steps that were supposedly at the house of Pilate, where Jesus Christ was on trial, moved to Rome. You climb up this on your knees, one step at a time, saying the Lord's Prayer on each step, and at the end your grandfather's soul is supposed to be released from purgatory. Luther recalls later that when he got to the top of the stairs he asked himself, "Who can tell if it's really true? How do you know?"

There's a real crisis brewing here. The Roman Renaissance papacy gets its funding, a lot of it from Germany, based on a piety that is this late medieval anxiety about your souls in purgatory, the possibility of going to hell because you're not in a state of grace, and these pious Germans are not finding the Renaissance papacy very convincing spiritually. Let's think about this medieval piety, where you're concerned about the state of your soul after death, your concern that you're in a state of grace when you die, not a state of mortal sin, but if you've done some really terrible sin and haven't confessed it, your soul is in a state of mortal sin and you go straight to hell.

You need to confess your sins, get in a state of grace, and then probably you'll go to purgatory, not heaven; you'll get punished, but at least you get a chance of getting into heaven. It might last a while, this punishment, but at least you get to go to heaven, and you can get help from people. You can have your heirs say a Mass for you; you pay for this Mass and you get help after death. There are other forms of help after death, like you can buy indulgences; we'll talk about that at great length. You get a piece of paper that says that someone you love gets freed from purgatory, or gets some of their sentence knocked off. There's this whole economy built on the anxiety the people had about the next life, a whole economy that is treated cynically by the folks in Rome, and these pious Germans are not happy. They're about to have a convulsion about it, and Luther will be at the very center of the convulsion.

They're anxious; their consciences are terrified of this judgment of God, and in this context, Luther's Gospel is like a bombshell. Imagine you're one of these people, worried about whether you're in a state of grace, worried about whether you can do something for your loved ones in purgatory, worried about whether your heirs will do something for you when you're in purgatory. Luther's message is you can have certainty about this; you can have certainty that God is gracious to you. How? Listen to God's Word, for heaven's sakes, believe his promise. Instead of being up at the top of the stairs saying: "Who knows whether any of this stuff really works," you have God's own promise. Trust in God's own promise; just believe that God isn't lying to you when he makes this promise, and you have what you need. You have God himself.

This is a spiritual thing that has enormous economic and political consequences. It means that you're no longer dependent on paying a bunch of clergy to say Masses for you, or buying indulgences, or doing all this economic stuff that funds the papacy. You no longer need to pay for that stuff. It's free, it's the Gospel, it's just Jesus saying: "This is my body; it's given for you. You believe that and it's true." It happens for you, and so what you have here in the Middle Ages is this particular tension. Think of it as German-Italian tension.

The Germans are pious folks. They're concerned about their state after death, and they're anxious, and they want something that really works, and they're paying through the nose to get something that really works, and their money is being shipped off to Italy, where it's used in cynical fashion by Renaissance popes to fight wars and build magnificent churches like St. Peter's Cathedral and Michelangelo's Sistine Chapel, and these cynical Italian priests are dropping children like flies. Good grief. What's happening from the German perspective is that these Italians are wringing money out of the anxious, terrified consciences of pious people. The pious people, beginning with Martin Luther, are about to say: "Enough. We don't need this. All we need is Jesus Christ and the Gospel." Once they hear that, an earthquake happens, and we call that earthquake the Reformation.

Lecture Three

The Augustinian Paradigm of Spirituality

Scope:

This lecture deals with the inner context for understanding Luther's experience of the Gospel. The kind of inner or spiritual experience the medieval church aimed to promote was broadly Augustinian, an earthly pilgrimage leading to eternal happiness via faith, prayer, love, and contemplation, all made possible by divine grace. Protestant theologians pick up on these Augustinian themes but ask a question that, in effect, disrupts the pilgrimage: How do I stand before God's judgment? This question becomes particularly urgent because of the way Augustinian spirituality went awry in the late-medieval theology in which Luther was brought up.

Outline

I. The Augustinian paradigm is a spiritual quest for eternal happiness with God.

   A. This paradigm is developed by the great 4th-century church father Augustine, who was influential for all of Western Christianity, both Catholic and Protestant.

   B. In the Augustinian paradigm, happiness (beatitude or bliss) means seeing God with your mind.

   C. Morality consists of the virtues needed to travel on the road to beatitude, our eternal home with God.

   1. Faith is the beginning of the road: You begin by believing what you're told by the appropriate authority (for example, the Bible), so that you might eventually see it for yourself.

   2. Love, a desire for union with God, is the crucial "engine" that drives us along this road.

   3. The only reward for loving God is that you get what you love.

   4. Salvation is not until we reach the end of the road, when we understand and enjoy God; that's what "heaven" really is.

D. Augustine believed we can travel this road successfully only by the divine inward help of God's grace.

    1. According to this doctrine, our love for God is a gift from God, because it is God who causes us to fall in love with God, giving us the delight and longing that pulls us along on the journey.

    2. Our unaided free will is not sufficient to create this love; therefore, without this gift of grace, we would perish in our sins.

    3. Augustine argued that if you tried to love God without grace, you would resent him rather than obey him from a loving and willing heart.

    4. The key task of faith is to pray for grace; thus, you receive the grace to love God.

    5. Love for God is obedience to the greatest commandment of God, that is, to love God with your whole heart, mind, and strength.

    6. Thus, Augustine traces an "order of salvation" from faith to love to happiness.

    7. Even our initial faith or conversion is a gift of God, not simply our choice (for without God's grace, we would not choose to have faith).

    8. As we grow in love for God and neighbor through the cooperation of grace and our own free will, we do actually become better and more worthy people—Augustine's doctrine of grace includes the concept of human merit.

    9. Nonetheless, all our merits originate from God's grace, without which we would not love and obey God.

II. The key Protestant departure from this Augustinian paradigm was in the matter of merit, as can be seen by contrasting important passages in medieval and Reformation theology.

    A. In the 12th century, Anselm prays a very Augustinian prayer about the misery of being far from God, as faith seeks but has not yet found understanding, salvation, and eternal blessedness.

    B. In the 16th century, Luther and Calvin both insist that if you want to understand why we cannot be justified by the merit of our own works, you have to imagine what you will say before the judgment throne of God.

C. Though doctrinally close to each other, these two views are imaginatively and emotionally far apart: Anselm is miserable because his earthly desires keep him far from God. The Reformers are afraid because they are sinners who must face God's judgment.

D. With their imagination focused on judgment, not journey, Protestants found nothing attractive in the notion of human merit.

III. What intervenes between the 12th and 16th centuries is the development of the penitential conscience, a heart whose concern is increasingly wrapped around issues of sin, judgment, and forgiveness.

A. *Conscience* is the target of medieval penitential practices tied to the sacrament of penance.

    1. Originally, the word referred to someone who knows your secrets and is aware of evils you had done.

    2. Later, it came to mean the inner witness in your heart, which knows what you have done.

    3. For Luther, when the conscience is aware of sin, it does not have guilt feelings but, rather, feels terrified of God's judgment.

B. The new thing in the Middle Ages was the practice of private confession, which was required of all Christians by the fourth Lateran Council of 1215.

C. Private confession meant probing one's conscience not just for notorious sins but for evil desires and thoughts that might be mortal sins and could bring about damnation; this became a kind of trial run for facing God's judgment.

D. Hence, the medieval conscience was an anxious and terrified conscience, as illustrated by Margery Kempe in her autobiography.

E. Luther's doctrine of justification can be thought of as growing out of one of the deepest moments of medieval piety, the art of dying well: For when facing the hour of death, a Christian was to be directed by the priest to trust Christ alone, not his own merits or even the saints.

F. The greatest fear of all was sudden death, when you had no chance to confess your mortal sins and attain a state of grace.

Essential Reading:

Augustine, *On the Spirit and the Letter*, in *Later Works*, chapters 1–32.

Supplemental Reading:

Anselm, *Proslogion*, chapter 1.

Calvin, *Institutes* III, xii, 1.

Kempe, *The Book of Margery Kempe*, chapter 1.

Lewis, "Conscience," in *Studies in Words*.

Questions to Consider:

1. Which picture of the spiritual life, the Augustinian Catholic or the Protestant, is more attractive to you?

2. How *should* we imagine God's judgment—if at all?

Lecture Three—Transcript

The Augustinian Paradigm of Spirituality

We were talking in the last lecture about the historical context for Martin Luther's theology and his life. In order to do that, we dwelled on the institutional structure of the church, and we dwelled especially on things going wrong, on abuses, on ways that the popes especially did things wrong, extracting money from terrified consciences is the way I put it, and we'll see how that works in a little bit more detail. But it's important to realize the medieval church is not just abuses. There is, in fact, a deep and wonderful spirituality of medieval Catholicism, and I want to give you some taste of how that works because medieval Catholicism at its best is where Luther starts, but it's also what he departs from, in the sense of that's where he starts and that's where he leaves.

Even medieval Catholicism at its best is something Luther parts company with. One of the questions is, in fact, "Will this have to divide the church? Do you have to have this split of the church because of this?" It is important; Luther disagrees with Catholic spirituality at its very best, at its most inward, and that's what we're going to look at in this lecture—the more inward, experiential, and deep side of Catholic spirituality, where it's not just about money, it's not just about exploiting people, it is about adjourning to God. Let's see how that journey works.

The journey is what I will describe as the Augustinian paradigm of spirituality. It's a paradigm for the spiritual life that goes back to Augustine, the great 4th-century church father. Think of him as just prior to the Middle Ages. He's not a medieval theologian; he's living at the end of the Roman Empire, but he establishes the fundamental theological categories for medieval thought. All of the medieval theologians are living and thinking in an Augustinian framework. The Augustinian paradigm is more or less everyone's paradigm, although there are some variations. In the Augustinian paradigm, we've got a form of spirituality in which life is a journey toward God. What it's all about is finding happiness, or what some translations will call beatitude, the bliss—there are several names for it: the blessed life, happiness, ultimate happiness, eternal happiness means finding God.

What else would it mean? It means, for Augustine, seeing God. This is a metaphor. You don't see God with the eyes of your body, and in the Augustinian paradigm there's a strong distinction between body and soul—outer and inner. The vision of God is inward; it's a vision of your mind and your heart that I've described in a previous Teaching Company lecture as intellectual vision, and it's seeing with your intellect, like seeing an eternal truth in a moment of "Now I see it." Let me give you a sense of what I think many medieval theologians were after. Think of yourself working on a mathematical proof, and you're breaking your head over the proof, you can't figure it out, and then all of a sudden, you have a moment of illumination, you call it, a moment of light. You say "Now I see it, now I get it, now I understand it. Yes, I get it."

Imagine you have that experience, but what you're seeing is not some mathematical proof, but God, the eternal truth, which contains all that is eternally true, Augustine will put it, so you're seeing the truth at the center of the universe from which all things come. Imagine that it's possible to see such a thing. Imagine that this "Aha!" becomes the very basis of your being, your mode of being. It's what you are; it's this joyful embrace of eternal truth. That's what's the Augustinian paradigm of spirituality is aiming toward; it's aiming toward that happiness of seeing God eternally. That's what an Augustinian theologian means by talking about "heaven," for instance. It's not just a place where you're up on clouds playing with harps and things; it's seeing God with your mind's eye. That's the end of the journey.

Meanwhile, here on earth, we don't see God. We might have glimpses, moments of "Aha!" but they're not the whole nine yards. It's a long journey, and what's needed for the journey is morality, virtues. What's needed for the journey is not vision, because that's at the end, but faith and hope and love—the fundamental Christian virtues. These are moral characteristics of the soul that power the soul on its journey. The journey begins with faith. That means essentially believing what you're told because the goal is to see for yourself. If you're in a math class, sometimes you begin by believing what you're told, you copy down a formula, but you want to understand it for yourself; you want to really see it with your own mind's eye.

Likewise, in the Augustinian paradigm, you begin by believing what you're told. You believe what the Bible says, you believe what your priest says, you believe the church, but that's only the beginning. Like in a math class, you want to actually see it for yourself. You want to see God for yourself. That's what everybody really wants; that's our deepest desire, so we start by believing what we're told, that's only the beginning. What moves us along the road, interestingly, is not faith but love. Love, for Augustine, in this whole Augustinian paradigm means desire, desire for union.

Let's start with a physical analogy. What does an alcoholic desire? He desires union with alcohol, and he unites himself with alcohol in the most simple and obvious way possible; he pours it down his stomach. What does a lover desire? Union with his or her beloved. What do all human beings desire? Union with God. Love is this desire, which is like a magnetic force, almost like a gravitational force pulling you upward—Augustine would compare it to. It's this force of attraction that draws you to what you want to be one with. You want to be one with God, and this love for God pulls you along. That's the engine that drives you on this journey. It's love, not just doing good work so you'll be rewarded.

In fact, the only reward for loving God is that you get what you love. You're not loving God so that God will give you a cookie called heaven; heaven is just another name for being with God, being united with God in this vision. That's the deepest desire of your heart, Augustine thinks, and what the Augustinian spirituality of the Middle Ages is about is cultivating this desire, cultivating this longing for a God that we have not yet arrived at. We're on the journey; we're on the way. We're not yet saved, Augustine will say. That's something for those of you Protestants in the audience to get used to. For Catholics, we're not yet saved; we're on the way. Augustine will say we're saved in hope, but not yet in reality. We're on the road, but we're not home yet, and there are many dangers yet. What salvation alternately means is this seeing of God.

Don't think that Catholics are all salvation by works; that's one of those Protestant simplifications. Catholics believe in grace because Catholics are all Augustinians, and Augustine believes very strongly in grace. What that means is your love for God is a gift of God. You love God because God gives you the gift of loving him. It's as if God had the power to make you fall in love, and that falling in love with

God is the delight and the longing that pulls you along the journey, so the very love that draws us to God is a gift of God and a gift of God's grace. That also means for Augustine that you don't simply choose to do the right thing and God rewards you. There's more than just our own free will involved. When we love God, Augustine thinks, our own free will is in fact engaged. We freely and longingly and gladly love God, but that gladness, that delight, is itself a gift of God.

That's how it actually works. If you're a monk in the Middle Ages and you find yourself delighted in the thought of God, you thank God for that delight. When you find yourself growing in the love of God, you thank God for that because that's God's own gift. The whole journey is full of grace. It starts with faith, and in faith you pray for grace. This becomes a very important theme, you pray for grace, and that deepens you in a love of God, and then you pray more. You can imagine you're a monk. Your life is spent in prayer, and you pray for more and deeper grace to love God more, and your whole life is loving God more deeply, more intensely, with more delights and longing, and that's how you get closer to God.

Augustine has an argument for why grace is so necessary that becomes very important for Luther, and let's work through this. This is a psychological argument that becomes very important in Luther's psychology. Augustine argues that if you didn't have grace and you were trying to love God with your whole heart, mind, and strength—the way you're supposed to—what you would end up doing is resenting it. Imagine that you've got this rule that says you have to love me, and you don't really feel very loving, and you've just got to work at it, and you get kind of tired of it. You'd rather be doing something else, maybe alcohol, or your physical loves on earth, or your wife or your husband is more attractive than this God that you've never seen yet, and you get tired of it, and you'd rather be doing something else.

Augustine proposes a kind of counterfactual test. Suppose that there was no command of God. Suppose God didn't give you this law that says: "love me." What would you rather do? Would you rather love God or would you rather do something else? If you would rather be doing something else, if you would do something else if you could only get away with it, then your love for God is not genuine. Genuine love for God is delight, and gladness, and joy, and longing *goal of seeing God*

coming from the depths of your heart. You can't produce that just by choosing it. Free will is not enough. Free will is part of it, but you need that falling in love, that delight. That doesn't come just because you choose it. We don't delight in something just because you choose to delight in it; it has just kind of overcome you.

We know what it's like to fall in love, or to hear a piece of music that the last time you heard it, it fell on deaf ears and didn't mean anything. This time, all of a sudden you've got chills up and down your spine. It's a gift; it just happens, you don't choose it. That's what loving God is like; that's why it's got to be grace, so the key task of faith, the key task of Christian belief, is to pray for grace because, of course, you can't pray without believing in the one you're praying to. Thus, by praying for grace, you receive grace that strengthens you in love, that pulls you closer to God, it gets you along this journey. You can imagine how a monk's whole life is structured in this way. *charity*

This love for God, I'll mention, is obedience to the great law of God, the great law that Christ summarizes in two commandments, "Love God with your whole heart, mind, and strength, and your neighbor as yourself." That's the love that pulls you along toward your goal of seeing God. There's this kind of "order of salvation," it's called, an order of salvation in Augustine. You start with faith, believe in what you're told, you pray for grace, that leads to love, that leads ultimately to happiness—the ultimate happiness of seeing God—so, you go from faith, to love, to ultimate happiness.

Then comes a crucial moment that not all medieval theologians agreed with, but Augustine came to the conclusion that even the initial faith is a gift of God. Even the initial choice to believe in God is a choice that's impossible without God's grace helping you; Augustine insists this is very important, that grace and free will are compatible. God's grace never takes away your free will. It helps your free will; it gives you what your free will is ultimately most longing for. But it does mean that free will by itself is not enough. Augustine is what the philosophers call a "compatibilist"; he believes that God's grace, or even God's determining what you're going to choose, is compatible with your free will. God will give you the gift of faith, and you get the gift of faith. You believe because God chose to give you that gift, and he gives you that gift and you have that

longing for

gift; you have faith because God chose to give you that gift. That doesn't take away your free will, says Augustine.

Not everyone agrees about that. Some people feel very threatened by this. Lots of medieval theologians said: "Wait a minute, it can't be that simple," or "Maybe it's got to be more simple than that. Maybe our free will needs to be free from grace in order to choose for God." That's a road that Luther will firmly reject. Luther is a very big grace guy and doesn't really have much use for free will. We'll talk about how that issue arises too, and how that plays out in the Middle Ages.

One more issue now about grace and free will. For Augustine, one of the reasons why we have to have free will is because we have to have merit. Only what we do by our own free will deserves praise or blame, condemnation or reward. If we don't do something of our own free will, we can't be blamed for it, and we also can't be rewarded for it, and Augustine does believe that we merit some reward. There are all sorts of language of reward in the Bible, after all, that we are in charge according to our works and rewarded according to our works. Augustine takes that quite straightforwardly. We do earn reward.

This earning of reward—this merit—is entirely by grace, Augustine will say. Any merit we have is by grace because you get merit by loving God and doing works of love, and since the love that we have for God is a gift of grace, all of our merit, which comes from this love, comes from God's grace. There's no merit apart from grace for Augustine, and that's a crucial principle for most medieval theology and certainly for Luther, although in fact what Luther will do is say, "We don't have merit at all," and Protestants are more or less allergic to the term "merit."

Let me say a little bit in its favor before I go on because we're going to hear a lot against it. What Augustine is thinking is as you get closer to God along this long journey, becoming fuller and fuller of the love of God—because that's how you become closer to God—you don't become physically closer (everywhere in the physical world is close to God), it's by loving God more and more that we become more like God and, therefore, closer to God. The deeper, the more ardent our love is, the more we are like God, the closer we are to God, and the more worthy we are of being with God. That's where merit comes in. To get closer to God is to be more worthy of God.

worthy

fit

Shouldn't it be so? As our love gets deeper, don't we in fact become better people? Shouldn't that be what's happening?

That's what merit is; it means that as we're on this journey toward God, we're on this journey home. When we get home, that's where we belong. We deserve to be there. We wouldn't be there if we didn't deserve to be there. We're now fit and worthy of the place we come to, this place called "heaven," which is really the place where we see God. That's the notion of merit. It's not some awful notion about earning brownie points. It can degenerate into that, but it's not that way in Augustine, it's not that way in the best medieval theologians. We'll get to that merit in a minute. I want to talk about why Protestants became allergic to the notion of merit, but to set up that contrast between Protestants and Catholics on merit, let me read you one more Augustinian Catholic in the Middle Ages, a man named Anselm, writing in the 12th century, but very much a representative of this Augustinian paradigm at its best.

He writes a treatise that begins with a prayer, and let me read you from this prayer. This will give you a wonderful example of Augustinian spirituality. Anselm says in his prayer:

> What shall I do, O Lord most high, what shall this exile do, so far from Thee? What shall Thy servant do, tormented by love for Thee, and cast so far from Thy face? I pant to see Thee, and Thy face is too far from me. I long to come to Thee, and Thy dwelling-place is inaccessible...I desire to seek Thee and do not know Thy face. Lord, Thou art my God, Thou art my Lord, and never have I seen Thee. It is Thou that hast made me...and yet I do not know Thee. I was created to see Thee, and I have yet done that for which I was created.

> O miserable condition of humanity, who have lost that for which we were made! ...We have lost the blessedness for which we were made, and found the misery for which we were not made. ...Humanity did once eat the bread of angels...now it is the bread of sorrow...O the universal lamentation of the children of Adam. He was filled with abundance, we sigh with hunger. He had plenty, we beg and pray. He possessed happiness and abandoned it, we suffer need and unhappiness, and feel a miserable longing, and

tree of life

remain empty…How miserable! Think what we have lost, being driven from paradise [That's original sin; this loss of our fellowship with God and all the rest of our lives is an attempt to get back to what we've lost, to get back home.] …cast out from our homeland into exile, from the vision of God into blindness…Look with grace upon us, O Lord [Anselm resumes]…take pity upon us as we strive after Thee, for without Thee we can do nothing [That's the doctrine of grace.]…O come help us Lord [the help of grace]…O Lord I am bent down, looking only earthward; O raise me up, so I might turn my gaze upward…and see Thee. Let me look up at Thy light…Teach me how to seek Thee, and show Thyself gracious to me when I seek, for I cannot seek Thee unless Thou teach me to seek, nor find Thee unless Thou show Thyself. Let me seek Thee by longing for Thee, and long for Thee as I seek; and let me find Thee by loving Thee, and let me love Thee when I find Thee.

Notice how this prayer works. Anselm is not afraid of hell. He's dealing with the misery of his present life far from God. That's the problem he has, not how to escape going to hell, but how do I get out of my current misery, my farness from God. I'm so far away from God, I'm an exile. How do I get home? The keynote here is not fear, but longing, desire. What he's afraid of is where he is right now in the misery of this earthly life—now contrasted different, a paradigm for the end of our lives. This is a paradigm shared by Luther and Calvin, the two great Protestant Reformers. I'll give you a version from both.

Here's Luther. He says (I'm paraphrasing here) suppose we take St. Peter or St. Paul, and they're doing some good work like preaching or praying. If it's really a good work, faultless, without any sin, then they should be able to stand with due humility before God himself in judgment and say something like this:

Lord God, behold this good work, which I have done—with the help of Your grace. [It's Augustinian there.] There is in it neither fault nor sin, nor does it need Your forgiveness or mercy. I'm not asking for forgiveness or mercy, for I want you to judge it with Your strictest, truest Judgment. I can glory in this good work before you, because You can't condemn it, for You are Just and True. Indeed, I'm certain that You cannot condemn it without denying yourself [as Truth]. There is no need here for mercy, such as we pray for in the Lord's Prayer (when we say, "Forgive us our trespasses"), for all that's needed here is justice to crown and reward this good deed of mine.

Luther concludes, "Latimus, doesn't this make you shudder and break out in a cold sweat?"

Latimus is the guy he's writing against. Do you really want to go in front of the judgment, in front of God, and talk like that? That's crazy. You can't earn God's respect like that; you can only come before God as a sinner. *as a saint*

Here's Calvin. Calvin says if we're going to understand the doctrine of justification, we have to lift up our minds to God's judgment seat that we may be firmly convinced of his pre-justification. Indeed, one can see how there's no one more confidently, as they say boisterously chattered, over the righteousness of good works than are they who are the worst sinners. That happened because they do not think about God's justice, which they would never take so lightly if they were affected by even the slightest feeling for it. We surely are undervaluing the justice of God if we don't realize that it's so perfect that it can admit nothing that is not whole, and complete, and undefiled by any corruption whatsoever. That's not the sort of thing that's found in any man and never will be. It's this we have to inquire about, he continues elsewhere, what continence can we bring to our defense before the judgment seat of God, not what we can talk about in the schools on the corners.

"Let's get serious," Calvin is saying, "You're going to face God, you're going to say that you merit and you deserve God's goodness and God's favor as if you've earned salvation, in front of the judgment seat of God? That's crazy; nobody would say that." See the difference. They're both Augustinian, both Anselm on one hand and Luther and Calvin on the other hand. They both believe in the doctrine of grace. But Luther and Calvin are rejecting the notion of merit. Luther and Calvin are rejecting the notion that we can stand before God having earned a reward. They've got a different paradigm at this point. The journey paradigm drops off because when you get home, you have to face judgment. That metaphor of facing God's judgment is not there in Anselm's prayer. Anselm believes in the judgment of God, but it's not at the center of his imagination, his theological imagination, the way it is for Luther and Calvin. Facing the judgment of God is what it's all about.

What's happened between Anselm and Luther and Calvin is the development of the late medieval conscience; something has happened. Anselm is early in the Middle Ages. What's happened in between Anselm and Luther and Calvin is the medieval conscience, the conscience that is concerned about the judgment of God. "Conscience" is an interesting word, actually. It originally meant someone who is in on a secret with you, literally someone who knows something with you, *conscientia*. You see the word "science" is in the word "conscience"; science means knowledge, so a *consciuse* in Latin was someone who knew with you some secret. Suppose you had committed a crime, you had an accomplice; he knows what you've done, and he can be a witness against you at a trial.

The "conscience" eventually came to mean the inner witness inside you who knows what you've done, who will bear witness against you in the judgment throne of God. Conscience is your awareness of where you stand before God, your awareness that you're a sinner, that you've got something in your own memory that will testify against you, in front of the judgment in front of God, and that's why, for Luther in particular, conscience doesn't feel guilty. I don't think Luther ever felt guilty in this life, this sense of "I'm a failure, I haven't done the right thing." It's terror. Luther speaks of the terrified conscience, the terror of facing the wrath of God and facing that judgment, that scenario where you're facing the judgment throne of God, which is so central, this scenario of conscience, and that has developed in the way that didn't happen for Anselm.

What happened in between, what made the difference, is the practice of private confession in the Middle Ages, the penitential practices of the sacrament of penance, where you go to private confession and you probe the inmost secrets of your heart and find if there's anything in your heart and memory that is offensive to God. You're probing your conscience and trying to find if there's this sin, whether you've hated your neighbor in your heart, whether you've done anything wrong that could be a cause of condemnation of front of the judgment throne of God. This is a deepening sense of "inwardness" that drives medieval piety; you're searching the depths of your heart.

It's not just outer worl
somebody; it's whether yo

You have these convers
whom you confess, and w
kind of questions are they
confess? To probe thei
questions like this, imagir
hear this kind of questior
alms, and religious acti
impress others than to ple
or other creatures more
Scripture, the sacraments,
first commandment. "F
goodness when you lost
because of bad weather, _____,

It's the art of dying well; that's th
books written with that title in
dying. You're about to die, a
will picture you being sur
conscience saying, "Di
sin there. Why don't
hell." It's understo
life is put to th
they're goin
here, the C
is not i
Yo

friend?" That's a sin against the second commandment. "Have you
skipped Mass on Sundays and holidays without a good excuse?"
That's a sin against the third commandment. "Have you insulted or
cursed your parents, forgotten them in their old age, wished them
dead? Have you insulted, cursed, or wished a clergy dead? Have you
failed to offer prayers, give alms, and endow Masses for people who
have departed?" These are sins against the fourth commandment.
There's a long litany of questions that can drive you increasingly to
anxiety and fear. Each one of these sins can get you in hell, and
you've got to make sure that you root them out of your heart, or else
you're going to die in a state of mortal sin rather than a state of
grace, and then there's no help for you.

One medieval penitent, a woman named Margery Kempe, who wrote
an autobiography about this, describes how, when she tried to bring a
secret sin to her confessor he started berating her, terrifying her, and
she literally went crazy. She had apparitions of demons and she was
tormented for a year until finally she had a vision of Jesus, who
comforted her and said "Daughter, I want you to know that Master
Robert, your confessor [she had a new confessor by this time],
pleases me very much when he assures you that I love you." That's
what Luther calls the Gospel. Think about this focal point of
medieval piety, late medieval piety, which is now a different sort of
piety from that Augustinian paradigm that we ran into in Anselm.

...e center of it. There are actually ...the late medieval history, the art of ...d these manuals about the art of dying ...ounded by demons who are probing your ... you do this or that? You have some mortal ...you despair and curse God and come with me to ...od that in the moment of death, everything in your ...e test, and the devils are going to be tempting you, ...g to be assaulting you. Luther used the word *Anfechtung* ...German word for "assault." The devils assault you, and this ...st Luther, this is late medieval piety all around.

...u're lying on your deathbed, and there are woodcuts of this, these ...devils are probing your conscience and trying to get you to despair of the mercy of God. You know you're about to face that judgment, and do you really have the grace you need? Have you really lived well enough? Have you really merited? At that moment, any ordinary medieval priest will give you the advice: "Don't trust in your good works; trust in Christ alone." That's advice that was there before Luther. Don't trust in your good works, they're not good enough; just trust in Christ alone. That's what you've got to trust in at the moment of death. That's the only thing that is strong enough, that's good enough to get you through the terrible trial of death. That's the matrix for Luther's theology, the late medieval matrix. It's the moment of death, where your conscience is at its most terrified, its most anxious. It's wondering, "What can I hang onto? Where can I turn?"

Let me mention one particularly terrifying thing. There's nothing worse than sudden death because you want to be able to confess your sins before you die, so if you have any of those mortal sins that will condemn you to hell, you can get rid of them by confessing them and receiving forgiveness. Sudden death is awful because here you are maybe harboring resentment of your parents or hatred for the clergy in your heart, and you haven't had a chance to confess your sins, and then you die. Suddenly someone stabs you in the back, or a thunderbolt comes from heaven and kills you, and you've got this mortal sin; you haven't had a chance to cleanse your soul. You haven't had a chance to get to a state of grace, and now there's no help for you. No matter how many Masses they say, you're toast. It's gone.

There's this anxiety, this uncertainty. How do I know I'm in a state of grace? And, especially, what am I going to do if I suddenly die? Luther's Gospel addresses that anxiety in a powerful way because Luther himself felt it in a powerful way, as we'll begin to discover as we acquaint ourselves with the life of Martin Luther, beginning in the next lecture.

Lecture Four
Young Luther Against Himself

Scope:

Against his father's wishes, young Martin Luther became a monk, seeking to give all his love to God and, thereby, become righteous in God's sight. But that very seeking comes to look to him like a damnable form of self-love. As he works out his doctrine of justification in his early lectures as a Bible professor, he concludes that the only way to become truly righteous is to hate oneself and wish to be damned, agreeing with the righteous God who hates sinners and damns them. Not surprisingly, this early doctrine appears to lead young Luther to experiences of deep terror, as well as hatred of God. From this terror of conscience only the Gospel can rescue him.

Outline

I. In the late Middle Ages, the Augustinian picture of life as a journey of love toward God gave way before the fear of facing God and his judgment, inculcated by the practice of confession.

   A. Private confession could be a terrifying experience, as priests led penitents to probe their hearts and consciences for sins that could get them damned.

   B. Sudden death (for instance, in a thunderstorm) was especially feared because it left no time for repentance.

II. Why did the young man Luther become a monk?

   A. Caught in a thunderstorm, he prayed for help to Saint Anne and promised to become a monk.

   1. For Luther, the most fearsome possibility was to die in a state of mortal sin, which meant eternal damnation.

   2. To face death is to deal with the uncertainty of whether one is in a state of grace or a state of mortal sin, an uncertainty Luther later identified with the experience of purgatory.

   3. This state of fear and uncertainty seems to have been a fundamental experience of Luther's life throughout his time as a monk and beyond.

B. Becoming a monk did not solve Luther's problem of terror and uncertainty in the face of God.

    1. Becoming a monk displeased his father, a hard-working businessman who expected his son to go to law school and earn worldly success.

    2. A fundamental aim of monasticism is to give up one's own will (by a vow of obedience to one's superiors), yet Luther came to regard his entering the monastery as itself a willful act of disobedience to his father and, therefore, to God.

    3. Luther went on to get a master's degree and a doctorate in theology and became a priest.

III. Luther's early doctrine of justification was a form of self-torture or torment of conscience.

  A. We have manuscripts of Luther's lectures on Paul's letter to the Romans from when he was a little-known monk teaching Bible courses at the University of Wittenberg in 1513–1516, working out a distinctive doctrine of justification that is not yet that of the mature reformer.

  B. The problem was how to come to love God.

    1. The state of grace desired in Augustinian spirituality was a state of charity, pure love of God for God's own sake.

    2. Luther's early theology was also indebted to Bernard of Clairvaux, the great 12th-century monastic writer who traced how we move from self-love to love of God for his own sake.

    3. But young Luther made this problem intractable, because he argued that the sinful heart is inherently "curved in on itself," seeking only itself in all things, so that every desire for good things (even blessedness and salvation) became evil.

    4. The only remedy for this evil self-love is self-hatred, which thus becomes the essential road to salvation.

  C. The search for grace in Luther's early theology was never-ending.

    1. In Augustine's *On the Spirit and the Letter*, which was extremely influential on Luther, the grace of God operates deep within the human heart, turning it from an outward obedience out of fear to an inward obedience out of love.

2. We are to seek grace by prayer and, the later Middle Ages added, acts of penance and confession.

3. The late-medieval theology in which Luther was trained taught that we must do our best to love God by our own natural powers, eliciting love for God by a sheer act of will so as to earn God's grace through "the merit of congruity."

4. But Luther, who always insisted that it was presumptuous for a man to claim any merit before, thought we must never believe we truly love God.

5. As a result, in his early theology, the whole life of a Christian is spent seeking grace but not finding it.

D. Luther's early doctrine of justification centered on self-accusation and self-hatred.

1. Young Luther taught that the just man always accuses himself.

2. Luther tried to deepen self-accusation into self-hatred and even the desire to be damned, because we are to please God by confessing that his judgment against our sins is true. To love God is to hate yourself.

3. Justification is, thus, hidden under its opposite: By agreeing with God's wrath against us and feeling it in our hearts, we justify him and he justifies us.

4. The problem was that this led to deeper fear of God rather than greater love for Him, thus setting up a vicious cycle of fear, resentment, and despair, leading to anger and hatred of God.

IV. What Luther's early theology was missing was the Gospel as God's kind word of promise.

A. Some Protestant scholars admire Luther's emphasis on pure, unselfish love.

B. Others focus on early Luther's "theology of the cross" (1518), in which God can be found only in suffering.

1. Luther spoke of finding God hidden under the opposite. For example, you find the grace of God hidden under an accusation; you find the love of God in hatred of self.

    2. Thus, the "theology of the cross" meant: All good things were found under an evil exterior.

C. The key insight of Luther's so-called "tower experience," concerning the righteousness or justice of God, was already present in this early theology.

    1. In this experience, Luther realized that the righteousness or justice of God is not the justice by which God punishes sins but the justice by which he makes us just.

    2. But the way God makes us just, according to the early Luther, is by getting us to agree when he accuses and condemns us.

D. Likewise, Luther's early theology already included the doctrine that justification is by faith alone. However, it is not justification by believing in the promise of the Gospel—as in Luther's mature theology—but by believing that God is true in judging and condemning us.

E. The mature Luther, the one who changed the world, emerges only when he learns to distinguish between Law and Gospel, the word that accuses and the word that is kind and gracious.

Essential Reading:

Bainton, *Here I Stand*, chapters 1–2.

Luther, "Lectures on Romans," in *Luther's Works*, vol. 25, esp. pp. 151–154, 197–206, 210–222, 237–248, 379–384.

Supplemental Reading:

Augustine, *On the Spirit and the Letter*, in *Later Works*, chapters 1–32.

Bernard of Clairvaux, "On Loving God," in *Selected Works*.

Questions to Consider:

1. What do you suppose would have become of Luther had he not been caught in the sudden thunderstorm and bargained with Saint Anne to save him?

2. What are some of the defining moments in Luther's spiritual life thus far?

Lecture Four—Transcript
Young Luther Against Himself

We were talking in the last lecture about the art of dying well, of how to face death in the late Middle Ages, when you've got a serious worry about God's judgment, and contrasting that with the earlier medieval piety that I called the Augustinian paradigm of spirituality, where life is a journey and you're getting better all the time, and eventually you get home and you belong there, you actually deserve to be there.

That journey metaphor is, in one way, less personal then his terror of facing God, which I've suggested to you (in the very first lecture) was a little bit like a little kid opening the door to his father's study or her father's study and having to face the judgment of his or her father when he or she has done something awful. It's very personal. What will you hear from this person who matters the most to you in the world? Suppose this father is God. What will you hear? What will you say? How can you possibly be justified in God sight? That is really an overriding concern of late medieval piety, and it really gives you a different paradigm for spirituality than this journey metaphor.

Let's think about this new paradigm, this paradigm that I associated with the late medieval conscience, and the practice of penance and confession, where you're exploring what's in your heart, and you're worried that what's in your heart is going to get you damned, that what's in your heart is something God will see and be offended at. The terror of this is literally cultivated in the spiritual practice of confession; you learn to be terrified in this way. People aren't born with this kind of terrified conscience; you learn it by going to a confessor who helps you probe deep into your heart to find things that offend God, and if that's not bad enough, there's something that's even worse we mentioned, and that's the terror of sudden death, when you don't have the chance to explore what's in your conscience and your heart, and you might discover after dying that you were a mortal sinner. You had a sin that was so offensive to God that you are in hell, and you can never get out.

Sudden death is the most terrifying thing of all for a late medieval person. That's why the late medieval folk were terrified, especially of thunderstorms. Being in a thunderstorm was a little bit like the way it would feel to us to have a gun put to your head. Imagine this, you've got a gun facing your head. Within one second or two seconds, you might be dead. That's what it felt like being in a thunderstorm; God is hurling these things from heaven, these lightning bolts, and in the next moment you may not have another breath to your name. You may be facing the judgment of God, and you may be a mortal sinner, and you may be past hope. What do you do?

A young man named Martin Luther, early in the 16th century, was caught in a thunderstorm. He was on his way to his second semester of law school; he was going to become a lawyer and make some good money. His father wanted that. He was going to be an obedient son, but he was caught in a thunderstorm, caught in that moment of terror, the possibility of sudden death, the gun pointed at his head. What can you do? You don't have time to confess your sins. You may have mortal sin in your soul, not being in a state of grace, and you will be utterly helpless to do anything about it. What can you do? What young Luther did is he prayed, "Saint Anne help me! I will become a monk." It's a famous vow; these are the first words we know of from Luther's lips, "Saint Anne, help me! I will become a monk." He recalls this many years later.

Why Saint Anne? Why not God? Saint Anne is a patron saint, and a patron saint is someone in medieval Catholicism who might be an intermediary between you and God. You go to a patron saint the way you would go to someone who has some pull at City Hall and you need a favor from the mayor. You go to someone who's connected with the mayor, and he gets some pull, and he helps you get what you need, and then you owe him a favor. He prays to Saint Anne to be his patron—he says, "Help me, I'm helpless, I can't do anything about my state of sin. If I die this moment, I'm going to hell. Please, put in a good word with God so the thunderbolts don't strike me." And then, of course, he owes the patron saint a favor. And that's why he says, "I'll become a monk; I'll make it up to you."

Think of that—the facing of death and the desperate search for something to hang onto, and the desperate uncertainty about whether it's going to do any good. Years later, his father, who is mightily displeased about this, says: "This vow of yours, I hope it wasn't just an illusion." After all, his father reminds him, you are supposed to obey your father and your mother, and honor your father and your

mother; that's what the command says. The command of God, Luther is thinking, is certain; this prayer to Saint Anne, that's not so certain. That's what his father reminded him of. His father was displeased; he wanted a son who would go to law school and make some money and get married and give him grandchildren. Luther entered the monastery against his father's wishes.

He entered the monastery, he later thought willfully, in disobedience to God, who commanded him to honor his father and his mother, so it turns out becoming a monk didn't really solve his problem. It didn't solve this problem of terror and uncertainty in the face of the judgment of God. First of all, it was against his father's will. Let me say a little bit about his father. His father is the son of a peasant; he's a social climber; he's working really, really hard. He can't inherit the family's property, so he goes off because he's not the younger son. He's the inherited son in this setup, so he leaves the farm and he gets involved in mining, which is a booming operation at this period in German history. He eventually becomes a mine operator and owner. He makes a decent living by working very hard, and he wants his son to go further than he does.

He sends his son to the university. He didn't get a university education, Hans Luther didn't, but Hans Luther's son Martin is going to get a university education and go to law school. Except then he becomes a monk; that spoils everything. What's happening here in Martin's standpoint is he is becoming a monk against his father's will, and this spoils everything because the whole purpose of monasticism for Luther is to give up your will. That's why you have this vow of obedience that I mentioned in the second lecture. You give up your will to your superior so that everything you do is out of obedience and not out of your own self-will. And here, Luther enters monasticism out of his own self-will.

Luther, in fact (we discovered in his later writings), really wants to get rid of self-will in a deep way. It turns out Luther not only becomes a monk, he becomes a priest, he has this clash with his father about the Ten Commandments when he's saying his first Mass; then, he goes on and he gets a master's degree and a doctorate in theology. He becomes a professor of Bible at the University of Wittenberg, and we have some of his early lectures on Paul's letter to the Romans, where he focuses on getting rid of this self-will. It's almost as if Luther just wants to get rid of his will altogether. Luther would be happiest if he was just listening to music and floating on the joy of good music; we'll see this later. But instead, he's trying his hardest to work to earn grace. There's a real problem here.

Let me say a little bit about these lectures on Romans, which we have manuscripts of from 1516. He didn't publish them, but he wrote them out, and we have these things now, and they're published in German and English. Remember—let's think about the Augustinian paradigm that he's working within here. You want to be in a state of grace rather than a state of mortal sin. A state of grace is a state of love for God, pure love of God for his own sake. There's the worry about willfulness, we'll see, and what happens is Luther wants to go from a kind of progress, where you start out loving God for your sake because you want something from God, and then you move to loving God for God's sake, loving God not for selfish reasons, not for what you can get from God, but for God's own sake. Eventually you love yourself only for God's sake, so you're loving yourself for your own sake, then you move to loving God for your own sake, then you move to loving God for God's sake, then you eventually even love yourself only for the sake of God.

This is a progression in the writing of a monastic writer Bernard of Clairvaux, writing in the 12th century, much admired by Luther, so he's trying to progress to the stage where his love for God becomes less and less selfish, less and less self-willed, less and less "curved in on itself." This is a term that Luther uses in these lectures. He's worried about how even when we seek God, we seek God for our sake, for what we can get out of it. This love is "curved in on itself"; we now say "selfish." That's a word that was invented after Luther, and Luther didn't have that word, so he talks about being "curved in on yourself." Because we're curved in on ourselves, because we're always seeking ourselves, even when we seek God we're really seeking God for ourselves—then everything that God does that's good becomes evil for us

Let me read to you from the lectures, and we'll get a good dose of what's going on in Luther's thinking in 1516; this is before he becomes a Reformer, before he publishes anything. This is before he discovered the Gospel, and I'll talk about why. Maybe you'll hear it as you hear. Here's Luther lecturing in 1516:

> For even though [God created] all things very good [this is what Genesis says], yet they are not good for us; and even if

> there were no things which were in any way evil, yet everything is evil for us...because we have sin [in our hearts]. So it is necessary to flee the good things and take on evil things. And we must do this not only with our voice and with a deceitful heart [saying it without really meaning it] but with our whole mind we must confess and wish that we might be damned and destroyed.

He means that you're supposed to wish to be damned. This is at the heart of his spirituality.

Let's read on:

> For we must act toward ourselves...in the same way that a man does who hates another man. For he does not hate him in imagination, but...sincerely desires to destroy and kill and damn the person whom he hates. Therefore if we so sincerely want to destroy ourselves that we offer ourselves to hell for the sake of God and His righteousness, we have already made true satisfaction to his righteousness, and He will be merciful and free us.

We're going to have to unpack the statement. Luther is saying that if you hate yourself enough, God will save you. That's how you save yourself, salvation by self-hatred. Many scholars have called this Luther's early theology of humiliation. I think it's just masochistic and horrifying.

There are some scholars who actually like the stuff; I don't understand why. It's this desire to be unselfish cranked up to such a level that you shouldn't even want anything good, which I think is crazy. If you're so unselfish that you don't want anything good, then you're insane, and you can't make any sane decision in your life. So why did he get to this point of thinking that the way to please God is to hate yourself, to indeed sincerely desire to be damned? That's the spiritual achievement that young Luther's trying to get to in 1516. That's the pinnacle of spiritual maturity.

Why in the world would he think this? Let's think about the search for grace in the Augustinian paradigm and how it might go wrong when it's combined with the late medieval penitential ethic of confession and probing your conscience. We go to Augustine again in the treatise *On the Spirit and the Letter* he writes, which is very extremely influential on Luther, and the grace of God is what inwardly turns the human heart from a mere outward obedience to God out of fear to an inward obedience out of love. Instead of just being afraid of God and doing what we're told because we're afraid of hell, we love God for his own sake. Grace causes us to delight in God. We seek this grace by prayer. In faith we pray for more grace. In the later Middle Ages, this prayer involved lots of penance, confession, accusing yourself of being a terrible sinner.

Penitential works come along with prayer as a way of seeking grace. You seek a state of grace by confessing what a sinner you are so that God will forgive you and give you grace, so penitential works come alongside this prayer for grace in Augustine and become a way of seeking grace. So, what you're doing is you're seeking grace by works, and this becomes the key to what Luther rejects in late medieval Catholicism—trying to do good works, penitential works, in order to seek grace, as if good works came before the gift of grace, which is not how Augustine thought about it, but it was how some late medieval theologians thought about it. Luther used Augustine against them.

Here's how the late medieval theology in which Luther was trained does this. What you're supposed to do is by prayer, penitence, fasting, and going to confession and accusing yourself, you're supposed to elicit an act of loving God above all things by your own natural powers (it's a technical term from the Middle Ages)—that is, you're supposed to, just by sheer force of will, make yourself love God more than anything else. You have to do the best you can; you have to do what is in you to love God above everything else. Even without grace, you can do the best you can; you can fight as hard as you can to love God, and then, these medieval theologians said (late medieval theologians): "God won't deny grace to someone who's doing the best that is in him, and then God will give you grace."

So, first, you have to work as hard as you can to love God with your whole heart, mind, and soul, and then God will give you the grace to really like loving God and delight in loving God, and to love God as if you really liked him instead of just trying it. You know what it's like to just try to love someone; it doesn't work. You need this delight, like when you listen to a piece of music and it washes you over with delight and gladness. Loving someone just by sheer force of will, you can do that in order to do outward works and help someone, but you can't just love someone by willing it. Luther found this a deep problem, but he was supposed to. He was trying to work to love God above all things so that God would give him grace, and he did so by confession, by penitence.

What that means is that because you're not ever supposed to believe that you have grace, you're always supposed be confessing your sins, always supposed to be seeing yourself as a sinner, you can never get to the point where you can relax and say, "The love of God is in me; I'm in a state of grace." Your whole life is going to be, and I'm quoting from Luther now:

> ...nothing else but prayer [for grace], seeking, and begging by the sighing of the heart, the voice of their works, and the labor of their bodies, always seeking and striving to be made righteous, even to the hour of death, never standing still, never possessing, never in any work putting an end to the achievement of righteousness, but always awaiting it as something which still dwells beyond them, and always as people who still live and exist in their sins.

That's how holy people behave, Luther thinks, always seeking grace, never finding it. You're not supposed to believe you've found it. It's wrong to believe you've found grace because that's presumptuous. That's like standing for God and saying, "See what a state of grace I'm in. I'm doing all these good works out of the love of God, thanks to your grace, and now you've got to reward me." Luther doesn't want to be in that position; he's terrified of being in that position. You can't possibly do that; that would be dreadful, so you have to believe that you're never in a state of grace, that you're always a sinner, that you will always deserve God's damnation.

If you want to help yourself realize that, just do that counterfactual test that I mentioned from Augustine. Suppose you're a penitential monk engaged in all these penitential acts—accusing yourself, fasting, praying. It's a lot of hard work; you're seeking justification, and it's so tiring, it's so exhausting, and you hate it. You'd rather be doing anything else in the world than what you're doing. That shows that you're mumbling against God, that in fact you resent God, rather than love God. Now you've got it; now you've got a sin to confess. Keep on that track. Keep on noticing how you hate God, how you really resent doing this stuff, and now you've got something to confess. Now you can really accuse yourself, see what a sinner you are, and come to realize that you deserve to be damned and really embrace that damnation. Now you're getting somewhere.

Luther quotes a proverb in the Bible that says, in the Latin translation he uses, "The just man accuses himself." That's what justice is, Luther suggests. Justice is self-accusation. What is a just man? Someone who accuses himself. Why? Because he anticipates the judgment of God and condemns what God condemns—that is, himself, and therefore in all things agrees with God and his judgment. That's where you get onto this road to self-hatred. Luther's assuming that when you get to the judgment of God, God wants to condemn you, and the way to be justified before God is to agree with him in advance. "Yes, I deserve condemnation. Yes, I'm doing my utmost to confess my sins, to accuse myself, to blame myself, to just terrify myself with guilt so that I might agree with what God thinks about me because God damns sinners, and I'm a sinner so I ought to damn myself." This is agreeing with God.

He actually quotes a parable from Jesus in the Sermon on the Mount, where Jesus says, "You need to agree with your enemy before you get to court." Jesus is saying seek peace, seek reconciliation, don't go to court with your enemy, give in and admit you're wrong, and then you don't have to go to court and fight with your enemy. You're supposed to love your enemy, but Luther interprets this to mean that your enemy is God. God is your cosmic enemy, and you need to agree with him before you get to the judgment day; that is, you need to condemn yourself, accuse yourself, damn yourself, and that's how you become a just and righteous person. A just man accuses himself.

In a nutshell, he says to love God is to hate yourself. True love of God is hating yourself. Why? Because God means to damn sinners. That's God's fundamental will towards you, and you ought to agree with it. That's how you end up becoming like God, is by hating yourself just as God hates you. This is awful stuff. I can't see why any scholar would find anything redeeming in this stuff, a kind of hopeful masochism, and you can see how profoundly self-defeating this would be, how profoundly self-undermining, a kind of vicious circle.

Think about how it goes. You're supposed to love God with your whole heart, mind, and strength with a kind of delight, says

Augustine, longing for God, delighting in God, looking forward to seeing God with your whole heart. You're not supposed to love God out of fear; that's precisely the motive you're not supposed to have because that means you resent God, you're behaving like a slave who outwardly obeys his master and inwardly resents his master. You want an inner delight; way from deep within, you need to delight in God, like a son who loves his father, not like a slave who is knuckling under resentfully and obeying only outwardly and not in his heart, so you don't want fear, you want love.

How do you build up this love for God, rather than fear? By hating yourself, by accusing yourself, by looking at your sins and constantly reminding yourself what a terrible sinner you are, how you deserve God's wrath, how you love God by saying what God says about you, which is by hating yourself, and that's, of course, what that does is it makes you terrified. If you were to follow this out, constantly looking at the sin in you, at the "bottomless iniquity of your heart," as Luther puts it, you would only grow more and more terrified, more and more resentful of how God is bearing down on you and means to destroy you, and it's your job to agree with that, to say, "Yes God, you're right. I should be damned. I want to be damned. I really want to be damned. If I only want to be damned hard enough, then you'll love me, right?" Imagine how much someone like that hates God.

His confessor at the time it turns out is a man named Staupitz, who says, "Martin, you say that God is angry at you, but you're the one who's angry at God. Your problem is not that God's angry at you, but that you're angry at God." You can easily see how that might be. You must be furious at God and terrified of him, and it must just get worse, this practice of constantly trying to find all of the evil in yourself and to hate yourself can only make it worse, because you're not meant—we're not made—to hate ourselves. We're not made to love evil things for ourselves rather than good.

We are not made to be unselfish in such a deep way that we don't even want good for ourselves. The Augustinian paradigm is right about this; what we want in our deepest way, in the deepest depths of our hearts, is the ultimate good, is God. We want good things, not bad things. To try to train yourself to want bad things, to hate yourself, doesn't work. It goes against the very grain of our souls in the way God made us, so I think, and so does Luther at the end of the day. But right now, here in 1516, he's trying to justify himself by self-hatred. Why? What's going on here?

I think there's one more missing piece to the puzzle. He believes at this point that faith means faith in God's Word (we'll see that this is, of course, always true for Luther); faith means believing what you're told when God speaks to you and God's Word, but he doesn't have the notion of the Gospel as a gracious, kind promise. He's thinking that the word of God is a word of condemnation, a word of accusation. He's supposed to agree with his enemy, who is God, but what his enemy is saying is: "You damn sinner, you go to hell." That's what he's supposed to agree with; that's the word that he's supposed to have faith in. In fact, he'll talk about being justified by faith alone in these lectures, but he means faith in this word of accusation.

Here's another quotation from the Roman lectures in 1516; this is about the word of God now. Think of how different this is from the Gospel that we spoke of earlier: "The word of God," says Luther "as often as it comes [to us] comes in a form contrary to our own thinking, which seems in its own opinion to have the truth [we always think that we're right], so our own thinking judges the Word which is contrary to it as a lie." We're constantly talking back to God; we're saying, "God, you're wrong, I'm right"; we always disagree with God's Word, Luther thinks. "And so much so that Christ called his word our enemy in the Sermon on the Mount, telling us we must 'agree with our accuser before we get to court.' " Luther is applying this to the word of God, which is a word (he thinks) of accusation. God is our enemy; he's accusing us; we have to agree. That's why we have to try to damn ourselves; the just man is the one who accuses himself, who agrees with God by sincerely hating himself and wanting to damn himself.

What's fascinating about this is that in Luther's early theology in 1516, he has a lot of the pieces of the puzzle that would become familiar from later Lutheran theology. Almost all the pieces of the puzzle are there, I think, except the notion of the Gospel, the notion of the Gospel as a promise, a gracious and kind word. That's why I tend to disagree with a great many scholars about how to read this document, Luther's lectures on Romans. There are some scholars who really think Luther is so great; he's pushing the issue of pure unselfishness. He's morally serious. He wants us to be unselfish. I've already suggested this seems to me to be a really bad idea.

We were meant to love good things, not bad things. We were meant to have a certain kind of self-loyalty to want good things for ourselves, rather than bad things. It doesn't work if you don't want good things for yourself. Augustine is right; the good thing we want most is God, for heaven's sakes. We ought to be terribly ambitious in the good things we want. I, myself, think that unselfishness is a really bad idea and, by the way, it seems to me there's nothing more selfish than the project of being unselfish. It's all about the self. Leave that stuff behind and try to learn to love people and forget about the self. But that's just me; if you really want to be unselfish, if you want to be systematically unselfish, Luther just might be your guide in these early writings, but I think it's crazy.

There's another bunch of theologians who focus on what they call Luther's "theology of the cross," a phrase that Luther uses in 1518, around about this time. It doesn't actually turn up a lot in later Luther. A lot of scholars are enamored of this. He talks about how God can only be found in suffering and on the cross. This is in 1518 that Luther is saying this. He talks about finding God hidden under the opposite. If you look for the grace of God; you find it in an accusation. If you look for the love of God; you find it in hatred of self. To love God is to hate yourself. All good things are found under an evil exterior, like the mercy of God is found under the cross of Christ.

This theme survives in later Luther, but it doesn't survive in quite the form that you have it in this early theology that I'm suggesting to you, where you find the grace of God under the accusation of God. I don't think that works. The cross of Christ is meant to be something gracious, not accusing, and Luther in his early writings finds the grace of God under the accusation. Christ is on the cross telling you what a sinner you are: "I have to die for you; look at what your sin does." Christ is an accuser. Christ calls his word "our enemy," Luther says. I don't think this is the key to Luther's love of the Gospel and to the Reformation.

There's another key element of Luther's later theology that's already present here, and that's, in fact, the notion of justification by faith alone. The phrase "justification by faith alone" turns up in these lectures, but—as I've suggested—it's justification by faith in this word of accusation. You're supposed to believe that God hates you, and the more sincerely and deeply you believe that, the more justified you are, so you're justified by faith alone, not in a Gospel promise, but in this accusation. You've got this key formula of the Lutheran Reformation, but you don't have the notion of the Gospel. That's what you need.

Another element in Luther's later theology is the notion of the righteousness of God. Let me say just a little bit about that; we're going to be running into it a lot. "Righteousness" in Latin, and in Greek. and in German is the same word as "justice." We get these two words in English, but in Luther it's the same word, so the righteousness of God is the justice of God. When Luther thinks about the righteousness or justice of God as a monk, he's thinking of God punishing us—God is just, he's a just judge; therefore, he has to punish us. Somewhere in the 1510s—maybe 1513, maybe 1516, maybe 1518—scholars disagree about this. Luther had what he calls a "tower experience," an experience in the tower. At least that's what it's called by scholars. I don't know if it's a definite experience at a definite date, but many scholars try to say that.

There's a kind of obsession with when does Luther have the Reformation discovery, when does he have this conversion experience? I'm not sure he does have such an experience. I think he's just a guy trying to figure stuff out, and the insights come at various times. But if there's one moment that makes all the difference, then it's a moment that Luther talks about late in his life, when he's sitting in the tower of the cloister, the monastery, maybe where the study is; it may also be where the bathroom is (one of the texts suggests he was sitting in the bathroom when this happened), and he has this insight about the righteousness of God.

The righteousness of God, the justice of God, is not justice by which God punishes sins, but the justice by which God makes us just. God is the source of all justice; he gives his justice to us; his justice means that we share in—and participate in—his justice, which makes us just. Luther loved this insight; he got his insight when he was probably just reading Augustine. It's right there in Augustine; it's not hard to find. It's a platonic insight, where the justice of God is the eternal form of justice, and we share in it, and so justice of God does not just punish us, it makes us just. That's a key insight in

Luther's doctrine of justification, but again—in 1516, in the Roman lectures—you become just by believing God's accusation.

I don't think you have the Luther who changed the world, the Luther who believes in the Gospel, until you recognize that the word that we believe in by faith alone—and are justified by faith alone—is a promise. It's a kind word; it's not God accusing us; it is God saying, "This is my body, it's given for you. Take, eat," or "I baptize you in the name of the Father, the Son, and the Holy Spirit." Luther thinks that that is God's Word. God is interested in saying kind things, and in making us glad, and giving us joy, and peace, and comfort—and until you get that note of comfort, and peace, and joy, I don't think you've got the Luther of the Gospel and the Luther of the Reformation.

Lecture Five

Hearing the Gospel

Scope:

For Luther the Gospel is a story that includes a divine promise of forgiveness, which forbids us from regarding ourselves as God's enemies. Instead of submitting to a judge who condemns, as in Luther's early theology, we must agree with a father who is kind and full of mercy. Though we remain unworthy sinners throughout our lives, the Gospel remains for us a word of comfort and joy, a promise of grace that gives what it promises to whoever believes it. As Luther describes it in his 1520 treatise *The Freedom of a Christian*, it is like a wedding vow that gives us a divine bridegroom, God's own son, together with all that is his: the righteousness of God, blessing, and eternal life. This modifies the Augustinian paradigm of spirituality, because Christ is not just the way, the road we take on our pilgrimage to God, but God coming to us and making himself ours.

Outline

I. The crucial proposal in the mature Luther's theology is to distinguish Gospel from Law.

  A. Gospel and Law are both God's Word but are two different genres with two different purposes and two different effects on those who believe them.

  B. The Law tells us what to do and, therefore, cannot save us (because our works can't save us).

   1. The Law is God's commandments, to which are attached threats and accusations.

   2. The Law's first purpose is its "civil use," which is to restrain evil outwardly by punishment and fear.

   3. The Law's second purpose is its "evangelical use," which is to humble, terrify, and spiritually "kill" the sinner; this is "evangelical" because it is the true preparation for the Gospel, a preparation performed by God, not us.

   4. In Luther's early theology, this spiritual humiliation is how we are justified, but the mature Luther gives an account of justification based on the Gospel instead.

C. Whereas Law is about what we do, Gospel is about what Christ does.

   1. The Gospel is not a technique for getting saved, because that is something we would have to do, and Law, not Gospel, is about what we have to do.

   2. The Gospel is not "practical" in the sense of giving us practical advice about how to apply God's Word to our lives, because that would be more talk about what we are to do.

   3. In another sense, the Gospel is profoundly practical (Luther thinks) because it changes us from the inside out.

D. The Gospel is not "mere words" but a word that changes those who believe it.

   1. The Gospel contains promises that give what is promised (for example, "This is my body, given for you.").

   2. Justification is by faith alone, apart from works, because you receive what is promised not by doing something about it but simply by believing it is true.

   3. The foundation of believers' confidence that they are justified is the certainty that God does not lie.

   4. Luther's famous motto, "Believe it and you have it," makes sense only if the object of belief is a promise.

   5. A more revealing motto is "The promise [of God] gives what the commandment requires."

   6. With this motto, Augustine's exhortation that we flee to grace by prayer mutates into Luther's preaching that we flee to grace by taking hold of God's promise.

II. Luther's mature doctrine, set forth in *Freedom of a Christian*, argues that God justifies us by giving us Christ in his promise.

   A. The Gospel is like a wedding vow in which Christ is the bridegroom giving himself to believers.

   B. But in receiving this bridegroom, believers also receive all that is his, including the divine attributes of righteousness, holiness, blessedness, and so on.

   C. The other side of the coin is that Christ the bridegroom receives all his beloved's debts, wounds, and sins, in what Luther calls a "blessed exchange."

D. On the cross, Christ fights what Luther calls a "mighty duel" and, by dying, defeats death.

E. Because the Gospel is a kind and comforting word, it also fills believers with comfort, good cheer, and gratitude, so that they are glad to love and obey God.

III. Luther's fixation on the Gospel has distinctive consequences for his view of God and humanity.

    A. The most scandalous consequences have to do with his profound insistence on human sinfulness.

        1. We're not ready for the Gospel until we give up all hope of justifying ourselves by works ("evangelical despair").

        2. Even believers remain sinners, unable to find any merit or justification in themselves apart from Christ: They are, thus, "at the same time righteous and sinners" (the phrase is extremely important and usually given in Latin: *simul justus et peccator*).

        3. Because all our righteousness comes by faith, all sin is unbelief.

        4. Believers who look away from Christ are prone to *Anfechtung*, temptation or spiritual assault, in which all one sees in oneself is sin and unbelief; the anxious conscience returns and fatal despair becomes a real possibility.

    B. Luther modifies the Augustinian paradigm of spirituality in other ways as well, which are subtle but profound.

        1. The spiritual life is less like a journey, because Christ is a gift we receive rather than a road we travel.

        2. Love for God is less like a longing and desire for our heavenly home and more like gladness and gratitude for a gift already received.

        3. The contemplative notion of seeing God tends to drop out of Protestantism, because God is known by hearing his word.

Essential Reading:

Luther, *The Freedom of a Christian* (first half), in *Luther's Works*, vol. 31, pp. 343–358; Lull, pp. 595–610; or Dillenberger, pp. 52–66.

Supplemental Reading:

Althaus, *The Theology of Martin Luther,* chapters 18–19.

Rupp, *The Righteousness of God*, chapters 5–6.

Questions to Consider:

1. How similar is Luther's doctrine of justification to the way you usually think about Christianity (or the way you were taught in church)?

2. Is Luther's doctrine of sin really bearable, in light of his doctrine of the Gospel?

Lecture Five—Transcript
Hearing the Gospel

In our last lecture, we looked at an unfamiliar Luther, not the Protestant Luther—the father of the Lutheran church who believes in justification by faith and a gracious Gospel—but, rather, a Luther who believes that you're justified by hating yourself. The way that you please God is to try to hate and damn yourself, and then you get justified by faith alone, in this very unfamiliar way—by believing in an accusation. Faith means faith in a God accusing you, and believing that God is right to accuse you, and agreeing with God that you're a terrible sinner, and that's what faith does is it tells you that you're a terrible sinner, and that's how you justify it. You hate yourself because you're such a terrible sinner.

That's 1516 in Luther's theology. This is the early Luther. It's before we have the Protestant Luther, the Luther of the Gospel. Because what, in fact, Luther adds to this picture in 1516—in order to become the mature Luther, the Luther that we all know—is nothing less than the concept of Gospel, the concept that the word of God can be a gracious, kind promise in Christ, so that believing it is not believing in accusation, not hating yourself as a terrible sinner, but believing that God is kind and merciful. Luther in his mature work always insists on a distinction between Law and Gospel. Gospel is this kind word of promise; the Law is also God's Word, but it contains accusations and threats because the Law is fundamentally a command, just as the Gospel is fundamentally a promise. The Gospel is both a story and a promise.

You can think of this as a genre issue. The Gospel is a story and a promise; the Law is commandment, and threat, and accusation and, of course, if you read the Bible, you'll find a lot of both in the Bible—promises as well as threats, accusations, and commandments. That's why Luther insists when you're reading the Bible—when you're reading God's Word—make this distinction. Always beware that there's this distinction. The Law has a purpose; it has a function, but it's not what saves you. You don't get justified by faith in the Law; you get justified by faith in the Gospel of Christ. We do have to think about what purpose, what use, the Law has. Luther doesn't simply abandon the notion that God accuses us; that's there in the Bible—it's very important. So what good does it do for God to give laws, give commandments, that we cannot keep, that we can never ever do all that God commands us to do and do it right? Therefore, we're always under this accusation if we're looking at the Law. What's the purpose of this? What's the good of it?

Luther thinks that there are two uses of the Law, two purposes of the Law. The first is a rather external kind of use; he calls it a "civil use." You can also think of it as the political use of the Law, where the Law outwardly restrains criminals and evildoers by threatening them, by saying, "You commit murder, and you're God's enemy, and you'll be punished in hell." That might make some people think twice about committing murder. It has some use. It doesn't make people into righteous people. It will get you to stop committing murder; you still want to commit murder, but you're scared to, so that doesn't make you a good person, but at least it helps in the ordering of society. It's an outward use of the Law.

But the Law's main purpose for Luther—its spiritual and central purpose—is what he calls its "evangelical use," which is a striking phrase because it means the Gospel use of the Law. The Law serves the Gospel in a particular way. This is its inward and spiritual use, and what that does is it humbles, terrifies, and spiritually "kills" you. Luther loves the Old Testament phrase where God says, "I kill and I make alive." God kills us inwardly and spiritually by the Law, and he makes us alive again by the Gospel. God does both those things, so there is a purpose for this word of accusation that terrifies us, but it's not a purpose that leads us to justification. It's a purpose that leads us to something other than the Law, to something better than the Law, to something kinder and more joyous than the Law—and that is the Gospel. For what in the early Luther was the fundamental basis of all theology, which was this humiliation, becomes in the mature Luther a preparation for the Gospel. It's what the Gospel and faith are all about.

Let's think a little bit about how this Law-Gospel distinguishes works in the mature Luther. I suggested that it's a genre distinction—that the Law is commandment, and the Gospel is promise and story. The Gospel is about what Christ does; it's a story about Christ, and it's a promise of Christ because one of the things he does is make promises; whereas, the Law is about what we do, and that's the fundamental distinction for Luther. Gospel is about what God does through Christ in his promises; Law is about what we do. The Law tells us what to do; it gives us commandments. That's why it's useless, spiritually speaking, other than to drive us to the Gospel because we don't do what we're commanded to do. Telling people what to do is one of the most useless things in the world in spiritual life, Luther thinks, because you tell people what to do and they can't do it. They're sinners. In that sense, the Gospel is different from the Law because it's about what Christ does, not what we do.

Let me dwell on this a minute. Anything that tells us what to do, for Luther, is Law, not Gospel. For instance, if some preacher tells you: "This is what you do to get saved," that's Law under Luther's classification because it's about what you do to get saved. Anything you do to get saved is Law, not Gospel. It's Christ who does stuff to get you saved, not you, and if you're talking about what you do, then that's Law—so the Gospel's not a technique for getting saved. The Gospel is not something you do; even faith is not something you do to get saved; it's just believing what Christ does. Likewise, the Gospel is not the "practical" part of a sermon. The practical part of a sermon in most sermons nowadays is where the pastor tells you what to do. I think pastors are told that that is the practical thing, that's where everything really important happens when you apply it to your life. But that's just more telling you what to do.

The practical part of the sermon is, for Luther, quite useless because it's telling you what to do, and you can't do what God tells you to do; you can only hate it, so in another sense the really practical part of the sermon for Luther, the profoundly practical part, the part that makes all the difference is not the Law, but the Gospel, precisely because the Gospel doesn't tell you what to do. The Gospel is not advice about how to live your life, how to be spiritual, how to be a better Christian. All that is Law. The Gospel is about Jesus; the Gospel is telling you what Jesus does. That's what's profoundly practical because it's not about what you do; it's about what Christ does, and that's what changes everything. What changes everything is not what you do, but what Jesus Christ does, and that's what makes you a new person, that's what changes you from the inside out, and in that sense, the Gospel is the practical part.

It's not like this later Protestant scheme of sermon, and you can see this in Protestant sermons for the past 200 to 300 years, where the first part of the sermon is doctrine and the second part is application, and the application part is all about us, and that's where it all gets practical, and that's where all the change happens in our lives. No, for Luther, what changes you is the doctrine of the Gospel; for Luther, what changes you is hearing what Christ does, not doing anything, not applying it to your life; what changes you is hearing what Christ does. That's because the Gospel word is a word of power, for Luther. This is something you've got to get used to. For Luther, the Gospel does stuff, the Gospel changes everything because the Gospel is God's Word, and God's Word is not "mere words." God's Word is a deed. God's Word does something. God's Word accomplishes something—it's efficacious, effective, powerful. We'll talk all that sort of way about the Gospel.

Most of all, most fundamentally, the Gospel's a promise that gives what it promises, the way a wedding vow does, I suggested earlier. There are lots of words where the word does what it says. If I put a ring in your hand and say, "Look at this ring," then my words are mere words, but if I put a ring in your hand and say, "I give you this ring," then my words do what they say, and through my words I give you the ring. Likewise, when God promises you forgiveness of sins in the Gospel, he does what he says. The word accomplishes what God says; that's Luther's notion, so when you hear about the Gospel in Luther, you've really always got to be aware this is not a theory, it's not a doctrine, it's the word that accomplishes something.

If it was merely a theory or a doctrine, then we would have to make it live in our lives. We would have to apply it to our lives, as the pastors like to say, and therefore we would be what makes the theory come alive; whereas, for Luther, it's the exact opposite. It's the Gospel the makes you alive. We are dead; we don't make the Gospel alive. The Gospel makes us alive because the Gospel is God's Word, and it's powerful and it changes everything because it's about what Christ does. Why is it that you have this word that does what it says? Behind it all is the notion that this is God's Word, it's God's promise and, of course, he keeps his promises. He does what he says; God does not lie. When you read Luther, look for the part where he says "God doesn't lie." He always says that; whenever he's talking about justification by faith, there's always a point where he says "and God doesn't lie." That's why the Gospel word is powerful. God tells the truth.

That's also why faith is certain, Luther thinks. After all, you can be sure that God will keep his word. Luther loves the saying of Saint

Paul in the letter to the Romans, "Let God be true and every man a liar." I might be a liar; my faith is full of lies, self-deceit, unbelief, inadequacy, and doubt, but God keeps his own word, so I don't even trust in my own faith, Luther says. Don't trust in your own faith; trust in God's Word. That's what faith does. Faith doesn't trust in faith; faith is not about "I believe." Faith is about God tells the truth, so the basis of your faith isn't "I believe," but rather "God doesn't lie." It's all about God; it's all about what God does. Faith is passive; it simply receives what God does.

But because it's about what God does and God keeping his word, faith is enormously powerful, precisely because it doesn't do anything but believe what God does. Luther has this famous saying, quite striking, and he repeats it many times, "Believe it and you have it," *Glaubst du, so hast du* in German, "Believe it and you have it." What that means is because God's Word is a promise, if you believe it then you get what God promises because he keeps his word. It's not this silly self-help notion where if I really believe in it, it happens just because I believe it so much. That's childish wishful thinking. You believe it and you have it because God keeps his word. The basis of it all is what God does, not what we do because it's a promise.

Even more revealing is another motto, which is less well known. It comes from Luther's treatise called *The Freedom of a Christian* in 1520, where a lot of this thinking about the Law and Gospels worked out in a powerful way for the first time. Luther says "The promises of God give what the commandment of God requires," and the promise, of course, is Gospel and the commandment as Law, so the Law requires us to do stuff. That doesn't give us the power to do stuff; that's why the Law is so impractical. Telling people what to do doesn't help them because they can't do what you tell them to do because they're sinners. The Gospel is what changes things, so the Gospel promise gives the obedience, and love, and good works that the commandment requires.

What's profoundly revealing about this motto is that it's actually a variation or modification of a motto that comes from Augustine, from that Augustinian paradigm of spirituality that I mentioned. It's about Augustine's doctrine of grace, where Augustine talks about how we pray for grace; I mentioned that before. We need grace in order to obey God's Law, so we have to pray for it, Augustine says.

So the prayer of faith, praying for grace, sounds like this, Augustine says: We say to God "Give what you command and then command whatever you want." Give what you command—that is grace, obedience, love—and then go ahead and command us to love God with our whole heart, mind, and strength. We can't normally do that, but you give us grace so that we can do it, and then go ahead and command anything you want. Just give us the grace to do it. That's the prayer of faith. You start with faith so that you can make that prayer and receive grace to obey God's command.

See the difference between Luther's motto and Augustine's? For Augustine, we get to obey the command of God because we're praying. We need to seek grace; Augustine will say we flee to grace by prayer. For Luther, we also flee to grace. Luther loves this notion of fleeing to grace; he picks it up from Augustine; he picks up lots of stuff from Augustine; he loves this notion, but you don't flee to grace by praying for Luther. You flee to grace by hearing. It's not what we say, it's what God says, so it's not our prayers or words, but it's God's Word, the Gospel. We flee to grace by hearing the Gospel, not by praying. We are supposed to pray, of course, Luther thinks that, but that's not what makes a difference—God's Word always, it's God's Word. Luther is absolutely obsessed with God's Word. It's all about what God does and says.

Another way of putting this: If you want to flee to grace, where do you go? Augustine doesn't give you a concrete "place" to go to; you pray and you expect that God will indeed answer your prayer. Luther gives you a very concrete thing to hang onto. He says if you want grace, your prayer's not good enough. Remember in the previous lecture, you're seeking grace all the time, you're always praying, and it's never good enough. You even have the doubt "I pray to God, but is my prayer sincere enough? Is it real enough? Is it faithful enough? Is it loving enough?" The answer is no, of course not, for Luther. Your prayer is a prayer of sin; it's never good enough, but the Gospel is good enough. The Gospel is God's Word, so just believe it's true. You're justified by faith alone.

So the Gospel is the concrete "place" you go to in order to find grace. It's God's promise of grace; you hang onto that promise for dear life because it saves you, and when God says: "This is my body, given for you," believe it's true. That's where you find grace; that's where you find God. There's something external and concrete, external meaning, "It's out there in the world; it's reverberating off the walls of the church, sound waves and all." It gets into your heart, but it doesn't start there. When Luther talks about God speaking, he's not talking about God speaking deep in your heart; he's talking about the preaching of the word—this external, oral word preached and spoken so you can hear it with your literal, physical ears. That means there's a concrete place you can go. If you're anxious about whether God really loves you, go and hear someone say: "This is my body, given for you"; that's where you go; you have a place to run to, something external to cling to.

That's the notion of Gospel as a powerful word. You have to get used to that notion to understand why Luther's Gospel works the way it is, why it's not our technique, why it's not merely a doctrine that you have to apply to your life. It's God speaking; it's God doing something. Luther works out this doctrine of the Gospel in its deepest and most systematic way for the first time in 1520 in *The Freedom of a Christian*. There's a number of things that happened earlier, and I'm going to talk about the first time he talks about the Gospel as a promise, but the first time he got a full-orbed, full-fledged sort of systematic theology based on this notion of Gospel and the contrast between Gospel and Law is in 1520 in this lovely treatise called *The Freedom of a Christian*. It's one of the favorite Lutheran treatises, and there's good reason for that. It's lovely and beautiful in all sorts of ways.

Let me tell you about the first half of *The Freedom of a Christian*; we'll talk about the second half of it in the next lecture. The first half is all about the Gospel, all about faith. Luther compares faith in the Gospel to a wedding. He compares it to taking hold of your bridegroom. I'm going to fill out this picture just a little bit from some other of Luther's writings because I think there's a whole set of systematic metaphors here. I suggested the Gospel is like a wedding vow. It's a promise that effectually gives you another person who is your beloved. Luther compares this to a king who gives his son in marriage to a prostitute. We're the prostitutes, folks, all of us, but we become the bride of Christ. The prostitute becomes the bride of the king's son, so that changes who she is.

She gets married, she gets cleaned up, she gets dressed in gorgeous glorious robes, and she gets all the wealth of the king's son, which it turns out then is her job to distribute to everyone else. She gets saved and then cleaned up so that she can help everyone else. That's where good works come in, which we'll talk about later. But think, first of all, now about the transformation. We are this prostitute. She hears this wedding vow, and she believes it, which means she no longer believes she's a prostitute. We don't have a right to believe anymore that we're sinners because this beloved, this son of the king, says: "You are my beloved, and I am yours." That's the wedding vow; it comes from the Song of Solomon. "You are my beloved. You are my beloved, and I'm yours."

You're supposed to believe that, which means you're supposed to believe you're no longer a prostitute anymore—you're a queen, you're royalty, you're glorious. You're not supposed to believe in the old self, the old sinner. You have received Christ; you are now the king's beloved, his son's bride. That means, of course, also in receiving nothing less than the son of a king himself, which, of course, means nothing less than God in the flesh; you have received also not only all that he is, but all that he has. You receive righteousness, justice, sanctification, holiness, blessedness, all that other stuff—big long words, justification. That comes second; that's like you marry the king's son, you get his wealth, but why would you want to marry him for his wealth? He's much better than all the riches in the world.

If you're a prostitute, you might have to learn a little bit about that, loving someone for themselves, but, after all, the king's son is glorious and wonderful, and we get used to the idea that having God is better than having anything that God has. We don't go to heaven in order to get some kind of giant cookie or something. We go to heaven so you have God; that's the very best thing. Who cares about this other stuff—justification, righteousness, sanctification? That all comes along, but that's not what it's all about. It's all about God; it's all about Christ.

The other side of the coin, after getting all that belongs to the king's son so that you have not only Christ but all that is his, the other side of it is that all that is his becomes yours. That's the first side; all that is his becomes yours. The other side is all that is ours becomes his. There's a "blessed exchange," Luther calls it; what is his becomes ours, what is ours becomes his. And what is ours? Sin, death, the devil, suffering, the cross. That's why he's on the cross, because he bears all that is ours—our sins, and death. That's the "blessed exchange"; we get what's his, he gets what's ours. It's like the prostitute gets all the wealth of the kingdom, and the king's son takes on all her debts, and wounds, and sufferings, and anguish.

And on the cross, one other thing that happens, in addition to this blessed exchange is what Luther calls a "mighty duel." Luther loves battles. "Thus ask who that may be, Christ Jesus it is he, and he must win the battle," says the favorite Lutheran hymn, *All Mighty Fortresses of God*, which Luther wrote. He must win the battle. On the cross is a battle, and Jesus wins. It might look like he loses, he dies, but this is God who is dying and therefore he defeats death. He takes death into himself, and death is swallowed up by life because this is God who is dying on the cross, and therefore in taking all that is ours—our sin, death, and suffering—he swallows it up in victory, and that happens on the cross, where the victory is hidden under its opposite.

That's what happens to that theme of being hidden under its opposite, which used to mean in the early Luther that justification is hidden under the accusation of God, who terrifies you. Now it means our salvation is hidden under the suffering of a crucified God. One last thing the Gospel does, Luther mentions, the Gospel cheers us up; it comforts us; it consoles us. Luther loves these words— cheerfulness, comfort, and consolation. The Gospel makes us feel better. Instead of terrified, we are comforted and cheered up because this is a kind word, and it's nice to be cheered up by a kind word from no less than God. So that's all the good stuff.

Let me say some things about some consequences of the Gospel that take a little getting used to. These are distinctive consequences of Luther's notion of the Gospel that sometimes run contrary to the way that other Protestants, as well as, of course, Catholics think. It's not just Catholics who sometimes don't get this stuff; other Protestants sometimes have a hard time. One thing is that the Gospel is closely connected to the notion of sin because the Gospel is good news for sinners. You're only in a good position to understand why the Gospel is good news if you regard yourself as a sinner. The king's son wants to marry a prostitute. If you think you're a great person who is a high and mighty princess, then the king's son isn't interested in you. He marries prostitutes; he marries sinners, but you've got to be thinking of yourself as a sinner.

That's why the Law is so important. That evangelical use of the Law gets you to realize "I'm awful. How can God possibly love someone like me?"—then you're ready to hear the Gospel. Then you're ready to hear: "Yes, you are beloved, precisely you, the one who's so sinful." When Luther talks about sin, I don't hear something nasty in it. He's always trying to get you to be in a position where you can realize that you're the kind of person for whom Christ died. That's why he wants you to recognize you're a sinner, you're one of those folks for whom Christ died. He's not trying to say, "I'm so much better than you because you're a sinner and I'm not so much of a sinner as you are." Some preaching works like that, but not Luther. Luther is just thinking we're all in this boat together; we're all deeply unworthy sinners. I want everyone to recognize this so they can all hear the same wonderful good news that I'm hearing.

He'll call it "evangelical despair," another strange saying, "Gospel despair." What the Law does is it drives you to despair of all of your works. You're trying to be a princess; you're a prostitute trying to be a princess. You try to think of yourself as a princess. It's not working, so the best thing to do is give it up—despair, and give up all hope of becoming a princess by your own efforts. Now you're ready to hear that the king's son wants to say: "You're my beloved." If you were still intent on becoming a princess by your own efforts, you wouldn't be welcoming this good word. "Evangelical despair" is what it means to think of yourself as a sinner, and that's why Luther thinks he's helping you by getting you to think of yourself as a sinner.

Another point about sin, and this becomes a deep point that we're going to have to get back to several times, Luther says that we are at the same time sinners and righteous. Even after the prostitute becomes the queen, she's still thinking like a prostitute, it's still part of her. She has to overcome that old self, but, of course, fundamentally she's the beloved of the king's son because that's what the king's son says; he says: "You're my beloved." She's fundamentally the queen, the bride of the king's son, and that's what the king's son says. That's who she really is, but there's still all sorts of sin left in her, and that's us again, for Luther. We're still unrighteous, Luther will say, this thing that is just so offensive to the Catholics of this time.

"The good works of a righteous man," he says, "are mortal sins." All our good works are always mortal sins in and of themselves. The prostitute, apart from the king's son's love for her, still thinks like a prostitute, lives like a prostitute. Apart from that good wedding vow, that promise, she's a prostitute, but because of the promise she is the queen. She is queen and prostitute at the same time. It takes a while for her to get used to the fact that she's not a prostitute anymore, so for the rest of her life she's got to fight with that. Likewise, we're sinners, we stay sinners. All of our good works are sins in God's sight apart from the mercy of Christ—but, of course, they're not apart from the mercy of Christ, so we're constantly having to go back and forth, realizing you look at yourself—you see a sinner; you look at Christ, your bridegroom, your beloved—and you see that you are, in fact, the bride of Christ—justified, sanctified, and holy.

One way Luther puts this is: "I am a sinner in and by myself apart from Christ. [but] Apart from myself and in Christ I am not a sinner. In myself, I am a sinner; in Christ, I'm not a sinner." And who is my real self? Not who I am in myself, but who I am in Christ. Who's the real woman here? Not the woman who looks at herself and says, "I look like a prostitute," but the woman who looks at her bridegroom, her beloved, and says, "He says I'm his beloved, so that's who I really am. I'm really the beloved of the king's son." You define yourself, for Luther, by what the Gospel says about you. The Gospel has the power to say who you really are.

Don't try to find out who you really are by looking at yourself. Your own self-perception, your own self-knowledge, will only be self-knowledge of a sinner, at least if it's accurate. If you're honest and you're self-knowledgeable, you will think of yourself as a sinner. But that doesn't define who you really are; who you really are is defined by God's Word, by his promise, by his Gospel, by the king's son saying, "You're my beloved. That's who you really are. Will you please believe that?"

On the other side of this, Luther will say something striking about sin, a third point about sin. All sin is unbelief, Luther will say, a famous and striking thing, all sin is unbelief, which is to say just as all of our righteousness comes by faith, all of our unrighteousness comes from lack of faith. That's why we are, in fact, both justified and sinners at the same time. We are justified by faith, but we're also full of doubt, we're full of unbelief, and therefore that's sin. We're always believers and unbelievers at the same time, not just justified and sinners at the same time, but believers and unbelievers at the same time. Psychologically, I think this is profoundly realistic. All believers are also unbelievers; all righteous people are also sinners. That, I think, is really good news, but we should contrast it with the Augustinian picture.

Augustine has a version of this being righteous and a sinner at the same time, but it's more progressive. It's "We're righteous, we're making progress, we're getting better but we're not perfect yet, so we're still sinners to some degree, but we're getting better all the time. We're righteous, but we're getting better and we're gradually overcoming sin." Luther thinks that's true, but that's not really the key point. It's not just that we're making progress; it's that we are the beloved of the king. That's simply who we are down to the depths of our soul because that's what the Gospel says, and the Gospel is true, and we ought to believe it. We're also sinners, because that's what we see when we look at ourselves, this *simul justus et peccator* in Latin, "at the same time righteous and sinners," just and a sinner, the *simul* in Latin, "at the same time."

This *simul justus et peccator* is fundamentally about how we look at ourselves. We look at ourselves in Christ, and we see a blessed and beloved child of God. We look at ourselves in ourselves, and we see sinners. That's why when we look at ourselves in ourselves, we're prone to temptation, to *Anfechtung*, Luther calls it, giving us this vivid German word meaning "assault," the devil's assault. The devil's assault doesn't tell us "You're a sinner, God hates you." That's what happens if you look at yourself and try to judge yourself by what you see. Don't judge yourself by what you see in yourself; judge yourself by the Gospel, by that beloved word. For Luther, the Christian life is full of this back and forth, just and sinner at the same time, this *Anfechtung*, which drives you away from looking at yourself to look in Christ.

The spiritual life is less like a journey, as in Augustine, and more like a gift that you receive. That's why Protestants will talk about "accepting Christ." This is not how Augustine talks about it. For Augustine, you're on this road trying to get to God, and you haven't gotten there yet. For Protestants, you've already received the most important thing, which is the gift of God in Jesus Christ. It's as if you've already gotten to the end of the road and, indeed, according to the Augustinian paradigm, that's what must have happened if you already have God in your heart in the deepest possible way. If you already have received or accepted Christ, you're already at the end of the road; what else is there for you to do? That's the topic of the next lecture.

But meanwhile let me say just two things about what implications that has. It means that the Christian life is less like this longing and desire as of Augustine and more like gratitude for a gift already received. It's not an aching longing; it's gratitude, it's gladness—and the goal is not seeing, not contemplation as in Augustine: "Now I see it, now I see the truth behind all things." Rather, the goal is to believe what God has to say and, thus, know God by believing what he tells you. That's how you know a person, Luther thinks, by believing what they say about themselves.

Lecture Six
Faith and Works

Scope:

Luther systematically distinguishes Law and Gospel: The one is God's commandment telling us what to do; the other is his promise telling us what he does for us. Because salvation comes simply by believing the Gospel, a question that inevitably arises is: What need is there for us to do any good works—especially works of love? Luther's answer, in the second half of *The Freedom of a Christian* and in other writings, such as his *Treatise on Good Works*, is that works of love make no contribution to our salvation or our righteousness before God but are needed by our neighbors. God saves us through faith in order to give us in love to our neighbors. It is as if the gift of Christ fills us to the brim and overflows in gifts and service to other people. This is what Luther calls our "proper righteousness," the imperfect but real change for the good in our lives as a result of the "alien righteousness," which is Christ given to us in the Gospel.

Outline

I. For Luther, what matters most in the Christian life is faith, not how Christians live out their faith—that is, good works.

    A. Hence Luther's key formulation, that we are justified by faith alone, apart from works of the Law.

    B. Faith alone re-makes us inwardly from the bottom of our hearts by changing our conscience, our awareness of how we stand before God.

    C. Good works are how we live out our faith outwardly, in works of love for our neighbors.

    D. Luther organizes the treatise on the *Freedom of a Christian* around these two points about faith and good works, which he states as two paradoxical theses.

        1. "A Christian is perfectly free, lord of all, subject to none" because Christians are inwardly freed by faith from sin, death, and the devil.

2. "A Christian is a perfectly dutiful servant of all, subject to all" because Christians serve their neighbors outwardly with works of love.
3. The first half of *Freedom of a Christian* explains the first thesis; the second half explains the second thesis.

II. If we are justified by faith alone, then the question inevitably arises: What are we supposed to do with our lives once we are justified?

    A. Luther's way of posing the question is: "Don't Christians have to do good works—works of love?"
1. For Luther, this is a question about what we are going to do now that we are free from sin and damnation.
2. It is as if a slave sold into prostitution has suddenly been given the king's son to marry: What does she do now that she is queen and disposes of all the wealth of the kingdom?
3. The answer is that the queen serves everybody in the kingdom, using her newfound wealth for the good of all her neighbors.
4. A favorite metaphor of Luther's is that the love of God poured into us from above overflows in good works to one's neighbor.
5. In doctrinal terms, the point is that anyone with true faith does works of love, not in order to be justified, but because she already is justified.
6. In one of his deepest formulations, we become Christs to one another (as the queen represents her husband when she gives his wealth away to others).

    B. Good works serve both one's neighbor and one's own body.
1. Good works discipline the body, mortify the flesh, and fight against the sin that is still in us.
2. The fight against sin in us is cheerful, because we are to identify ourselves with Christ in us, not with "the old Adam" that still remains in us; hence, in contrast to Luther's early doctrine of justification, we are not to be our own enemies.
3. Good works do not help the soul, but they do help us outwardly.

    C. In all this, the Law comes in to guide us in external ways.

1. The Law must not be allowed to touch the conscience, except to terrify us and drive us to the Gospel (the evangelical use of the Law).
2. The Law of God does not instruct believers how to be better Christians (that is, to become more righteous).
3. While we are in this life, we remain righteous and sinners at the same time. Everything we do is sin, including our good works, but our sin is not imputed or counted against us.

D. Why does Luther avoid speaking of the Law as a means of teaching Christians how to live better lives?
1. For Luther—as opposed to the doctrine of later Lutheranism—the Law has no third use beyond the evangelical and civic uses.
2. Luther wants Christians to focus on the Gospel, not the Law, as the catalyst for making them better Christians.
3. Luther's *Treatise on Good Works* clarifies the role of the Law in the Christian life.
4. The Law of God frees Christians from the burden of "self-chosen works."
5. Self-chosen works include any form of moralism or spirituality that adds extra duties to what is required by the Ten Commandments and other Scriptures.
6. Because of the command "Honor thy father and mother," a housemaid obeying her master has more certainty that she pleases God than the monk pursuing all the spiritual disciplines he imposes on himself apart from the requirements of Scripture.

III. To clarify the relation between faith and works, Luther distinguishes different kinds of righteousness.

A. The crucial distinction is between person and work, who we are and what we do—symbolized by tree and fruit.

B. As the tree must be good before the fruit is, so the person must be righteous before he can do good works.

C. What makes the person good is *alien* righteousness (literally, the righteousness of another), which is Christ in the heart; the good works one does are *proper* righteousness (literally, one's own righteousness), which has nothing to do with justification.

D. Alien righteousness is the righteousness of God in us, making us a new kind of person.

E. Alien righteousness is *passive*, in that it is God's doing, not ours; proper righteousness is *active* because it consists of works we do.

Essential Reading:

Luther, *The Freedom of a Christian* (second half), in *Luther's Works*, vol. 31, pp. 358–377; Lull, pp. 610–629; or Dillenberger, pp. 66–85.

Supplemental Reading:

Luther, "Two Kinds of Righteousness," in *Luther's Works*, vol. 31, pp. 297–306; Lull, chapter 11; or Dillenberger, pp. 86–96.

Luther, *Treatise on Good Works*, in *Luther's Works*, vol. 44.

Questions to Consider:

1. Do you find Luther's critique of "spirituality" freeing or suffocating?

2. On the issue of how we become virtuous, do you prefer Luther to Aristotle or Aristotle to Luther—or do you think both are right in some sense?

Lecture Six—Transcript
Faith and Works

In our last lecture, we were trying to get at what is really central and at the very core of Luther's thinking, this thing called the Gospel. It turns out that as you think through it conceptually, it can be very puzzling. At one level, it's very obvious and very simple, and Luther tries to make it as simple and obvious as possible. At another level, it's very puzzling because you have to get used to thinking in a way that's rather unusual and rather unfamiliar. You have to get used to thinking that the really important thing is not what you do, but what God does. The really important thing, therefore, is not what to do but what you believe, that merely believing is really the crucial thing, not doing anything about it, not putting in the practice, not living out your faith in your life. That's important, but it comes second.

The really important thing, the thing that comes first and is at the core of everything, is believing what God does, not what you do, and believing what God does rather than trying to do something yourself is what makes all the difference for Luther, and that really takes some getting used to. Luther admits this is a hard idea to swallow, and you have to spend the rest of your life as a Christian trying to live this out, to get used to the idea that it's not how you live it out that matters, but rather what you believe about what God is doing. Luther has this formulation, this famous formulation, in which he tries to sum up this kind of paradox that we are justified by faith alone, apart from works of the Law. Works of the Law means the things that we do in obedience to God. The things that we do in obedience to God are not the important things. They don't justify us, they don't make us Christians, they don't make us holy, and they don't get us in right relationship to God.

None of that is what does the important thing of getting us in the right relationship to God. Faith alone does that, just believing it, simple as that. It's not what we do; it's what we believe. That takes a lot of getting used to, and that's what the Christian life is about is getting that thought, that belief, that good news as deep into our hearts as possible. For Luther, what changes us inwardly, what makes all the difference from the bottom of our hearts on upward, is faith in God's Word, because by faith you receive God's Word, God's Word gets into your ears, the Gospel that is, not the Law, but the Gospel (Law also does this), but the Gospel is good news. It get into your ear, gets into your heart, it changes things for good. The Law gets into your ear, gets into your heart and terrifies you, so you want the Gospel. This good news becomes spoken orally. It's preached; it's external; it gets into your ears and then down into your heart, and then from the very bottom of your heart it makes everything different because it's the good news about Jesus Christ.

The other side of it, after faith, is good works. There is a place for good works in the Christian life. You are justified by faith apart from good works, but good works have a place in the Christian life. There is a role for living out your faith. It's second, not first; it's secondary, not primary; it is outward, not inward, Luther will say. Faith inwardly changes us from the bottom of our hearts; good works are how we live out the faith outwardly in works of love for our neighbor. Faith is inward; good works are outward. Luther's whole theology is organized around this contrast. We'll find this same contrast when we get to his political theory, for instance, but that's a little bit later.

Right now, let's think about this contrast. This kind of faith is inward; good works are outward. That's the organizing contrast for the treatise called *The Freedom of a Christian*, which we started discussing last time, this very important 1520 treatise, a very crucial document for Lutheran theology. It begins, in fact, by setting forth these two points in two theses that look very paradoxical. Here's thesis one: "A Christian is perfectly free." That's the theme of *The Freedom of a Christian*: "A Christian is perfectly free, lord of all, subject to none" but thesis two: "A Christian is a perfectly dutiful servant of all, subject to all" and then Luther notes cheaply, "You might think that these look like they are contradictory. Let's call it a paradox, not a contradiction."

In fact, Luther tries to show that they're quite compatible with each other as soon as you make this distinction between inward and outward, between the inner change that faith makes and the outer works of good works for our neighbor because the Christian is perfectly free. Why? Because of faith, which brings the good news of Christ into your heart and therefore frees your conscience from fear and terror, frees you from sin and death and the devil; you're free from all ills and perfectly in love with your bridegroom. That's freedom, not servitude.

Meanwhile, the other side of it, the outward side, a Christian is a perfectly dutiful servant of all because what do you do with your faith? You serve your neighbor in love, so the Christian is perfectly free by faith; the Christian is a perfectly dutiful servant in love because good works are works of love, and that's the outward side. Love is the outward sign of this Christian life, for Luther. Faith is what's inward; works of love for your neighbor are outward. We need to talk about how you get from faith to good works because although you justify that faith apart from good works, nonetheless faith leads to good works, and they're inseparable as the outer and inner are inseparable.

What happens, in fact, is that the first half of the treatise on *The Freedom of a Christian* talks about this inward gift of faith, which makes you free of all ills, and the second half is about these outward good works, so now what we're doing in this lecture is talking about that second half of the treatise on *The Freedom of a Christian*, which is about the outer works of Law, where you serve your neighbor— not trying to set things right with God, that's the inner freedom of faith, that's an inner relationship, faith is all about that. Your neighbor, doing things for your neighbor, that's what love is about. That doesn't make you a good Christian; that doesn't set you right with God, it doesn't justify you, but your neighbor needs your good works, and that's why God saves you and gives you faith so that you can serve your neighbor.

Let's put it this way, suppose you ask the question, "What are we supposed to do with our lives now that we're justified and saved?" like that Augustinian paradigm, where you're heading toward salvation, you're not saved yet, says Augustine. Protestants say you are saved; you've received the gift that Augustinians think that you're heading for all of your lives, and in one sense it's already happened for Protestants. You've already received the gift of God himself. You're united with God by faith; you've gotten to the end of the road. What are you going to do now? Another way of asking the same question is: "Don't Christians have to do good works? Don't they have to do something? It's not just believing something, it's doing something, isn't it?" It is really a question, what do we do now, now that we're freed from sin and damnation.

Let's go back to that metaphor from the previous lecture. Suppose you're a prostitute who gets married to the king's son. What do you do now? You are now no longer a prostitute; you're the queen, you're glorious, you're happy, you're wealthy. You're the most beautiful, and glorious, and wonderful person in the kingdom. Everyone loves you. What are you going to do now? You're going to behave like the wife of the king's son. You're going to behave like the king's son himself behaves. You're going to serve the whole kingdom, that is to say you now have all the wealth of the king's son, and it's your job to give it away. You don't become queen by behaving like a queen. You become queen by believing the king's son when he says, "You're my beloved."

But now you've got all the wealth of the king's son, and you've got to do something with it. You've got a life to live and you have to live like a queen, which is not selfishly, not by just enjoying yourself. God saves you in order to give you to your neighbor; God frees you from sin, and death, and the devil to make you a servant of your neighbor. God makes you a king or a queen so that you may serve everyone else in the kingdom. That's the way of love. That's what good works are. All the wealth of the kingdom is yours; it's now your job to use it well, the same way that Christ does. You're married to him, so behave the way he does. Do his work; do the work of Christ for your neighbor.

Another way of putting this, and here's a favorite metaphor of Luther's. It's as if the love of God is poured down into the bottom of your soul by faith in God's Word, and it wells up and overflows so that God pours all this good stuff into you—all this love, and glory, and blessedness, and happiness—and it overflows outwardly toward your neighbor. You have been justified; you have been saved; you don't have to worry about those things anymore. Now you've got nothing to do with your life but being like God is, loving your neighbor, doing good for your neighbor, doing what Christ does. Luther will say, in one of the most profound formulations, "We become Christs to our neighbors"; that's what happens to your faith. You get married to Christ, and you become like him, you do what Christ does.

You receive all this goodness in God's love for you in the Gospel, and then you share it with people. That's your job now; you've got all the goodness and happiness you need to share with everyone. In doctrinal terms, what you can say is faith does good works. Luther will say this all the time—faith does good works. Faith creates works of love. We don't do good works by trying to obey God; you do good works by hearing the Gospel and believing, and then faith itself does all the good works. That means, of course, good works don't justify you, don't make you righteous in God's sight. You get married to the king's son, not by becoming a good person, but by believing what the king's son says and his wedding vow, but now you get to be a good person.

What's the purpose of being a good person if it's not for the sake of justifying yourself before God? God doesn't need your good works, but your neighbor does. Your good works are needed outwardly. Actually, there are two ways in which your good works are needed. God doesn't need them, but your neighbor needs them and your body needs them, Luther will say. Good works are done to discipline the body, mortify the flesh, fight against the sins that are still in us because, remember, we're both sinners and righteous at the same time; we're still sinners all the time. You could say the prostitute still has the prostitute's thoughts running in her head, and she has to remind herself "I'm the king's beloved, I'm not who I used to be. I have to fight against that old self."

Luther will say you have to fight against "the old Adam" in you; that's the old self; it's not who you are anymore, so you fight against that, but the fight is cheerful. It's not like in the early Luther's writings, where he's trying to hate himself, accuse himself, damn himself. You fight against "the old Adam" in you because that's no longer who you really are. You fight against "the old Adam" in you cheerfully, the way if you were a prostitute who gets married to a king, you have to remind yourself "I am not who I used to be anymore. I don't have to think like that. The news is better than that; I'm a better person than that because that's what my beloved says, and I have to remember that so I can keep on remembering the good news instead of the bad news about who I used to be."

Good works do discipline your life, especially outwardly. You remember "I don't behave like that anymore because I'm not that kind of a person anymore, because I'm now the person that the Gospel says I am." There's all sorts of disciplines; there's fasting, and prayer, and spiritual discipline, and all those sorts of things, which don't make you a good Christian; only faith makes you a good Christian, only believing makes you a good Christian, but those good works are a good discipline. They help your body; they help outwardly; they don't help your soul. Good works don't help your soul, don't help your heart, don't help your conscience, don't help you inwardly, but they help your body outwardly. More importantly, good works help your neighbor. Good works are fundamentally works of love, and you serve your neighbor as Christ serves your neighbor. That's why God saves you, so he can give you to your neighbor in love.

In all this, the Law comes in to guide us in external ways, but, for Luther, the Law must never get into your conscience unless it's going to terrify you and drive you to the Gospel, that evangelical news. But the Law is not there to tell you who you are inwardly. The Law is not there to say: "Be this kind of person"; that would be like telling a prostitute: "Behave like a queen." That doesn't help. The Gospel tells the prostitute: "You are my beloved. You're married to the king's son, would you believe that," and if you believe it, that's what changes you, so the Law is not supposed to tell you who you are; it just guides you outwardly, in outward deeds, in outward good works, so Luther makes this inner-outer contrast, and we'll be seeing that contrast over and over again later on in his works. The Law is outward; the Gospel is inward. Faith is inward; good works are outward.

Likewise, outwardly, while we're in this life, we remain sinners. We are sinners and righteous at the same time; the righteousness is the inner part, the righteousness by faith, but we're also sinners still. Outwardly, we still have those bad habits from "the old Adam"; we still sometimes think like prostitutes rather than royalty, and God says we're royalty, so we have this unbelief that doesn't take in the Gospel and believe what God says about us, so we behave like we were sinners, and we do release sin, but here's the last point about this outward stuff—our sin is not counted against us, Luther says. It is not imputed; this is technical language, the sin is not imputed, it doesn't count.

We do really sin, all the good works of a righteous person (or sins, as Luther says), everything we do considered in and of itself apart from the mercy of Christ is sin, but because the mercy of Christ is real and really governs our lives, the sin isn't counted against us; it's not imputed. Inwardly, we are freed by faith; outwardly, our good works aren't good enough to justify us, but they don't count against us because of their sinfulness.

This is all aiming at a very technical point, which I want to get to. The later Lutheran tradition spoke of a "third use" of the Law. Remember I mentioned two uses in Luther. Luther will typically identify two uses. There's the external use of the Law, the "civil use," which terrifies evildoers and threatens murderers so they won't commit murder; that's merely outward. Then, there's an inner spiritual use of the law, which terrifies you in your conscience so you'll go to the Gospel. It doesn't make you a good person, and you shouldn't let the Law define who you are, but it does scare you enough that you go back to the Gospel all the time.

Quick note, we'll get to this a little bit later, but Luther doesn't think that you have one conversion experience and then you never have to deal with the wrath of God again. That's a Calvinist view. Luther's thinking you're always over and over again hearing the Law. It gets into your conscience; it terrifies you; it drives you to the Gospel. That's how you become a Christian is continually going through this process of being terrified, of going back to God. Every time you look at yourself you get terrified, and you go back to God. That's the Christian life; that's what forms you as a Christian, not attempts to do good works, but what you hear. It's not what you do that makes you who you are; it's what you hear. You hear the Law, and that terrifies you; you go to the Gospel, and that comforts you, that reminds you who you really want to be and why you want to be the king's beloved and not who you used to be.

The Law is not supposed to do this third thing, the third use of the Law, which is defined in later Lutheran theology as teaching you how to be a good Christian, giving you instruction about how to live the Christian life. Luther doesn't talk that way about the Law. It's striking; I can see why the later Lutheran tradition wants to add that third use of the Law. It certainly makes obvious sense that when God tells you what to do, that ought to help you figure out what to do. But it doesn't quite work that way for Luther. At least I think there are reasons why Luther himself does not talk about a third use of Law. Let me try to explain why I think that's true.

First of all, it has to do with how the Law is not supposed to shape our conscience, shape our heart. The Law is not supposed to get at us inwardly other than to terrify us and drive us back to the Gospel. For Luther, he really wants you to get this notion that the Gospel is what changes you, not the Law. He doesn't want to you to think, "If I practice doing what the Law tells me, I become a better person," as if that would change you. It's the Gospel that changes you. He's really serious about that, and he wants you to think that through. Let's see if we can think that through with him. He says the Law must touch the conscience. That means the Law of God builds up the Christian life not by instructing believers how to be better Christians, but by doing something else.

Here's the positive function of the Law in the Christian life, and we run into this in a treatise called the *Treatise on Good Works*, also written in 1520. What the Law does, the Ten Commandments in particular, is it says these are the good works that Christians do and not anything else. What the Law does, Luther's equivalent of the third use of the Law, how the Law helps you in the Christian life, is by telling you all the good work you don't have to do. At the beginning of his *Treatise on Good Works*, which is a long exposition of the Ten Commandments, in 1520, he says this: "The first thing to know is that there are no good works except those works that God has commanded."

What Luther's doing with the Law of God at this point is saying it frees us from all these other works, and we do need to be freed from all these other works, the kind of works that Luther was doing as a monk, these penitential works, these works of praying, and fasting, and spiritual discipline—all of which are attempts to please God quite apart from God's Word. Remember how Luther wanted to become a monk originally in order to give up his own will and obey the will of his superior, but he became a monk willfully against his father's will, against the command of God, which says: "Honor thy father and thy mother," so he had this problem as a monk. He wanted to give up his own will, but that project of giving up his own will was willful, and he became a self-contradiction in a vicious circle. How do you willfully give up your own will?

What I suggested about what doesn't work about the notion of unselfishness is that there's nothing more self-centered than the project of becoming unselfish. It doesn't work. What can you do to make yourself a better Christian? You can't do this stuff of always this spiritual discipline, that spiritual discipline, this prayer, that prayer. That's what the monks were thinking; that's what Luther was thinking when he was a monk, and Luther wants to be free of those things. He calls them *Menschenlehre*; that's German for the "doctrines of men." That's a quotation from a passage in the New Testament, the doctrines of men. They're not the command of God. Remember, for Luther, it's all about hearing what God has to say.

The problem with the works of the monks—with all this penitential fasting, and prayer, and all that sort of stuff—is that it's stuff that human beings invent in order to justify themselves before God. It's self-chosen works, he'll call it, self-chosen works, *Menschenlehre*, doctrines of men. You try to justify yourself that way and you just can't do it. It's just one form of torture after another, as we discovered when Luther tried to torture himself into being just before God, hating himself enough.

The wonderful thing about the command of God, Luther thinks, is it tells you all the good work you don't have to do. All you have to do is follow the Ten Commandments, and Luther thinks that's enough for a lifetime. You can work on learning to follow the Ten Commandments, this external obedience to the Ten Commandments, which is what you're going to be doing, and that's going to take all your life. You're never going to get good at it. You're never going to cease to be a sinner and be free of sin in your own life apart from your faith in Christ. So, by your deeds, you get better, you practice at it, but that's only external, and it doesn't make you righteous and just and, thus, by being aware that this is the work of a lifetime, you don't have to go on to something more holy and spiritual.

It's like this, the monks are thinking, "The Ten Commandments, that's pretty easy. I've got that under my belt. I've figured that stuff out. Now I need to go on to something better, something more spiritual," something that Luther would say is self-chosen works, willful, doctrines of men. Luther says you never graduate beyond the Ten Commandments; you never outgrow them. You're going to spend the rest of your life trying to learn to become someone who obeys the Ten Commandments. That's OK; you're not supposed to make yourself perfect by your deeds, after all. You're not supposed to be justified by your works, so it's OK if you spend the rest of your life learning the Ten Commandments. Luther will insist on this. We're always learners; we never graduate to something more spiritual, more inward, because no good works are inward. Only what God does in faith is inward.

An example he gives (we'll run into this later) is an example of the housemaid who sweeps the floor. The housemaid who sweeps the floor, Luther thinks, is obeying the commandment to honor father and mother. I need to say a little bit about that. The command to honor father and mother, Luther thinks has to do with all relationships of authority. When you obey your king, that's honoring your father. When your housemaid obeys the father of the house telling her to sweep the floor, she's honoring her father. In general, this is typical of Christian readings of the Ten Commandments; you always expand the Ten Commandments.

"Thou shalt not kill" doesn't mean just don't be a murderer; it means help your neighbor, be friends to your neighbor. We'll see that this is how Luther reads the Ten Commandments later, but it's a typical Christian reading of the Ten Commandments. It's not just a bunch of narrow prohibitions. It's a whole ethic for Christian life. It's enough to learn for your lifetime. So, the command to honor your father and your mother, he expands to mean all relationships to authority, and he's saying every time you obey a legitimate authority like a housemaid sweeping the floor because the father of the house tells her, then you're pleasing God. God is pleased by your obedience. You don't justify yourself before God, but God is happy that you're doing this because he's told you to do it.

Every time you obey the commandment of God and do the good works that God gave you to do, you're pleasing him, not justifying yourself in his sight, but it's like the king's son takes delight in everything that his bride does. Even though in and of themselves they might not be worthy of passing judgment, nonetheless, he delights in everything she does, so when she learns obedience, even though the obedience is imperfect, he's pleased with it. Husband and wife are pleased with each other. That kind of situation is what our good works are like when faith does them. We do them simply to please God, simply because God takes pleasure in us and we take pleasure in pleasing God. We're married here.

Likewise, suppose you've got a father of the household who thinks that the housemaid is a worthy and good person, and he says: "Yes, I think you're great. Please help us with the house and let's sweep this stuff up," and she's glad to do the work. She pleases the master of the house and, therefore, she pleases God because she's honoring father and mother. Luther will say this housemaid sweeping the floor pleases God more than all the works of the monks, because all the works of the monks are self-chosen works, willful—whereas the housemaid is obeying God, and therefore she's more spiritual than all those monks. You can see here why the Reformation ends up becoming very powerful in the minds of ordinary people sweeping floors, rather than the spiritual people in the monasteries.

I want to now introduce a complicated topic that's going to come back for us later on in these lectures when we talk about the doctrine of justification once again by contrasting Luther and other Protestants. I want to talk about Luther's way of distinguishing two kinds of righteousness or two kinds of justice. Remember, righteousness and justice are the same word in Latin, German, and Greek, so Luther doesn't make any distinction whatsoever between justice and righteousness. I will use the two terms interchangeably. Luther wants to distinguish two kinds of righteousness because he wants to distinguish what he calls person and work. This is another version of that inner-outer distinction. The person is who you are inwardly; the work is what you do outwardly. The person is changed by faith; works are works of love, that same set of dualities that we'll be running into over and over again in Luther for the rest of these lectures.

He'll compare it to a tree and fruit. What he says is this: A good tree bears good fruit, and that's how you get good fruit, by having a good tree. You don't get a good tree by growing good fruit. The tree does not make itself good by growing good fruit; the good fruit is good because the tree is good, so the person has to be good before the work is good. Inwardly, you have to be justified by faith in Christ before the outward works are any good. The outward works, the fruit, is what Luther calls *proper* righteousness. This is a technical term. Proper comes from the Latin word *propria*, which means "your own," as in "appropriate" or "property." Proper righteousness is one's own righteousness. It's your own property; it's what you do; it's what you actually do in your own person—not in your own person actually; it's what you do outwardly. What you do in your own person is God's. Let me get to that.

The outward righteousness, the righteousness of good works, is proper righteousness. It's your own. The inward righteousness, the righteousness that changes you from the bottom up through faith, he calls *alien* righteousness. This has got to be confusing, and I want to say just a little bit about this. Alien righteousness comes from the Latin term meaning "other"; *alien* means "other." The alien righteousness is the righteousness of Christ deep in our hearts. It's not apart from us; it's not far from us. It's in our hearts, but it is alien in the sense that it comes not from us but from Christ. It's a gift of God through the Gospel, so the alien righteousness is righteousness deep within us. He said it in this quote I gave you before: "Apart from myself and in Christ, I am righteous. In myself and apart from Christ, I'm unrighteous." So, apart from myself and in Christ, I am righteous, but that means deep within when I believe in the Gospel, Christ is in my heart and that's my righteousness.

What you've got to get used to is this notion: In faith, we look away from ourselves at Christ, over and over again. Don't look at yourself; you see a sinner. Look at Christ, you see yourself justified because Christ died for you. You believe Christ's story; he died for you, so Christ's story tells about who you are. You look at Christ away from yourself and you discover who you really are. Deep within, who you really are is who you are when you're looking away from yourself at Christ, which is another way of saying Christ dwells deep within you. This is hard to get used to. Christ dwells deep within you because you look away from yourself; you don't look inside yourself to find out who you are. You don't look inside yourself to find Christ. You look away from yourself; you pay attention to the Gospel story, which isn't about you, but about Jesus, but because he died for you, it changes you from the inside.

This is for you; it starts with the very depths of your soul, and what's in the very depths of your soul? Christ. How do you know that? By looking at yourself, by looking deep within, by experiencing it, by feeling it? No, by believing it, by believing this Gospel that comes to you from outside. So, what comes to you from outside is an alien righteousness that gets deep within. Precisely by looking away from yourself, you have Christ within your heart. You don't find Christ in your heart by looking in your heart; you find Christ in your heart by looking at the Gospel. So, you don't know that Christ is in your heart except that he promised. That's how you know; he promised; he keeps his promise so you know he's in you. You don't feel it; you don't experience it; you don't look within. You look outside yourself, and that's how Christ is deep within.

That pattern of getting Christ in you by looking away from yourself, looking to something external in order to have the deepest gift of all deep within, that takes getting used to. I'm going to be coming back to it from several different angles later on in the lectures. I think if you don't get this part right, you're not going to get a lot of other things right in Luther. In particular, we have to notice that this notion of righteousness as deep within through the gift of the Gospel is very different from the notion that you train yourself by doing good works, by becoming virtuous, by practice. That goes back to Aristotle; that's a Catholic view that Luther rejects, and we're going to have to see how that works when we get to further discussion of the doctrine of justification in a later lecture.

Lecture Seven
The Meaning of the Sacraments

Scope:

For Luther, the Gospel is an external word that gives believers what it promises, which means that word and sacrament are parallel: Both are outward signs that give the inward gift they signify. Indeed, Luther first works out his concept of Gospel as a word of forgiveness in writings on the sacrament of penance, where he identifies the word of absolution as a sacramental sign—so that in this case, the word *is* the sacrament. This lecture traces Luther's sacramental concept of the word of God in his earliest treatises on the sacraments, dealing with penance, baptism, and the sacrament of Christ's body.

Outline

I. Luther develops his mature concept of the Gospel via the Catholic notion of a sacrament—an *external* thing that can make an *inward* change in a person.

    A. Luther has two ways of dealing with "externals."

    B. On the one hand, he treats external things as secondary or worthless.

        1. While faith changes the heart within, works are outward deeds needed by our body or by our neighbor.

        2. The righteousness that even pagans are capable of is outward, a righteousness of deeds before men, rather than the heart before God.

        3. The more superstitious aspects of late-medieval piety (pilgrimages, indulgences, Masses for the dead) are mere outward works with no power to change the heart.

    C. On the other hand, there is a sense in which Luther's faith is directed wholly at external things.

        1. Though we must not trust outward works, even more emphatically, we must not trust ourselves.

        2. When we look at ourselves apart from Christ, we see only sin; thus, we must continually look away from ourselves to find Christ in the Gospel, which is an external word.

3. The sacraments are part of the story about how we look away from ourselves to find Christ.
4. In fact, Luther first developed his understanding of the Gospel (as a gracious promise that gives what it promises) when he was thinking about the sacraments.

II. The sacraments for Luther have the same basic structure as the Gospel: They are signs that give the gift they signify to those who believe.

    A. The theory of sacraments in Western Christianity stems from Augustine's theory of sacraments as signs of grace.
        1. For Augustine, both sacraments and words are external signs signifying something inner.
        2. Words signify the thoughts of the heart; sacraments signify an inward grace.
        3. Medieval theologians added to this a theory of sacramental efficacy: Sacraments are signs that not only signify but confer grace.
        4. Thus for Luther, the power of the Gospel is similar to that of a sacrament: The Gospel is a sign (promise) that gives what it signifies (promises) to those who believe it.

    B. Luther analyzes the sacraments in terms of their sign structure.
        1. The sacrament itself is an external sign (for example, the water of baptism).
        2. It signifies and confers an inner gift (as baptism signifies and confers death and rebirth in Christ).
        3. It does no good except when received in faith.
        4. It is accompanied by a word without which the sign is a mute material object, not a sacrament (for example, "I baptize you in the name of the Father, the Son and the Holy Spirit").
        5. It has its power or efficacy because of Christ's promise (for example, "whoever believes and is baptized is saved").

III. Luther first describes the Gospel as a gracious and efficacious promise when discussing the sacrament of penance.

    A. This turn to the sacrament to find the Gospel happens in 1518–1519, after the Reformation is already under way.

1. Despite his dedication to a penitential life, Luther shows no interest in the *sacrament* of penance prior to the indulgence controversy, which began the Reformation.
2. Given that indulgences are theologically part of the sacrament of penance, it was a topic Luther could not avoid once he began criticizing indulgences.
3. German scholar Oswald Bayer locates this crucial discovery in an untranslated and little-known set of disputation theses, *On the true way to question and console frightened consciences* (1518).
4. These theses form the outline for a sermon on the sacrament of penance (1519) that is available in English.

B. The sacrament of penance was traditionally divided into four parts.
1. Confession: The penitent confesses his sins to the priest (called the *confessor*).
2. Contrition: The penitent should be contrite, which means he hates his sin and seriously intends to sin no more.
3. Satisfaction: The penitent is assigned some works of penance to make satisfaction (that is, to make up for) his sins.
4. Absolution: The priest formally forgives the penitent's sins, saying the word of absolution: "I absolve you of your sins in the name of the Father, the Son and the Holy Spirit."

C. Luther's treatment of the sacrament of penance shifts the emphasis from the inward penitence of contrition to the external word of absolution.
1. For Luther, the word of absolution functions as the external sign of the sacrament of penance.
2. The penitent should hear the absolution as if Christ himself were saying it.
3. Christ himself promises, "what you loose on earth shall be loosed in heaven."
4. This "gift of the keys" given to Peter in Matthew 16:19 is not just for the pope or the priest but for all Christians—even women and children can absolve sins at need.

D. Luther's focus on the sacrament of penance stems from his concern with indulgences and marks a crucial turning point in his theology.

Essential Reading:

Luther, "The Sacrament of Penance," in *Luther's Works*, vol. 35.

Bainton, *Here I Stand*, chapter 3.

Supplemental Reading:

Luther, "The Sacrament of Baptism," in *Luther's Works*, vol. 35.

Yeago, "The Catholic Luther," in Braaten and Jenson, *The Catholicity of the Reformation*.

Questions to Consider:

1. If God is to be found anywhere, is it outside us or within us?

2. What do you think of sacramental piety? Does it seem to you lovely and comforting, or solemn and joyous, or ritualistic and empty?

Lecture Seven—Transcript

The Meaning of the Sacraments

In the last two lectures, we've been trying to look at the very core of Luther's theology, especially this key central notion known as "Gospel" and its implications for Christian life and for our hearts, souls, bodies, and minds. Now we're going to bring to a close in this lecture the initial treatment of Luther's theology and get ready for Part II in the next lecture, where we start talking about the Reformation, about how Luther's Gospel changed the world. Right now, we're still focusing on how Luther's Gospel changed Luther.

There's a kind of development that I want to sketch here, and I've been setting this up now by talking about the early Luther in 1516, when he's an unknown university professor lecturing at the University of Wittenberg on Paul's letter to the Romans and saying: "You're justified by faith alone"; that is, by hating yourself, by believing in an accusation from God and believing that when God accuses you of being a terrible sinner that that's true and, therefore, you should hate yourself just like God hates you, and if you could really try to damn yourself, then you would really be justified. I wouldn't like to be at those lectures, but then four years later, in 1520, you've got this treatise on *The Freedom of a Christian*, which we've been discussing for the past two lectures, where the word of God is not just this accusation (there is an accusation, this Law), but that's not what the Bible's all about.

What the Bible's all about is the Gospel, this good news about Jesus Christ, this promise of grace and mercy—which is good news, joyous, comforting, consoling. It's like we've got a different Luther in 1520 than we do in 1516, although not an entirely different Luther. I've tried to suggest there's a whole lot that Luther has in common in 1520 with the Luther in 1516. There's justification by faith alone; there's this notion that the justice of God, or the righteousness of God, becomes our righteousness. All the pieces of the puzzle are there except this central notion of Gospel. Once that central notion of Gospel drops into the picture, we have the Luther that we are now familiar with. So, I'm interested in how he gets from 1516, hating himself, to 1520, believing a gracious and kind word of God, a promise of Christ and mercy. How did he get from one to the other?

I think there's a central stopping point, a central way station. It's not a stopping point. It's in between 1516 and 1520. He gets from A to B through a crucial development that has to do with the sacraments. He becomes the Protestant that we know by first becoming more Catholic, that is, by first thinking more deeply about the Catholic notion of a sacrament, which is missing from 1516 and becomes absolutely central in 1520. It's one of the ways that Luther is a bit more Catholic than most other Protestants, which makes him very interesting; so, I want to set this up and think about what's going on.

My suggestion is that the Gospel is ultimately a sacramental concept for Luther; that is, it's a concept of how something external makes an inner change in you. Remember, at the end of our last lecture, we had this real puzzle. You're supposed to be looking away from yourself at an alien righteousness, a righteousness of someone other than you, namely Christ, and somehow that changes you deep *within*. How is it that looking away from yourself, at Christ and not yourself, changes you deep within? Looking inside yourself is just terror, and horror, and sin, and look away from yourself at Christ, of the Gospel, at this external word that's preached, and that changes you deep within. I'm going to suggest now that's a sacramental notion. It's a notion of an *external* word or sign that is a sign that signifies an inner gift, an inner transformation, and it helps bring about that inner transformation. That's a very Catholic idea; that's a sacramental idea.

How do we get to the sacramental idea? Let's think a little bit first about this puzzle about external and internal, and that will help us get to the notion of the sacrament because the sacrament is about external things that make an inner change, and Luther has this very distinctive way of talking about inner and outer, and we need to get used to it. What's so puzzling about it is there's two different ways of talking about inner and outer. Think about what happened when Luther talks about merely external things. On the one hand, he'll treat external things as if they're secondary, sometimes even worthless. Remember, faith is inner; good works are outer. Faith is an inward change; good work is an outward thing that you do. It's a good thing, you should do it, but it's outward, secondary; it doesn't change you from deep *within*.

Another example, Luther will acknowledge that even pagans are capable of certain kinds of righteousness, but it's an outward righteousness, a civil righteousness. A pagan Roman can be a good man who doesn't commit murder, is faithful to his wife, all that sort of thing, but inwardly he's a rebel against God because we all are— so, inwardly he doesn't have a righteousness before God, but outwardly he has a righteousness before human beings, a civil or political righteousness. So, even pagans are capable of a certain kind of outer righteousness; the inner righteousness is Christ in us through faith; so, once again, the inner is what matters most. It's the inner that's really important.

Likewise, there are some external things that are just downright worthless and wrong, like all that *Menschenlehre* that I mentioned before, the doctrines of men. *Menschenlehre* is German for "doctrines of men," self-chosen works, people saying Mass when there's nobody around—a priest is saying Mass, and there's not a single person listening to it. It's just an external work that is supposed to do some kind of magic that'll get somebody out of purgatory. Luther just hates that; he thinks that's terrible blasphemy. This external work is going to save somebody's soul? Forget it, so there's all this outward piety of Catholicism he rejects. What he doesn't reject is the outward sign called the "sacrament," which is very Catholic idea, so what's going on here?

Let's look at another aspect of outward things for Luther. On the one hand, outward things look secondary. You're inwardly free by faith, and you're outwardly the servant of everyone through good works. That's the structure of *The Freedom of a Christian* treatise in 1520. And yet, although we shouldn't trust outward works, we should also not trust ourselves, he says. You don't look inside yourself to find Christ; you look away from yourself, outside yourself, to someone other than you. That's why it's an alien righteousness; *alien* is basically Latin for "other." It's a righteousness that comes from outside you, from other than you. So, the sacrament seemed to be part of the story about how we look away from ourselves to find Christ. I mentioned the Gospel as a place to look to find grace. It's not just praying for grace, like Augustine, but you've got an external place to run to. That place is called the Gospel—a promise, a word. It's resonating in the air; it's the sound waves in the church.

But it also gets deep inside you. Think about music, for instance. Music is an external thing; it's sound waves, and yet it gets in your ears and gets in your heart, and music changes your heart. Luther's very convinced of this; Luther loves music. Music changes your heart; it cheers you up and makes you feel differently, makes you think differently about all of life, and it starts outside of you, a little bit like alien righteousness that way. So, we're getting used to this conceptual structure where something outside—turning away from yourself, outside yourself—changes you within because it's really all about relationship. The consciousness, or rather the *conscience* (actually the same word in Latin), the *conscience* is your consciousness of how you stand before God. The deepest thing within you is your consciousness, your *conscience*, about how you stand before what is outside you, namely God. There is nothing more inner in us than our relationship to what is outside of us, namely God.

We've got to think through that structure, and the best way to think about structures is to think about sacraments. The sacraments, for Luther, have the same basic structure as the Gospel. They're outward, and they give you an inner gift. The theory of the sacraments in Western Christianity and in the Catholicism that Luther was growing up with, stems from (once again) that crucial figure early on in the history of the church, Saint Augustine, who died in 430 AD, so he's a long time before Luther, more than 1,000 years ago. For Augustine, sacraments and words, interestingly, are both external signs. Words are signs that signify what you're thinking; so, they express what you're thinking—so they express what you're thinking by being signs that signify it.

Sacraments are external signs that signify an inner gift of grace. The notion is you've got an outer sign that signifies something inward, and in the Middle Ages, after Augustine, around the 12th century, this thing is added; the external sign of the sacrament not only signifies grace, but it confers grace. The sacraments give a gift of grace. They're an external thing that gives an inner gift. That's a striking idea, and I think Luther could not have come to the notion of the Gospel without that idea in the background. Luther's notion of the Gospel is a sacramental notion. It is, in that sense, a very deeply Catholic notion, and I'll try to show you why by looking at a key text in just a minute.

But let me also show you how Luther analyzes sacraments in terms of their sign structure, just like Augustine. I want to get used to this medieval notion of a sacrament and how Luther adopts it, especially in its Augustinian aspects. The sacrament itself is an external sign—so, for instance, you're baptized. That's a sacrament—so the sign is the water, or perhaps the action of dunking you in water, or sprinkling water on you. That's the external or material sign. What's signified by that sign is an inner gift; for Luther, it's the gift of being born again in Christ, having a new life in Christ, being joined to the church and, therefore, to the body of Christ, and then there's a third element, and actually Luther and Catholics—everyone—agrees about this.

There's the outward sign, the inner gift, and the third element is faith. Faith brings the outward sign and the inner gift together. In order for the outward sign to do any good at all, it has to be received in faith. Without faith, particularly imagine you're an adult getting baptized and you don't believe in this stuff; you're just doing it for show; then, the baptism doesn't do you any good at all. It's just like being splashed with water. You have to receive the sign in faith for it to do you any good, but, likewise, it's the same thing with the Gospel. The Gospel doesn't do you any good if you don't believe it; so, God can say all sorts of wonderful things to you in the promise and the Gospel of Christ, and if you don't believe it, it's like someone is just whispering in your ear, and you're deaf.

Two more points about sacraments. In addition to the outward sign, there's always a word. Conceptually, for Augustine, all words are signs, but in the sacrament you can distinguish the sign, which is the material thing like water, and then the word, which also signifies things—and in the baptism, for instance, you've got the water, which is the external sign, and you have this word such as: "I baptize you in the name of the Father, the Son, and the Holy Spirit." Without the word, the sign doesn't mean anything. If you splash somebody with water and don't say those words, it's not a baptism. The sacrament has essentially both word and sign in it. You can dunk somebody, and if you don't say: "I baptize you in the name of the Father, the Son, and the Holy Spirit," you're just dunking him—you're not baptizing him. Likewise, you can give them bread and wine, and if you don't say this thing about "This is my body, and this is my blood," you're just giving them bread and wine.

The power of the sacrament, for Luther, stems from the word, from the fact that this word is God's promise. Luther thinks that when a pastor or priest says: "I baptize you in the name of the Father, the

Son, and the Holy Spirit," he speaks for Christ. That's Christ saying: "I baptize you in the name of the Father, the Son, and the Holy Spirit"; that's God's Word; so, when you're baptized, you are receiving God's Word in that way. You're actually being named by God's own word: "I baptize you Philip in the name of the Father, the Son, and the Holy Spirit." You're normally named in your baptism, so that it's God in his own word calling you by name and saying: "This is who you are. You belong to the Father, the Son, and the Holy Spirit."

The power of the sacrament is fundamentally the power of the external word, which goes with the sign; so, it's not like you splash somebody with water and their life changes. You splash somebody with water, and you say Christ's word, and then their life changes if they believe it. Likewise, we can quickly sketch this in the Eucharist, the sacrament of Christ's body and blood. You've got the bread and wine; you've got the words: "This is my body, this is my blood"; and then you've got receiving in faith, and then your spiritually fit— that's the inner gift.

Penance is a sacrament in the Catholic Church, and it remained basically a sacramental idea for Luther as well, though not for most other Protestants. Here again, Luther is more Catholic than most Protestants. In penance, you don't really have an external sign apart from the word, so the only external sign in the *sacrament* of penance is the word itself, the word of absolution, which parallels the word in baptism. What the priest is supposed to say at the end of your time in the confessional is: "I absolve you of your sins in the name of the Father, the Son, and the Holy Spirit," so it's parallel to the baptismal formula. What ends up happening is Luther comes to the decision about 1518 that this word of absolution is Christ's word. It is Christ saying: "I absolve you of your sins in the name of the Father, the Son, and the Holy Spirit."

We don't hear Luther talking that way in 1516. We do hear him talking that way in 1518. I think that's the first time that Luther ever thinks of God's Word as a kind word, as a good word. In 1516, God's Word is always against us, an accusation. In 1518, when he's talking about the sacrament of penance and he gets to talk about this word of absolution, he has to say that's Christ's word, that's God himself saying my sins are forgiven, and I'm supposed to believe that. I'm supposed to receive that in faith like every other sacrament, so I don't have a right now to hate myself and think of myself as a damn sinner. I'm supposed to think of myself as a forgiven sinner. I've been spending all this time trying to convince myself that I will never ever have grace.

I'm seeking grace, but I'll never find it. Remember how that works in 1516? You seek grace, and you never find it? You must never presume that you have grace; you must never presume that God is on your side. You must always assume that God is against you because you don't want to say, "I'm OK, I'm good enough." You don't have to presume that, but you do have to believe God's Word, and in 1518, God's Word says, "You're forgiven; your sins are absolved; you don't have a right to think of yourself as a damn sinner anymore." That is where Luther, for the first time, works out the concept of the Gospel as a gracious and efficacious promise, a promise that gives what it signifies—a promise that gives what is promised. That happens when he thinks about the sacrament of penance.

This gets complicated because in 1518 the Reformation is already underway. It would be more convenient if Luther made this discovery before the Reformation began, and then we could talk about this now, and then in the next lecture we could talk about the 95 Theses, and we will talk about the 95 Theses in the next lecture. That's when he posts those theses on the church door, and that's when the Reformation begins, as good a time as any to date the beginning of the Reformation. But, in fact, this happens after that; the 95 Theses, it turns out, still has this theology of self-hatred in it, and then a few months later, he's dealing with the sacrament of penance, and he talks about penance or the word of absolution as a gracious promise of Christ.

He makes the fundamental theological discovery that makes him a Protestant after the Reformation has already begun. The 95 Theses are the old Luther, the Luther of self-hatred. The sacrament of penance ushers in the new Luther. You might think he thought about the sacrament of penance before, but, in fact, he didn't. We don't have any treatment of the sacrament of penance in Luther's writings prior to 1518. He doesn't think about penance as a sacrament, which is very strange because, after all, he's been talking about penance, penitential works, confession; he's been talking about that obsessively, but he's never talked about the sacrament of penance.

He's been interested in the inner penance, the inner change of heart by hating yourself; he never talks about the external word, the absolution that you receive by hearing it with your ears.

I follow here a German scholar named Oswald Bayer, who thinks that the crucial discovery that makes Luther who we now know Luther to be—Luther the Protestant, Luther the Reformation person—happens after the 95 Theses. That happens as Luther thinks about the sacrament of penance (as a result of the 95 Theses, he has to think about the sacrament of penance), and Oswald Bayer, this German scholar whom I follow in this, locates the first carefully worked out version of this notion of the word of absolution as a Gospel promise in a little-known set of theses in Latin that were used in a disputation in the university in 1518, and it's not translated, so I'm going to follow here a sermon on the sacrament of penance that came out in 1519.

I've checked it and compared it with these theses in 1518 in Latin, and it turns out the sermon is based on the theses. You can find most of the theses in 1518 in this 1519 sermon, so what I'm going to do is give you some stuff from this 1519 sermon on the sacrament of penance, which I think gives you the crucial discovery that Luther makes in 1518. Let's say just a little bit about the structure of the sacrament of penance, which is what Luther starts with in these treatises. Traditionally, the sacrament of penance is divided into four parts. There's the confession, the contrition, the satisfaction, and the absolution.

Confession means you go to your priest and you confess your sins. Contrition means that inwardly you should hate your sins. Contrition is inward penance; it's the penance in your heart, the attitude of penance where you hate your sins because you hate the fact that you've offended God. If you've ever done something that you really wish you hadn't done, you hate the fact that you've done it—that's contrition. Then, there's satisfaction. Satisfaction is literally doing enough. After your sins are forgiven, you still have to do something to make up for it. If you're a thief, for instance, you may confess your sins, your sins are forgiven, but then you have to return what you stole. That would be part of satisfaction and, typically, the satisfaction involves prayer.

For instance, if you're Catholic, if you're an older Catholic, you used to go to confessional. They don't tend to have them anymore, and you would confess your sins and the priest would give you what they called in those days "penances." "Say ten Hail Marys and five Our Fathers"—that's satisfaction; that's works of satisfaction. Contrition and satisfaction are both penitential works; they're something you do, and Luther the monk was really focused on contrition, on hating himself, confessing his sin, looking deep in his heart and seeing what a terrible sinner he was, and so he could hate that. He also did some works of satisfaction, but it was the contrition that had him tied up in knots because what he was in effect trying to do was to be so contrite, to have so much penance in his heart, that God had to justify him; so, it's this inner work of penance that was so deadly.

That's why the sacrament of penance was so good for him. He was too inward; he was too focused on this inward change in his heart by trying to do it by his own self, by looking at himself. You don't change yourself by looking at yourself, the mature Luther thinks. You don't change who you are by looking deep within. You look outside of yourself at Christ; so, something had to get him looking outside of himself, and what it was, was the fourth part of the sacrament of penance, the absolution, as I've mentioned, where the priest says: "I absolve you of your sins in the name of the Father, the Son, and the Holy Spirit."

Luther argues in his work on the sacrament of penance in 1518–1519 that that word of absolution is Christ's word. It's Christ saying that—so you don't have a right to say you're a sinner anymore because Christ says otherwise. You have to agree with him, for heaven's sakes, and he's saying that your sins are forgiven—so you'd better believe you're forgiven. In essence, you don't have a choice about it. Jesus is saying this to you, so you have to believe it. Luther never says: "Make a decision for Christ; make a choice; believe; make a decision to believe." Other Protestants say that; Luther never says that. You have to believe it, Luther says, because it's Christ saying it. You're going to call him a liar? Do you dare call God a liar to his face? Then you have to believe that you're forgiven.

It's actually very nice. If you're one of those people who has a hard time thinking: "How can I make a decision in faith? How can I be sure that my faith is real? How can I have a real choice for God?" You tie yourself up in psychological knots the same way you tie yourself up in knots when you're a young Luther trying to confess his sins so much, so that you need this external thing that says, "You don't have a choice about this. You're a forgiven sinner. That's what God says. You're going to believe that, or are you going to call him a liar?" So that's the way I put it from Karl Barth, who says: "It's a must in service of a may." You must believe that God loves you and you're a forgiven sinner, because he says so, and you don't want to call him a liar. That's rather nice. God twists your arm and says: "Are you going to believe that I love you down to the bottom of your soul or not? Or are you going to call me a liar? What's it going to be?"

It took that much pressure to get Luther out of his inwardness, this contrition where he's constantly looking at himself and trying to find all these sins. He needed someone to say: "Wake up Martin, listen to me. Stop looking at yourself, and listen to me. I absolve you of your sins in the name of the Father, the Son, and the Holy Spirit. Are you going to believe that for a change?" That's justification by faith alone. Why is it that this absolution, this sacramental thing that the priest does, is Christ's word? Why would you believe that? You look at the Bible, Luther says, and here Christ says to Peter: "What you bind on earth will be bound in heaven; what you loose on earth will be loosed in heaven," and the word for "loose" is the word for "absolution." "Absolve" comes from the verb "to loose." What you absolve on earth is absolved in heaven, Jesus says to Peter.

Luther thinks that means not just that Peter can do this, but that any Christian can do it. You don't even have to be a priest; you can be a woman or child, Luther says. He's getting radical already; he's already working on the notion of the priesthood of all believers. Any Christian can absolve you of your sins—can say: "I absolve you of your sins in the name of the Father, the Son, and the Holy Spirit," or can assure you your sins are forgiven in Christ's name. Christ himself says that's his word because he says if you loose someone's sins on earth, they're loosed in heaven. So, Christ's promise in the Bible backs up Christ's word in the sacrament. There are two words of Christ here—the promise in the Bible, which then authorizes this word in the sacrament. The sacramental word is not the priest's word; it's not the church's word; it's Christ's word because he said so, in effect. Just like in the Eucharist, when the priest says: "This is my body, given for you," that is Christ speaking, not the priest. Here is God's Word, Luther says.

What happens when you hear this is God's Word? Let me read to you how this sounds because I read a little bit of the lectures on Paul's letter to the Romans in 1516 all about self-hatred. Listen to how different this sounds; this is only two years later. When talking about the word of absolution, Luther says: "This holy, comforting, and gracious word of God must enter deeply into the heart of every Christian, where he may with great gratitude let it become part of him. Instead of identifying and agreeing with the word of accusation, you identify and agree with a gracious and comforting word." You're supposed to let yourself be comforted; God himself wants to comfort you. Who are you to disagree?

Notices it's an external word, this holy, comforting, and gracious word of God; it's a word of absolution—someone speaks it, and it must enter deeply into the heart of every Christian; so you've got this structure, this external word of absolution that enters deep into your heart, and you must, remember, you must let this happen so that you may with great gratitude let it become part of you. You may love God and be glad, and rejoice, and be comforted. You may do all those things; you have permission to do all those things because you have to. You don't have a choice. God's not letting you go out and hate yourself anymore. You don't have a choice about that; you are not free to hate yourself anymore. You must be comforted, and glad, and joyful. This is wonderful stuff.

Here's another way of emphasizing the outwardness of this. Luther says: "This is called a sacrament, a holy sign because in it, one hears the words externally that signify spiritual gifts within, gifts by which the heart is comforted and set at peace." That's what a sacrament does; it comforts you and sets you at peace with an external word, like the word of absolution in the sacrament of penance and, of course, it has to be received in faith. That's the must; you must believe this in faith, he says. He firmly believes that the absolution, the words of the priest, is true by the power of Christ's words. So, it's true, you are absolved of your sins. Why? Because Christ promised.

That means that these other parts of the sacrament—contrition and satisfaction, which are traditional parts of the Catholic sacrament of penance—are not nearly so important. Luther will say contrition and good works are not to be neglected, but one must not build upon them. You don't build your hope and your confidence on them, but only upon the sure words of Christ, who promises you that when the priest looses you, you shall be loosed. Your contrition and works may deceive you, you may try to be pure in your hatred of your sin, you may try to be pure in your works of love—but you're never good enough that way. These things will deceive you, and the devil will very soon overturn them in the hour of death and temptation.

Remember, this is problem with the art of dying; can you really trust that your good works are good enough? In the moment of death, you'd better not trust that. What do you trust? Christ alone; trust his word—that's worth trusting. Your good works are not good enough in the hour of temptation, the hour of *Anfechtung,* that German word for "assault," when the devils are hovering around your bed as you're dying, saying: "Your good works are not good enough. All your works are really mortal sin. Despair and die." That's what the devil's saying, and what you say to him in reply, Luther says, is "Christ says otherwise, and I'll believe Christ instead of you." Instead of trusting in your contrition and good works, you trust in Christ, your God, who will not lie to you, says Luther. That's how you answer the devil. It's God's Word; we don't have the right to doubt it, and we don't have the right to believe the devil instead.

Quick note, that also means you see forgiveness of sin doesn't really depend on human authority, and it is not the authority of the pope or the priest, but the word of Christ. This is where the Reformation side of it comes in. It's not on the pope's authority that the priest is absolving you, but on Christ's authority, and the pope has no say about it. This is actually different from the situation in the Middle Ages in Luther's time, when the pope actually reserved some sins to himself, which means if you go to confession and have certain reserved sins, the confessor, the priest, cannot absolve you of those sins. He has to go to a bishop or maybe even the pope, and then, typically, you have to pay to have your sins absolved. The only freedom from your anxious conscience is by cash payment.

Luther says no, it's all free because it's Christ's promise; the pope and the priests have nothing to say about it. Any Christian can absolve you of any of your sins because Christ said so; if it's loosed on earth, it's loosed in heaven, and so anyone, any Christian, including women and children, can assure your forgiveness of your sins in Christ's name because that's the Gospel. It belongs to all Christians, and that's why all Christians are priests, the priesthood of all believers, which we'll run into as a Reformation document just a little bit later.

Let's set the context for our next lecture just a bit. Luther came to this notion of sacrament of penance because he has to think about the sacrament of penance for the first time in his career. Why? It's 1518, and he's writing about indulgences. Those 95 Theses are about indulgences, and indulgences, it turns out, are all about penance, about what happens when there's some penance left over, there's satisfaction that you haven't completed yet, and you have to complete it in purgatory. Indulgences get you off the hook so you don't have to complete all those terrible satisfactions in the next life. In order to think about indulgences, you've got to think about the sacrament of penance; so when Luther is defending the 95 Theses in 1518, just a few months after he posts them in 1517, he has to deal with the sacrament of penance for the first time in his life. For the first time in his life, he has to deal with an external word that says: "Your sins are forgiven; you're supposed to believe that," and I think that changes everything.

Lecture Eight
The Indulgence Controversy

Scope:

The Reformation began with the indulgence controversy, when Luther posted his famous 95 Theses on the church door at Wittenberg on October 31, 1517. Luther's doctrine of the Gospel took shape as he considered what was wrong with indulgences and how they undermined true penance. While Luther was coming to ever more radical theological conclusions, the indulgence controversy exploded in public when Luther's earliest papal opponent labeled him a heretic because he questioned the pope's actions. This exaggerated papalism shifted the focus of discussion and helped turn an academic theological disputation about indulgences into a Europe-wide controversy about papal authority and the doctrine of justification by faith alone.

Outline

I. The beginning of the Reformation is traditionally dated October 31, 1517, when Luther nailed 95 Theses to the church door in Wittenberg.

    A. Yet no one, least of all Luther, expected a sweeping reformation of the church to come of this.

        1. The theses were not nailed up in protest against the church but were posted on the bulletin board on the church door, announcing an academic disputation in Latin that was unreadable to the laity.

        2. The theses concerned only the narrow issue of "the power and efficacy of indulgences."

        3. They were directed against certain local abuses by indulgence-sellers, which were corrected before the Reformation was even fully underway.

        4. They never question the authority of the pope and repeatedly insist that the abuses they critique are contrary to the pope's wishes.

        5. They are based on Luther's early theology of self-hatred and do not mention justification by faith alone.

B. Hence, there is a complicated story to tell about how an academic criticism of a specific local abuse grew into a principled alternative to the medieval Catholic form of ecclesiastical control over anxious consciences and, thence, into the Reformation.

II. The events leading up to the posting of the 95 Theses are a late-medieval story.

A. The story begins with Albert of Brandenburg acquiring the archbishopric of Mainz, which is very expensive, and funding it through a sale of indulgences, which went to pay off the pope and help build St. Peter's in Rome.

B. The indulgences were hawked by a traveling salesman, a Dominican named Tetzel, who is famous for the jingle "As soon as the coin in the coffer rings, a soul from Purgatory upward springs."

C. Tetzel's activities were banned by the elector Frederick of Saxony (where Luther lived) to keep people from being fleeced by Rome.

D. This was not a rejection of indulgences *per se*, which Frederick believed in, together with the power of relics, Masses for the dead, and so on; all were important to Wittenberg's economy.

E. By this time, Luther had been appointed town preacher, as well as university professor, and his public opposition to indulgences stems from concern for the spiritual health of his flock.

    1. The 95 Theses pitted his theology of self-hatred, which he thought of as true inward penance, against confidence in the uncertain promise of indulgences.

    2. Although reputable authorities never claimed indulgences could forgive sins but only remit punishment in purgatory, less reputable representatives, including Tetzel, were not always so clear.

    3. The 95 Theses strike at the heart of the theology of indulgences, arguing that the church has no power to remit the penalties of purgatory.

    4. In order to make this theological argument, Luther must think for the first time about penance as a sacrament, which results in a dramatic change in his theology, described in Lecture Seven.

III. Within a year after the posting of the 95 Theses, the debate came to center on papal authority and justification by faith.

    A. In 1518, Luther writes a defense of the theses in which the new theology of justification by faith becomes increasingly prominent.

    B. In October 1518, after the imperial Diet of Augsburg, Luther is interviewed by Cardinal Cajetan, the papal legate, for three days.

        1. Cajetan's brief from the pope is to secure Luther's recantation or have him arrested and sent to Rome.

        2. Against Cajetan's intentions, the interview turns into a debate, where Luther defends not only his criticism of indulgences but also his view of papal authority and justification by faith in the promise of God.

        3. Catching wind of the plans to arrest him, Luther escapes Augsburg by night and returns to Wittenberg a hunted man, a year after posting the 95 Theses.

    C. Suddenly, the issue of the authority of the pope becomes central to the debate.

        1. Prierias argues that because the pope is infallible, anyone who disagrees with him is a heretic.

        2. A year later, Prierias appeals to the canon law that says popes cannot be deposed, even if they lead multitudes to hell; this helps convince Luther that the papacy is Antichrist.

Essential Reading:

Luther, Ninety-five Theses, in Dillenberger, Lull, and *Luther's Works*, vol. 31.

Bainton, *Here I Stand*, chapters 4–5.

Supplemental Reading:

Luther, Proceedings at Augsburg, in *Luther's Works*, vol. 31.

Luther, "Explanations of the Ninety-five Theses," in *Luther's Works*, vol. 31 (for the emergence of the Reformation doctrine of justification, look at the explanations of Theses 7, 38, and 62).

Questions to Consider:

1. Is this story so far like the Luther you had expected to hear about?

2. Could or should Luther have managed to find some way to be critical of papal abuses without rejecting the papacy as an anti-Christian institution?

Lecture Eight—Transcript
The Indulgence Controversy

We're now starting Part Two of this series of lectures on Martin Luther, where we start looking at the course of the Lutheran Reformation and, indeed, the course of the whole Reformation—that huge social, religious, and historical movement that changed the shape of Western European society and religion—and Luther, more than anyone else, got that whole thing started. We've been looking previous to this time in our lectures (up to this point) at the notion of Gospel, which is the central notion in Luther's theology. Now we want to look at what happens when Luther's theology begins to enter the public stage, become an issue of public controversy, and what happens then to the rest of Europe as a result.

We'll start with the traditional starting point of the Reformation; it is really as good a place as any to mark the beginning of the Reformation. That happens on October 31, 1517, when Luther famously posts 95 theses on the church door in Wittenberg. (By the way, for those of you who don't know German, it looks like Wittenberg, but it's V-ittenberg in German.) That's where Luther lives; that's where he teaches in the university; and that's where he goes on basically Halloween, All Hallows' Eve, or the eve of All Saints' Day, and he goes to the church door and he nails up these 95 theses.

This event has sometimes been distorted. He's not nailing them up in anger and protest. You sometimes get this picture; Luther goes to the church door and says: "I protest this church," and he nails these 95 theses up. That's not what he's doing. The church door is where the bulletin board is, and he's tacking up a set of theses on the bulletin board. The theses are in Latin; they're not directed toward ordinary people, to the common folk; they're directed toward other scholars and priests, people who can read Latin. They're a university thing; what he's doing is he's announcing a set of public disputations in Latin about these 95 theses. He's not protesting the church. The word "Protestant" only comes into circulation about 10 years later, and it's not about protesting the church, but about protesting something the emperor does against the Reformation.

What he's doing is he's a professor announcing a public disputation that will be centering on 95 theses that you can argue for or against.

The theses are titled "Disputations on the Power and Efficacy of Indulgences"; that is, what can indulgences accomplish? So they're about the abuses of indulgences by local indulgence sellers, which Luther wanted to correct and, indeed, one of the odd things about this is that the abuses in the use of indulgences were corrected before the Reformation really got fully underway. This was a very temporary problem; it was almost over by the time you get to 1521 or so; so, by the time the Reformation really gets up a head of steam, the issues have changed. It's not about indulgences; it's about something much, much more.

In fact, Luther ended up being very surprised about what happened. He thought he was a professor trying to talk about a church abuse that needed to be corrected, and lo and behold, someone takes them down from the church door, publishes them, translates them into German, and people start reading them; they are very interested, and it becomes a huge controversy very quickly. But it's important to know something about the content of the 95 Theses. He's not protesting the church; he's not attacking the pope. He mentions the pope quite a bit in the 95 Theses, and he is always deferential to the pope. He says the bad things that are happening with indulgences are against the wishes of the pope; surely the pope doesn't want this to be happening; so, he never says anything but good things about the pope in the 95 Theses.

There's no attack on the church; there's no attack on the papacy and, also, as I've already suggested, the mature Reformation theology of faith in the Gospel of Christ is not yet present in the 95 Theses. The 95 Theses have this theology of self-hatred. In the fourth of the theses, Luther announces that true inward penance is self-hatred. It would be more Catholic to say true inward penance is hatred of sin—that's contrition—but Luther goes further. This is the early Luther, the Luther of self-hatred. True inner penance, true contrition, means you hate yourself; you want to be damned. That's the underlying theology of the 95 Theses. We're not yet getting Luther's Reformation theology; we're not yet getting the Gospel; we're not yet getting an attack on the pope; we're not yet getting an attempt to criticize the church. We've got this distinct local problem about indulgences, which Luther wants to correct.

Let's talk about his local problem with indulgences. What's going on with the selling of indulgences in Germany in 1517, when Luther tacks up the 95 Theses? This is going to be a late medieval story; this is going to bring us back to the themes of our second lecture about how spiritual power, economic power, and political power are tied up together in the Middle Ages in a way that we're just not used to nowadays, and we have to remind ourselves how this goes. Let's tell the story here a little bit.

We have to go back to a man named Albert of Brandenburg; sometimes the name is given in German, Albrecht, but Albert of Brandenburg. He is a member of the Hohenzollern family, almost as important a family as the Hapsburgs. These are important people; they are on the make—they are trying to consolidate their control of Germany as much as possible, so they want Albert—who's a young man—to get as much control, as much power, as possible by becoming a bishop in as many places as possible. Nowadays, of course, you're not allowed to be bishop except in one place; that's good church practice, and the Catholic Church insists on that.

But in the 16th century, things were different. Pope Julius II was bishop of about half a dozen places before he became pope. Albert is already, in fact, bishop of Halberstadt and the archbishop of Magdeburg, as well as the secular Margrave of Brandenburg; he's the secular prince of Brandenburg; he's the bishop of Halberstadt; he's the archbishop of Magdeburg. Being bishop of more than one place means that you are a pluralist in the medieval sense of the term; you hold more than one benefice. Remember, a *benefice*, like a *bishopric*, is a source of wealth and power, as well as a spiritual office. When you become a bishop, you get power, and you get wealth. That's what Albert is after; that's what his family is after. They want him to be archbishop of Mainz, in addition to bishop of Halberstadt and archbishop of Magdeburg.

How does he get to be archbishop of Mainz? How does he get to be archbishop of two places? It is irregular; even in the 16th century, that's an irregular proceeding; so, the pope has a chance to say: "This is not quite according to canon law, so you have to pay extra." Remember the business about annates. Annates are the tax that a bishop pays to the pope in the first year of holding a benefice as a way of paying for the benefice. He has to fund the papacy somehow; the bishop owes the pope, so part of the money of the benefice goes to the pope. It's a kind of tax, but when you're charging as much as the pope charged Albert of Brandenburg, it really does verge on the sin known as *simony*.

Simony goes back to Simon Magus in the Bible, who tried to buy spiritual power from the apostles. Albert is trying to buy a benefice from the pope. He's actually not very interested in the spiritual power of it; he wants the temporal power. He wants the wealth, the land, and the power. He will become the ruler of Mainz, the city of Mainz in Germany, by becoming the archbishop of Mainz. The archbishop of Mainz is the temporal prince over Mainz, but it happens a lot with archbishops in Germany. By becoming archbishop of the city, he becomes a prince of the city. He's going to rule Mainz. It's a plum—it's worth buying. It's expensive. Pope Leo X is the Medici pope; he is charging 10,000 ducats for this benefice—10,000 ducats in annates. That's a lot of money.

Albert doesn't have that much money, but this is a little bit like a takeover situation in our economy. If you're a corporation that wants to gobble up another corporation, you go into debt so you can buy that corporation. Albert, he wants to gobble up a new benefice; how is he going to do it? He goes into debt; he borrows money so he can buy the benefice. He borrows money from the Fuggers, the most important banking family of the 16th century. He borrows a lot of money, of course; he buys the benefice. Now he's got to pay them back. How is he going to pay them back? He's going to sell indulgences. For that, he needs a license from the pope, but the pope is willing to help him with that. The pope says: "You want to fund this? I like this 10,000 ducats you're giving me. I'm willing to help you fund this. You can sell indulgences."

The pope issues indulgences (only the pope can do this), and now Albert commissions a man named Tetzel, who's a Dominican friar, to go around Germany selling indulgences. The proceeds from the indulgences go half of them to the pope, who will use them to continue work on St. Peter's. You know St. Peter's in Rome, that huge magnificent church; it's built in part from money from Germany from these indulgences, and it helped start the Reformation (that church did). The other half of the money goes to Albert to pay back his bank loan. Albert has a lot riding on these indulgences; he's got to pay back this loan. He's got this Dominican friar going around in Germany named Tetzel selling indulgences.

What do indulgences do? Indulgences get you out of purgatory, especially *plenary indulgences*, which these are. A *plenary indulgence* is a full indulgence, and it means that all of your punishment in purgatory is canceled. Tetzel would go around with his little jingle, saying: "As soon as the coin in the coffer rings, a soul from purgatory upward springs." You throw the money in the chest, and as soon as it hits the bottom of the chest and clinks, there's a soul jumping out of purgatory and going to heaven. You get to pay to get your friends out of purgatory. You get your relatives, your dear ones, to heaven because you paid cash on the barrel. You can imagine Luther, who is so serious about inward penance, and what he thinks about that.

It turns out, in fact, a lot of people don't like this. You don't have to be a deep religious spirit to dislike this. Tetzel's activities were banned in Luther's territory, called Electoral Saxony. There's actually two Saxonies; one of them is run by a duke, and that's called Ducal Saxony—that's run by a man named Duke George. And then there's Electoral Saxony, which is run by his brother or cousin, Frederick. Frederick "the Wise" is Luther's ruler; he's the Elector of Saxony because he is one of the seven rulers in Germany who help elect the next emperor; so it's called Electoral Saxony.

Frederick "the Wise" is widely admired. He's widely thought to be wise—both in his time and by historians today. He was smart; he realized we don't want this guy fleecing our people. All he's going to be doing is making people anxious in their consciences and also selling them a bill of goods, and then exporting the money back to Rome. I don't need that. He's not allowed to sell that stuff around here. So there's no Tetzel in Luther's area, but it's just across the border, and there were people from Wittenberg, where Luther is living, going across the border to Ducal Saxony and elsewhere to buy indulgences. After all, it's a pretty attractive proposition. You get your mom, or your dad, or your grandma, or your grandpa out of purgatory; you pay and you send them to heaven. Isn't that nice?

Frederick, by the way, is not like Luther; he's not a Protestant yet. He is actually a very pious Catholic. He believes in relics; he believes in Masses for the day. Remember, there were 9,000 Masses being performed in 1519, two years after the 95 Theses were posted—9,000 Masses mostly at the side altars, mostly with no one there, a very Catholic thing. Frederick collects relics; the castle church has a vast number of relics—things like a bit of milk from the Virgin Mary, a nail from the cross of Christ, a thorn from the Crown of Thorns, a piece of Jesus's crib—all these holy things and, of course, people would go on pilgrimage, go to Wittenberg, to see these holy things and pray in front of them, and then make a contribution.

These relics were a moneymaking operation; pilgrimage was a moneymaking operation, sort of like tourism is today. Frederick's motives are always mixed. He wants to keep Tetzel out because he's got a religious economy going here. It's a good thing; he doesn't want that compromised by this guy, Tetzel. You want to keep the money in Germany, for heaven's sakes, not exported to Rome. As a matter of fact, the religious economy of Wittenberg is so focused on these medieval Catholic things that they have to do something quite striking.

You've got all these priests; they're all living off of endowments to say all these 9,000 Masses. It supports quite an economy, quite a large number of priests, but no one is preaching to the ordinary people of Wittenberg. These priests are paid to say Masses with no one listening. The town council of Wittenberg, as a responsible set of rulers, says: "We need a town preacher who will preach to ordinary people," and so, in 1514, they appoint someone to preach to the ordinary people in Wittenberg in the church, and guess who that is? It's Martin Luther.

Martin Luther, thus, feels responsible as a pastor about what's going on with the 95 Theses. He's, of course, appalled by the indulgences because he's thinking it's so hard to be justified by faith because you have to hate yourself, hate your sins, confess your sins when you're doing penance, and you've really got to get serious about this stuff, and here are these people thinking they can buy their way out of it. That's complacency, and it's not likely to work. Who can be sure that this works? Remember Luther at the top of those stairs; who can be sure if this really works? At this point, Luther is thinking, "Of course it doesn't work. Only true inward penance works." Buying your way out of purgatory isn't going to work, and people are going to trust in money when they should be trusting in true penance.

Luther decides to launch an attack on the power of indulgences. It's important to see that Tetzel is going a little far. The doctrine of indulgences had not been fully systematized and developed at this point in Catholic theology, so there are a variety of opinions. The reputable authorities never claimed that indulgences could forgive sins or buy grace. All they did was cancel punishment in purgatory. It's called remission of punishment, not remission of guilt; only the sacrament of penance remits guilt when the priest absolves you. But after your guilt and sin have been absolved, you also have these satisfactions to do, these works of penance that will be extended to punishment in purgatory.

What purgatory is is an extension of this satisfaction you're supposed to make. Your sins are forgiven; that's why you're in purgatory. If your sins weren't forgiven, you'd be in hell. Your sins are forgiven, and your guilt is forgiven, but you've still got some punishment to purify you and make you better. The indulgences are supposed to get you out of that. It's is kind of self-contradictory actually; if the punishment in purgatory is supposed to make you a better person, then why would you want to be released from it? In fact, the deeper Catholic notions of purgatory do not think of purgatory as a place of second-rate hell. It's actually a place of purification, a place of love and hope. If you read Dante, for instance, in the *Divine Comedy*, or Catherine of Genoa, who has a treatise on purgatory, purgatory is a place of love. The people who are in purgatory are living in hope.

There are no demons in purgatory; there are no hellish tortures; there's this purification out of love, and the people in purgatory don't want to leave purgatory until they're purified. People's prayers help, but you don't pay to get out of the only coherent notion of purgatory. But in the late Middle Ages, Dante's notion of purgatory, this humane and deeply spiritual notion of purgatory, is not the main notion of purgatory. Purgatory is a place of hellish torture; there are demons with pitchforks ripping the skin off your back, and again, in modern Catholic teaching, like in Dante, there are no demons in purgatory.

Purgatory is actually, Dante insists, part of heaven. Everyone in purgatory is forgiven; everyone in purgatory is in a state of grace; everyone in purgatory loves God. There are no demons there. But in the late Middle Ages, that's not how most people thought about purgatory. They pictured purgatory as a kind of junior hell. There are demons there; the only thing different between purgatory and hell, really, is that purgatory's not permanent, and so you really want to get out of there as soon as possible. If you can pay to get out, great, let's do it. Luther, looking at this, says one of the things he thinks is that real purgatory is not demons and all that sort of stuff. Real purgatory is fear and terror; real hell is fear and terror. The only difference is that purgatory is not permanent.

Luther's notion of hell is this notion of terror where all things accuse you, and they accuse you in the voice of God. That's real purgatory; Luther thinks he's experienced purgatory on earth. He thinks that that's what's going to help you. You don't want to actually escape from it; you want to keep on being terrified so that you can get thoroughly purged of your sin. Indulgence is a way of paying to escape from the hard work of penance and, therefore, it will corrupt ordinary people by making them think that they can buy grace, buy forgiveness of sins, get out of the serious work of penance by paying for it instead. Luther strikes at the very heart of the theology of indulgences. He argues that the church has no power to remit the penalties of purgatory, and it's in that context that he also has to, for the first time, deal with sacrament of penance, as we mentioned last time.

How is it that this discussion of indulgences and penance ends up becoming the Reformation? It turns out this way a few months later, in 1518, when Luther is writing an explanation of the 95 Theses. The 95 Theses are about seven pages long; the explanations are about a 180-page book—so he's writing a whole book defending them, and that's where he starts introducing the notion of the Gospel.

For instance, he says:

> You're justified when you're terrified by God, but there's also this word of absolution, and that comforts you, and so you're supposed to believe that you're forgiven because the word of absolution says so. You're not justified by the word; you're justified by the terror, but the word comforts you.

That's in the explanation of the seventh thesis. A little bit later, in the explanation of the 38th thesis, we get his mature view. We're justified not by being terrified; we're justified by a comforting word, by the Gospel and, in fact, in Thesis 62, in the explanation of that thesis written in 1518, we get an explicit contrast between Law and Gospel, and we have the mature Luther.

Interestingly enough, it's that book that gets things rolling. In 1518, in October, they have an imperial Diet, a kind of parliament of the empire, where the Emperor Charles V meets with the princes like Frederick "the Wise" and the Duke George of Ducal Saxony. They have this Diet of Augsburg, and afterwards there's a papal representative, a papal legate from the pope, a man named Cajetan. He's the most brilliant Catholic theologian of the time; he's the most able theologian. He's a legate because he's got some business to do at the Diet about crusades and things. But after the Diet is over, he also got instructions from the pope to talk to Luther. His job is to get Luther to recant, to revoke, to take it back, or else to get him arrested and sent to Rome. He's not supposed to debate with Luther; he doesn't intend to debate with Luther, but, in fact, that's what ends up happening.

It's hard to get Luther to shut up, and it's impossible to get him to retract. Interestingly enough, Cajetan has not just read the 95 Theses, he's read the explanations of the 95 Theses that Luther wrote in 1518, and he focuses some of the discussion, in fact, on Thesis 7, where Luther says, remember: "You're justified by being terrified, but the comforting word of the absolution is also something you should believe. You should be certain that the absolution is true because it's Christ's word [that's the mature theology coming through]. Cajetan says: "You're never supposed to be certain that the sacraments give you grace. That would be presumption," and that's the standard Catholic view to this day. You're not supposed to be certain you're in a state of grace; that's presumptuous. Luther says: "It's Christ's promise."

There, for the first time, you have a Catholic-Protestant disagreement. Luther's actually taking a higher view of the sacrament than the Catholic is. "You can be certain that the sacrament gives us grace. You should be certain that the sacrament gives us grace because it's Christ word." That's, of course, closely tied to justification by faith alone; believe it because Christ says it. Cajetan wants him to revoke it and to recant and, for Luther, that sounds like saying you can't believe the Gospel. That's how Luther hears it, in fact; it's as if: "This cardinal [and Cajetan is a cardinal; he's one of the highest bishops in Rome after the pope], this guy from Rome, is telling me I'm now allowed to believe the Gospel of Christ."

That's what the Reformation is about. Luther hears the Catholic Church saying: "You're not allowed to believe the Gospel. You're supposed to be in bondage to the pope. The pope gets to forgive your sins," especially those reserved sins that I mentioned that only the pope can absolve, but Christ? Christ doesn't get to say anything about this. What's this about believing the Gospel? Luther says to Cajetan: "I can't take these things back. To revoke those things, which I must believe according to the testimony of my own conscience, I can't do that. As long as these scriptural passages stand," says Luther, "I cannot do otherwise." We're going to run into that phrase again in a couple of years in another Diet, the Diet of Worms: "Here I stand, God help me, I cannot do otherwise."

This debate with Cajetan goes on for several days, and then Luther catches wind of the fact that he's supposed to be getting arrested. Cajetan evidently is setting up the arrest of Luther, and he escapes in the middle of the night. He has to sneak by the guards of the gate because they're looking for him. He escapes, and he goes back to Wittenberg. He, interestingly enough, arrives back on October 30, 1518, one year after the posting of the 95 Theses. It's a year later, and he's now a hunted man. He has now been condemned by the pope. He is supposed to be arrested; he's being labeled as a heretic. One year. Things go on from there.

Let me mention another thing that happens in 1518, another track, because in addition to the issue of justification by faith in the Gospel, which comes up in this Diet of Augsburg, when Luther's talking to Cajetan, another issue that comes up (big time) is the authority of the pope. The 95 Theses, as I said, did not attack the authority of the pope, but within a year, the authority of the pope has become a big issue in the indulgence controversy because the indulgence controversy really expands; it's no longer just about indulgences. The attack comes from Rome, from another theologian in Rome named Sylvester Prierias. He is not as able a theologian as Cajetan, but he is the official papal theologian. He is the chief theologian in Rome in service to the pope.

He replies to the 95 Theses in a book in 1518, where he attacks Luther for disagreeing with the pope. Luther didn't want to disagree with the pope, but Prierias is saying: "You are disagreeing with the pope, and that makes you a heretic." He clubs Luther; he says: "The pope is infallible." This doctrine of the infallibility of the pope had not been fully developed at this point; Prierias is a big advocate of this doctrine. He says the Roman Church and the pope cannot err when the pope is acting in his capacity as pope to make a decision, when he comes to a decision in consequence of his office. The pope can be wrong about whether it's going to rain tomorrow, but when the pope makes an official decision, he can't be wrong; he's infallible.

That was a relatively new doctrine at the time. Therefore, whoever does not hold to the teaching of the Roman Church and the pope as an infallible rule of truth, from which even Holy Scripture draws its power and authority, is a heretic. The Bible gets its power and authority from the pope, says Prierias. That's going further than the Roman Catholic Church does today. That's going beyond the line, and it's like saying the Gospel of Christ is truth because the pope says it is. Who gets their authority from whom, for heaven's sakes?

Luther does not like this at all. It goes a little further, "Whoever says in regard to indulgences," writes Prierias, "whoever says in regard to indulgences that the Roman Church cannot do as she actually has done (by issuing indulgences) is a heretic." If you question what the pope actually does when he issues indulgences, then you're questioning the pope. That means you're a heretic because the pope is infallible, a very blunt instrument for attacking Luther. If you disagree with what the pope does, you're a heretic. There's no dialogue here, and it's as if everything depends on what the pope says; so, it's the Roman Church that raises the issue of the authority of the church and, particularly, the authority of the pope. Luther did not attack the authority of the pope; the Roman Church insisted, Prierias insisted, it's all about the authority of the pope. You're a heretic because you question the pope's authority, and Luther says: "Maybe I should question the pope's authority."

In fact, in 1519, a year later, there's a public debate in Leipzig between Luther and one of his colleagues and some Catholics in Leipzig, and Luther's opponent in this debate in Leipzig says: "We could've agreed about this stuff about indulgences easily enough if you hadn't attacked the authority of the pope." The authority of the pope is now the issue. Indulgences? There's some abuses in indulgence, they can be cleaned up, most of the Catholics think, but attacking the authority of the pope—and the problem was that the pope himself commissioned this man, Prierias, to say it's all about the pope. The pope basically plays the pope card, and that was a mistake.

He should have thought: "Maybe we should clean up the sale of indulgences. It's not being done right; we can fix a few things." Pope Leo could've responded that way. "Tetzel's not doing it right; let's fix this. Martin, you're speaking up too loud, you're questioning the pope; cut it out, but, meanwhile, let's fix indulgences." He could've taken that tack, but instead they said: "You're questioning the pope. The pope is infallible; you're a heretic; cut it out." The authority of the pope becomes the issue. Luther didn't make it the issue; the pope made it the issue through this man Sylvester Prierias, who is the pope's chief theologian and was clearly acting on the pope's behalf.

In 1519, again, Prierias writes another document in reply to Luther's reply to him; so, there's a back and forth here, and this is the second time that Prierias writes about Luther, and he brings to Luther's attention a piece of canon law that reads like this: "If the pope were so scandalously bad that he led multitudes of souls to the devil, still he could not be removed from office." This is a papal decree; it's in the canon law. Luther reads this in the summer of 1520 because he doesn't get Prierias's reply in Wittenberg until 1520 (it's a very fateful summer), and he reads this and he wonders if everyone in Rome has gone crazy. If the pope leads people to hell, then you can't do anything about it? If the pope sells stuff, makes money by driving people to despair and to hell, and this is how he funds the papacy, that's OK? You can't do anything about it?

In his reply to Prierias in 1520, his comment is: "Be astonished, O heaven. Shudder, O earth. Behold, O Christians, what Rome is." It will take him a few months to get explicit about what he thinks Rome actually is; he'll say that Rome is Antichrist; Rome is the principal of the devil; it is an institution that is anti-Christian, that comes right straight from the devil because it's saying: "I, the pope, can drive everyone to the devil. Even if they all go to hell, I can make my money that way, and you can't do anything about it." Luther's conclusion at the end of all this, as he thinks this through in his second response to Prierias is this: "Now farewell unhappy, hopeless, blasphemous Rome. The wrath of God has come upon you in the end as you deserved."

He's decided that the pope is Antichrist; that's the deep decision that makes the Reformation necessary. You don't compromise with the

Antichrist. You don't try to reform the Antichrist. The Antichrist is no longer the church; the institution of the Antichrist can only be resisted. You break away from it; you have nothing to do with it; you start anew from the Gospel of Christ instead of from the word of Antichrist. That makes the Reformation necessary.

Lecture Nine

The Reformation Goes Public

Scope:

Under the protection of his prince, the elector Frederick "the Wise" of Saxony, Luther is kept safe from Rome and is able to develop a program of Reformation and advocate it in a voluminous outpouring of writings that start to change the religious landscape of Europe. His address *To the Christian Nobility* picks up age-old complaints of the nobility versus the clergy and transforms them into a radically new vision of church and society. By the time he must face trial as a heretic, it is not before the pope but the emperor at the Diet of Worms (1521), from which come the famous words "Here I stand. I cannot do otherwise." Declared a criminal by the Edict of Worms, Luther goes into hiding in the castle at the Wartburg, once again under Frederick's protection. The future of the Lutheran Reformation is tied ever afterward to the protection of rulers.

Outline

I. After 1518, the case of Martin Luther becomes increasingly public and political.

    A. Frederick the Wise, elector of Saxony, is Luther's indispensable protector in these years.

        1. Pressured by Cajetan to hand Luther over and uncertain what to make of Luther's teaching, Frederick nonetheless asks Luther not to flee and refuses to hand him over.

        2. Frederick can get away with these delaying tactics for quite some time, because the impending imperial elections make him the most powerful and sought-after prince in Germany.

    B. In these crucial years, Luther has a breathing space in which he out-writes his opponents.

        1. First of all, quantitatively: Beginning in 1519, Luther's literary output is vast and soon provides a small library of Reformation writings.

        2. The impact of these writings is vastly enhanced by the new technology of printing, which creates an entirely different social environment from any previous attempt by Rome to suppress heresy.

3. Luther out-debated his opponents, often getting straight to the point, where they dealt in scholastic technicalities.

4. Luther's style is direct and unadorned, yet emotionally convincing, and even in his Latin works, free of the pomposity and abstraction that burden his opponents' writing.

5. In his German works, Luther wrote with an unprecedented power, eloquence, and directness that brought the German language into its own for perhaps the first time in history.

6. In the astonishing year of 1520, he writes four treatises that become cornerstones of Reformation theology: *Treatise on Good Works*, *To the Christian Nobility*, *The Babylonian Captivity of the Church*, and *Freedom of a Christian.*

C. In 1520, the battle with the papacy resumes.

1. The papal bull *Exsurge Domine* is published, condemning Luther's teachings and calling for his books to be burned.

2. Luther responds by burning the bull, along with papal decretals and books on canon law.

II. The address *To the Christian Nobility* illustrates the appeal of Luther to his fellow Germans.

A. Luther appeals to the nobility as Christian princes responsible for both the temporal and spiritual welfare of their people.

1. Their concern should be for "the misery and distress of suffering Christendom," oppressed by "the popes and the Romanists."

2. Most fundamentally, Roman control of German benefices means that money flows from Germany to Rome while the people are left without pastors.

3. Also, church courts claim extensive jurisdiction, protecting criminal clerics and referring cases to Rome for settlement, providing ample opportunity for bribery and extortion.

B. Luther sides with the princes in the centuries-old medieval power politics between temporal and spiritual powers but gives the princes a radically new theological rationale that will re-shape the church itself.

    1. Luther rejects the very notion of a special social class of clergy as a "spiritual estate," because baptism makes all Christians spiritual and priests.

    2. The clergy have different work, not different status, called to be ministers of the Word of the Gospel for the good of others and to be supported voluntarily by the congregations.

    3. The humbler German clergy stand to gain from Luther's proposals, released from the burdens of clerical celibacy and the resulting tax on concubinage.

    4. For Luther, the papal system is Antichrist, functioning to funnel wealth to some by doing spiritual harm to others.

III. At the Diet of Worms (1521), Luther takes a stand before the emperor himself.

    A. Fredrick's efforts to get Luther a fair trial eventually land him in front of the emperor Charles V at the next Diet, held at Worms in April 1521.

        1. By this time, the issue is much more than just 95 Theses: The papal prosecutors point to a whole pile of books, ask Luther if they're his, and demand that he recant and retract them.

        2. His ultimate reply is not about freedom of conscience but about his conscience being captive to God's Word.

        3. The famous words "Here I stand. I cannot do otherwise," were probably added to the written account later.

        4. Nonetheless, they sum up his attitude well—not defiant but compelled to disobey even the emperor.

    B. The Edict of Worms issued at the end of the Diet makes Luther a condemned criminal, and he goes into hiding in the castle at the Wartburg.

        1. Though effectively in exile, Luther is in close contact with friends in Wittenberg as they begin the practical reform of the church according to Lutheran doctrines.

2. He also gets an enormous amount of work done, most importantly, the translation of the New Testament into German.

C. Thus begins the most intensive decade of the Lutheran Reformation, which will culminate with the Lutheran princes presenting the *Augsburg Confession* to the same emperor, Charles V, in the Diet of Augsburg in 1530.

D. Ever afterward, the Lutheran reformation thrives only under the protection of the state.

   1. In contrast to Reformed and Anabaptist churches, the Lutheran church is typically a state church.

   2. In the immediate aftermath, this means that wars between Lutheran and Catholic princes threaten Germany for more than a century.

   3. The year after Luther's death, Electoral Saxony and the town of Wittenberg are overrun by the soldiers of Emperor Charles V.

   4. Eventually, the Peace of Augsburg (1555) affirms that each prince will be allowed to establish his own religion while tolerating the other (*cujus regio, ejus religio*).

   5. This is, in turn, the basis for the Peace of Westphalia, ending the Thirty Years' War in 1648, which can be thought of as the end of medieval Christendom.

Essential Reading:

Bainton, *Here I Stand*, chapters 6–10.

Supplemental Reading:

Luther, *To the Christian Nobility of the German Nation*, in *Luther's Works*, vol. 44, and Dillenberger (under the title "An Appeal to the Ruling Class").

Melanchthon, *The Augsburg Confession*, in Leith and in Tappert.

Questions to Consider:

1. What were the losses and gains of Luther's blanket rejection of the papacy?

2. Can a church retain its integrity as a state church?

Lecture Nine—Transcript
The Reformation Goes Public

At the end of the previous lecture, I suggested there was a kind of inner decision that Luther made in the depths of his heart that made the break with Rome inevitable, the decision that the pope is Antichrist. You don't compromise with Antichrist; you don't try to figure out he might be right about a few things and wrong about other things, and can you come to agreement. No, you break with him; you flee from him. That inner decision took place in a context of very outward politics, and I want to look at the politics of the Reformation in this lecture.

The indulgence controversy that began when Luther posted the 95 Theses began as a theological controversy, but it didn't stay that way. It became a very political issue. Luther, it turns out, is very fortunate in his political circumstances because he lives in Saxony in Germany, whose prince or ruler is Frederick "the Wise." Everybody seems to think he's wise, people living at the time, historians; he certainly is astute as a politician because Frederick got pressured by the "Romanists," the pope, and especially the pope's legate, Cardinal Cajetan, the man who interviewed Luther there after the Diet of Augsburg in 1518. Remember, Cajetan was supposed to arrest Luther and send him to Rome.

There was a summons for Luther to go to Rome, and Luther fled from Augsburg in the middle of the night to escape arrest. He arrived back in Wittenberg just one day short of a year after posting the 95 Theses on September 30, 1518, and immediately Fred is under pressure (Frederick, I'll call him Fred); he's under pressure to hand Luther over from Cajetan and others, but Frederick is astute, as I say. He doesn't just say: "No, I won't do it." He delays; he sends it to committee; he wants to maybe have a panel of theologians convene to judge Luther because he is a responsible Christian prince. Frederick wants to do justice for his subject, and he knows that if Luther goes to Rome, he gets burned as a heretic; so, he wants to have some kind of judgment for Luther to happen on German soil.

It turns out he gets his wish at the next imperial Diet of Worms. By the way, it reads in English as the "Diet of Worms," but it's pronounced the "DEE-et of Vohrms" because "W" is a "V" in German. But that's in 1521. Meanwhile, Frederick delays, and his delaying tactics work, in part because Frederick has become a very powerful person rather suddenly when the Emperor dies, and they have to elect a new Emperor. Remember, there are seven electors, seven German princes, who elect the Emperor, and Frederick the Elector of Saxony, as he is known, is one of those electors. That makes him very powerful, and something more happens. There's a lot of maneuvering to prevent Maximilian the old Emperor's grandson Charles V from replacing him.

Old Maximilian, who's dying, really wants his grandson, Charles V, to become Emperor and, in fact, he does get his wish, but there's a lot of powerful people, like the King of France as well as the pope, who don't want Charles V to become Emperor because he would end up having too much power. He's already King of Spain; he's got lands in Austria, and Hungary, and in southern Italy. He's a Hapsburg; this is the Hapsburg empire; this is too much for the King of France and the pope. They would rather have Frederick himself be Emperor and, in fact, they woo him for the job of Emperor. So they're wanting to make nice with Frederick, and so they don't want to twist his arm; so, Frederick can succeed in delaying the handing over of Luther.

The pope actually sends another legate or, rather, representative, a man named [Karl von] Miltitz who takes care of some of the indulgence problem. He gets this monk, Tetzel, who sells the indulgences, to get basically fired and sent to a monastery and, in fact, there's also a *bull*, that's an official papal document written to clarify the issue of indulgences, and some of the worst of the indulgence doctrines that Luther attacks are cleaned up. The bull is actually written by Cajetan. The indulgence controversy is about to go away, but the politics, the theological issues—those won't go away. The indulgence controversy is getting cleaned up; the indulgence practices of the church are getting cleaned up.

Meanwhile, this man Miltitz, the pope's representative, comes to Luther and says: "Could you just be quiet for a while?" Luther says: "All right, if my opponents stop attacking me, I will stop attacking them." Fat chance. The opponents keep attacking; the pope can't control these Catholics who want to attack Luther, and Luther talks back. Luther becomes one of the great back-talkers of all time. In this breathing spell of 2–3 years, 2.5 years that are created by Frederick's delaying tactics, Luther writes, and he writes, and he writes, and he does not shut up. He does not keep quiet; so, in 1519–1520, the first part of 1521, Luther has this breathing space, and he out-writes his opponents. That's the simplest way to put it. He writes more; he writes better.

He creates a small library of Reformation writings in these years. His output is vast—lots of little books, often very pungent, powerfully expressed. Even Luther's Latin is simple and direct in a way that the Latin of his opponents isn't. His opponents are mostly professors; they write like professors—long-winded, technical jargon. Luther writes like a really good preacher, both in Latin and in German. Of course, he's actually proud of this. He says: "I teach my opponents how to speak German," because he writes in German that is really impressive, powerful, provocative, and vibrant, and in a very simple and direct way he explains the issues in a way that any ordinary townsman in Germany can understand him. Verbally, he's just very powerful.

The power of it is enhanced all the more by this rather recent invention, the printing press. You have to remember Gutenberg's Bible was printed in the 1470s, less than 50 years before the time that Luther is writing. So, the church has never had this experience of trying to suppress a heretic who is so eloquent, who writes so much, whose words disseminate throughout Germany before you know it because of the printing press. Because of the press, Luther's words are everywhere. Everyone can read them or have them read to them, and even if they're illiterate, they can at least hear it in German, very powerful.

The culmination of this astonishing productivity of Luther as a writer comes in the year 1520, a really good year for Luther as a writer. He writes the *Treatise on Good Works*, which we've mentioned before. He writes *The Freedom of a Christian*, which we spent two lectures discussing, a magnificent (brief) book. All of Luther's books are brief; he doesn't write long books; he just writes a lot of them. He writes a book called *The Babylonian Captivity of the Church*, which we'll talk about in the next lecture, and he writes an address to the Christian nobility (*To The Christian Nobility*), which we'll talk about in this lecture. But, first, let me say one more thing about the politics because in 1520, also another thing happens.

The battle with the papacy does resume. The Emperor gets elected, Charles V, and the pope comes down hard on Luther in no uncertain terms. He writes a bull. I have to mention this—a bull comes from the Latin word meaning "an embossing"; so, the papal decrees are embossed with a special *bulla* in Latin; that's why it's called a *bull*. So, the pope publishes a bull, which begins "Arise O lord, and judge thy cause…A wild boar from the forest has invaded your vineyard [that is the church] and seeks to destroy it." So, Luther is an enemy of the church. The bull includes a list of 41 teachings of Luther's that are condemned for all time as heretical. The writings are to be burned, and no Christian ought to read them or defend them, and it cites and invites Martin to Rome with safe conduct to have a friendly discussion with the pope. The bull doesn't say he'll get burned, but that's what everyone's expecting.

The bull is published in June; it reaches Luther in Wittenberg in October, and in December 1520, he takes it outside the city, and he burns it. That's when the public break with Rome becomes irrevocable. When he defends it, he once again comes back to that quote from canon law that the pope's theologian Prierias had brought to his attention: "If the pope were so scandalously bad that he led multitudes of souls to the devil, he still could not be removed from office," says the canon law. Luther brings it up again when he's defending his bonfire.

He says: "What a devilish un-Christian thing. What devilish un-Christian thing would they not undertake if they shamelessly hold and teach such frightful things. See there, Christian, what canon law teaches you," and then he drops the canon law into the fire, along with books of scholastic philosophy, the creedals of the pope, and the bull of the pope. His hand trembles a bit as he holds it over the fire, because now the break is irrevocable. It's not just in his heart; it's a public break. He's committed now to having a church that is different from the pope's church. If you want to find the true church, you're not going to find it in Rome. This is a different church now; the true church of Christ is not the pope's church.

What led him to this moment and got him through it is this decision that Rome is Antichrist. He writes in a letter to a friend around this time: "I feel much freer now that I'm certain that the pope is Antichrist. I feel much freer now that I know for sure the pope is Antichrist." It really does free your mind when you no longer have to try to figure out how to compromise with somebody that you think is just plain wicked, devilish. Quick note though, the pope is Antichrist not as a person, but as an institution. It's not like the popular American evangelical picture of the Antichrist as one individual. For Luther, it's the institution of the papacy that's Antichrist, and that becomes a fundamental, precipitating cause of the Reformation. You wouldn't have had the break—the split in the church—without that conviction that the pope is Antichrist, someone you don't compromise with.

We see that conviction set forth for the first time in a very public document in this address to the Christian nobility (*To the Christian Nobility*), which I'd like to spend some time on now, this 1520 treatise. "The Christian nobility should set itself against the pope as a common enemy," is the thesis. Isn't this interesting? He's addressing the Christian nobility; the subtitle is "Concerning the Reform of the Church." This is the first official Reformation appeal; we need to reform the church. Who's going to do it? Not the pope, not the bishops under the pope—so he appeals to the German nobility, to the Christian nobility of the German nation. It turns out the Christian nobility are going to act as emergency bishops to reform the church; the temporal prince will reform the spiritual estate. That becomes a characteristic feature of the Lutheran Reformation. The princes are the power that backs the Reformation. Who else are you going to turn to if he can't turn to the pope and the bishops?

What are the complaints that Luther makes in this treatise? It's interesting; he makes complaints that the German princes have been making about Italian clergymen for a long time. One of the central complaints is that the Romans have been getting control of German benefices. Remember the notion of the benefice—a crucial notion, this kind of ecclesiastical fief. When you're bishop you get this fief—this is land, wealth, and power. The benefices from Germany mean German land, German wealth, and German power in the control of a Roman or an Italian appointed by the pope who doesn't even go to Germany. He stays in Italy, in Rome, collecting the money—so it's exporting money from Germany to Italy.

You don't have to be a theologian to dislike this; all the German princes were making this kind of complaint and, in fact, there was a whole complaint composed by the German princes to present at the next imperial Diet of Worms in 1521—so, Luther's giving them a theological rationale to back up a complaint that is already on their minds in this ongoing politics between the princes and the popes. Luther says this is already happening in Italy; we've got all these pluralists, all these men who have many benefices. They control monasteries, bishoprics, and archbishoprics. They get all the wealth, and they stay in Rome getting rich, which means Italy is now almost a wilderness, Luther says, monasteries in ruins, bishoprics in spoils, land and people ruined because services are no longer held and the word of God is not preached, and why? Because the cardinals must have income. The money flows to Rome.

Even Italy is not benefiting from this, only Rome.

> Now that Italy is sucked dry, [he continues] the Romanists are coming into Germany [They're not actually coming into Germany; they're just getting the money from Germany]…The "drunken Germans" are not supposed to understand what the Romanists are up to until there is not a bishopric, a monastery…a benefice, not a red cent left. Antichrist must seize the treasures of the earth.

Those are stirring words, and a whole lot of German princes are about ready to hear them.

Notice he's attacking one of the fundamental fundraising activities of the Renaissance papacy, not just the claiming of benefices, but also the selling of offices. A rich Italian can buy a benefice, a German benefice. You pay the pope, and you get a German benefice—you get the German money. The pope needs a lot of money. This is one way that he raises money, and Luther is speaking for the German princes in saying: "We've had enough. Shouldn't we reform this? Shouldn't we change this?"

He also backs the German princes' claims to judge their own citizens. The attack is on the ecclesiastical courts, so that if a clergyman commits a crime against Germans, then the church will often say this is a clergyman; therefore, it's under an ecclesiastical court. The case goes to Rome; it's not tried in Germany. Clergy have exemptions from German justice. Again, there's this fight between German princes and the pope about this and, again, Luther's on the side of the German princes. Several things go on as well, more theological things. Luther is providing this theological rationale to underpin these political concerns of the German princes. The theological rationale goes deeper than just the surface here.

One thing he does is he attacks the very notion of a special spiritual estate, the clergy as having special spiritual powers; here he brings forth his distinctive doctrine of the priesthood of all believers. All Christians are priests by virtue of being baptized; that's what makes you a priest. The clergy do not have some kind of special spiritual status; they do not have special spiritual power. Remember that notion of spiritual power versus temporal power; the clergy don't have spiritual power. The only spiritual power is Christ's word, the Gospel, and clergy are ministers of the word. That becomes a key Protestant notion. A Protestant clergyman is a minister of the word, and "minister" means "servant."

The Protestant clergyman does not have spiritual power. He serves God's Word. He does things like pronounce that word of absolution; he doesn't control it. Luther is very indignant at the pope's claim, for instance, that certain sins, when you bring them to the confessional, cannot be absolved by the priest. They are *reserved* sins; they go to Rome, and only the pope can absolve them for a fee. Luther says: "No; no clergyman has that power. The clergyman is a minister of the word; he serves the word of absolution; he doesn't control it; he doesn't have power."

But he's not just attacking the clergy, either. A whole lot of priests are willing to hear this message too because, for instance, here's what he says about clerical celibacy, the rule that priests can't get married: "How many a poor priest," he says, "is overburdened with wife and child, his conscience troubled?" Everybody knows this; priests have concubines, priests have women living with them. They pay for that. There's a kind of cubinage fee or tax. Officially it's a fine because they're not supposed to do it, but really it's a tax—a fee. The priests pay this fee to their bishops—one more way the bishops get rich. In one large diocese, there were allegedly more than 1,500 children born annually to priests, "for each of which the bishop received a cradle fee"—one more way the bishops make money from Germans.

There were also concubinage fees for having a concubine, and legitimation fees to make the child legitimate rather than bastard. It's a great racket. "There are hardly two pimps in the whole diocese who take in that much money!" says one commentator. So, these poorer clergymen (for example, parish priests, many of the people who do the real work of the church) "were often as much victims as perpetrators of the church's policies, clearly a factor in their joining the Reformation in large numbers," says scholar Steven Osment. You don't have to be a prince to be on Luther's side; a whole lot of clergymen feel that they're victims of the system as well.

What ends up happening is the papal system is so greedy for money that it's willing to condemn people's souls for money. These poor priests, their conscience is burdened; they feel like they're sinning against God, even though they're doing what comes naturally and doing what is right. Clergy should have a right to marry, but against their own conscience they're living with a woman, and they can't honor her by marrying her. Another beneficiary of all this, by the way, is all these women living with these priests who get to be wives instead of a priest's woman. All these people whose consciences are burdened, who feel like they're heading toward hell, all in order for the Roman system to make money; that's why Luther is thinking this is Antichrist.

Once again, in fact, he quotes this canon law: "If the pope were so scandalously bad that he led multitudes of souls to the devil, he could not be removed from office," and in the treatise *To the Christian Nobility*, he says: "At Rome, this is the cursed and devilish foundation on which they build: They think that we should let all the world go to the devil rather than resist their dishonesty." He's stirring people up, and he's going to get a lot of people on his side. What kind of Christian leader is it who makes money by sending people to hell? In the next paragraph of the address *To the Christian Nobility*, he suggests an answer: "It is to be feared that this is a game of the Antichrist, or at any rate, that his forerunner has appeared." He doesn't quite come out and say that the pope is Antichrist, but the implication is very clear. "If an authority does anything against Christ, then that authority is the power of Antichrist," Luther writes, "the power of the devil."

So, the die is cast; we're going to have a break from Rome. You don't try to reform the Antichrist; you don't try to go into a back and forth with him. The Reformation wouldn't have happened without the conviction that the pope was Antichrist. What happens in our current ecumenical situation when most Protestants no longer think the papacy is Antichrist? It's actually a crisis for contemporary Protestantism. If the pope isn't the Antichrist, what right do you have to be split? You need something radical to force that break, and this is pretty radical.

Back to the politics. The delaying tactics only work so long. At the Diet of Worms, things come to a head. But Frederick does get his way. Luther doesn't go to Rome; the trial of Luther the heretic does not take place in front of the pope or an ecclesiastical court; it takes place on German soil in front of the Emperor Charles V, the Emperor of Germany. By this time in 1521, in April, at the Diet of Worms the Diet now is all these German princes getting together with the Emperor, figuring out imperial legislation. The Emperor is not a king; he doesn't make direct decisions for Germany. He has to get the cooperation of these other princes; so, they gather together in this irregularly scheduled parliament called the Diet, and the German princes are presenting their complaints against the pope, and also on the docket is the case of Martin Luther, the monk.

They pile up his books on a table. There are a lot of books now. They're not about indulgences, most of them. They are *The Freedom of a Christian*, *The Babylonian Captivity of the Church*, the address *To the Christian Nobility*, the *Treatise on Good Works*, lots of sermons, Biblical exegesis, and they say: "Are these your books, Martin?" He says: "Yes, all of them." "You ready to recant?" comes the next question. Luther does a bit of maneuvering. He says: "Some of these are sermons; they're just pastoral things. If I revoke them, I'm revoking the Gospel, and I can't do that," so there's some maneuvering about that and, eventually, they press him to answer without any of these fancy logical distinctions, "without horns or teeth" is the phrase. "Those are actually logical terms. Don't go making all these distinctions; don't try to make it difficult for us. Are you going to back down or not? That's the issue."

Strikingly, it's like the interview with Cajetan in that no one gives him a refutation; no one tells him why he's wrong. No one gives him a good argument, and that's what he points out in his reply. Here's his reply, in the face of the German Diet, standing in front of the Emperor, the most powerful man in the world, here's the famous reply, the monk Luther:

Unless I am convinced by the testimony of Scripture or by clear reason (for I do not trust either in the pope or in councils alone, since it is well known that they have often erred and contradicted themselves) I am bound by the Scriptures I have quoted and *my conscience is captive to the Word of God*. [Striking, not free, captive but to the Word of God] I cannot and I will not retract anything, since it is neither safe nor right to go against conscience.

Notice the appeal. He's not appealing just to Scripture; reason is good enough. Later on, he'll insist that Scripture alone is the basis for this kind of appeal, but an argument from reason would be good enough at this point. He's saying: "You've got to give me an argument either from Scripture or reason, but you're just demanding that I back down with sheer force, but I gave you reason. I argued from Scripture. Won't anyone address those issues? Until someone does, these Scriptures speak clearly enough to my conscience that I cannot abandon them. I cannot retract without calling God a liar, without saying God's Scriptures aren't true. I can't say that; my conscience is captive to the Word of God."

That's the key moment, "my conscience is captive." This is a great moment in the history of the freedom of conscience, but notice how it works. His conscience is free to defy even the Emperor because it is captive to a higher authority, and Luther really is an authoritarian down to his toes. You're always obedient to some authority, at least you ought to be, and you can't be obedient to the Emperor because you have to be obedient to God instead. Always, your conscience is captive to something. The best thing is to be captive to God's Word.

When this was reported in a written document a few months later, the following words were added. He probably didn't say them at the time, but they're the famous words. He says: "Here I stand. I cannot do otherwise. Help me God." Each time, *Ich kann nicht anders,* "I cannot do otherwise," eloquent German, "Here I stand." It's not a defiant moment. Luther doesn't want to be a rebel; he's an authoritarian down to his toes. He never says anything nasty about the Emperor the way he does about the pope. He's ready to defy the pope, not the Emperor; he wants to obey the Emperor.

I think he's terrified at this moment, not because he's afraid of death. In his letters, you see that he's figuring he's going to die. He's ready for that. He's a monk; he's been practicing death for a long time, fasting, prayer, and all that, but he's afraid of being a rebel because rebels are disobedient to God, as well as to their prince or their king. He doesn't want to be a rebel, but he doesn't have a choice. "Here I stand. I can't do anything else," really does express how he felt at the moment. I wouldn't be surprised if he was the one who added those words to the written account, "What else can I do? It seems to be very clear that this is what God is saying; I can't say God's a liar, and so, therefore, I have to respectfully decline the Emperor's request that I revoke my writings." It's a magnificent moment; it's a moment that everyone remembers. Roland Bainton's famous biography of Luther uses these words as the title, *Here I Stand*.

What happens as the aftermath? Luther doesn't win, of course. It turns out that he's got a safe conduct to Worms; that's very important, and so he's allowed to leave freely, and after he leaves— in fact, after a good number of the representatives at Diet leave—a rump Diet promulgates the Edict of Worms, where Luther is put under the imperial ban. He's an outlaw; anyone who helps him is an outlaw. He's now got to be protected by Frederick, not only from the pope but from the Emperor (the Emperor now becomes Luther's enemy), and Luther's riding off back home to Wittenberg, and everyone's worried about him, so Frederick arranges to have him "kidnapped," and in the woods near the city of Eisenach, a bunch of armed horsemen come and they grab him. Luther's in on this, it turns out, but his poor companion, this monk who was traveling with him, isn't in on this, so this poor monk runs away and says: "Luther's been kidnapped; I don't know what happened."

He's taken to a castle on a hill perched above the city of Eisenach, winding through the woods for an hour or so, many hours until about 11:00 at night they get to the castle. It's called the Wartburg, which shouldn't be confused with Wittenberg. This is the Wartburg; it's a castle. Luther's all alone there. It's not a city; he's basically in exile, hiding out, being safe. He stays in contact by letters with his friends in Wittenberg, but he's lonely. For a while, he doesn't even have any books. When he gets his books, he starts once again doing what comes natural to Luther. He writes, he writes, he writes; he starts translating the New Testament into German. Luther's pen is going to be very influential. This is actually a very productive time for him, but for a while nobody knows what happens to Luther because this is the only way to keep him safe.

What is begun at this point in 1521 is the most intensive decade of the Lutheran Reformation, the 1520s. It ends in 1530, when, once again, you have a Diet, once again the Lutherans are presenting themselves in front of the Emperor, but Luther can't come. This is the Diet of Augsburg in 1530, once again a Diet of Augsburg, but this is in 1530 in front of Charles V. Luther can't come because he's an outlaw. He's under the imperial ban; anyone who helps him is officially an outlaw also; so, a bunch of Lutheran theologians, led by Luther's best friend, Philip Melanchthon, present the Augsburg Confession in front of the Emperor in 1530 in Augsburg. It's rejected; once again, there's going to be warfare between the Emperor and the Lutheran princes, but the Augsburg Confession becomes the official confessional document of the Lutheran church—its creed, as it were.

Ever afterwards, the Lutheran Reformation is deeply involved in the politics and the warfare of German princes. The Emperor Charles V gets geared up to fight a war against the Lutheran German princes. Not all the German princes are Lutheran; some of them are on Charles's side; Germany is divided. The war doesn't actually come until the year after Luther's death, in 1547. Luther dies in 1546 at the age of 63. In 1547, Emperor Charles's troops take over Wittenberg; they depose and, in fact, capture the Elector John Frederick, who is Frederick's nephew, and people urge Charles to disinter Luther's bones and burn them as a heretic. Charles is a good man; he says: "I don't make war on the dead." Good for him.

The warfare is actually unsatisfactory it turns out. How do you get rid of all these Lutheran pastors when you don't have any Catholic priests left in those parts of Germany? You can't undo the Reformation, which has already been taking place now for about 25 years or so, in 1547—so Charles has to make compromises. In 1555, he makes the Peace of Augsburg, which organizes a kind of compromise where every Lutheran prince gets to have his territory be Lutheran; the Catholic princes get to have their territory be Catholic. They have to live in peace with each other; they have to tolerate each other, including Lutherans in Catholic territories, and Catholics in Lutheran territories.

The principle is called *cujus regio, ejus religio*—it's his region, therefore it's his religion. The territorial princes get to determine their own religion in their own territory. That becomes the basis also for the Peace of Westphalia, which ends the Thirty Years' War in 1648. That becomes the fundamental principle upon which Europe finds peace after the religious warfare that is unleashed by the princes for supporting either side of the Lutheran Reformation or the Catholic Counter-reformation.

Lecture Ten

The Captivity of the Sacraments

Scope:

Among the world-changing works Luther published in the amazing year of 1520 is a treatise on the sacraments, *The Babylonian Captivity of the Church*. In it, Luther criticizes the Catholic sacramental system on the basis of his understanding of the word of God. He interprets the Mass as a promise in which God gives us Christ, rather than a sacrifice in which the priest offers Christ to God, and he presents an epochal criticism of the Catholic concept of transubstantiation. He treats baptism and the Lord's Supper (and, in a way, penance) as sacraments but argues that the rest of the traditional seven sacraments—confirmation, marriage, holy orders, and extreme unction—are not properly sacraments, because they do not contain a divine promise plus a sign.

Outline

I. In 1520, Luther wrote a series of groundbreaking works.

   A. *The Freedom of a Christian* is about a Christian's inner freedom of soul.

   B. *To the Christian Nobility* is about Christian rulers' outward responsibility for the church.

   C. *The Babylonian Captivity of the Church* is not about inner freedom but outward captivity, that is, the corruption of the church's institutional life that "takes captive" the sacraments, which are external signs.

II. Most famously, Luther reduces the number of sacraments from seven to two.

   A. To do this, Luther uses a modified version of the traditional Augustinian definition of *sacrament*, adding an insistence on faith in Christ's promise.

      1. A *sacrament* is traditionally an external sign of God's inner gift of grace, which confers that grace.

      2. Luther adds: The sacraments are founded on Christ's promise and, therefore, to be received only by faith.

B. Using this definition as criterion, several church practices that Luther approves of are nonetheless not accorded the special status of sacraments.

  1. Confirmation (or laying on of hands) is a worthy church practice going back to the New Testament but with no specific promise attached to it.

  2. Extreme unction (or anointing of the dying) is a practice instituted in the New Testament letter of James, not by Christ himself.

  3. Marriage is a gift of God to the whole human race, not just to the church.

C. The Catholic sacrament of holy orders (ordination) is the only one Luther simply rejects, for reasons that display a crucial structure of Lutheran thought.

  1. Ordination is a practice not authorized in Scripture, neither by command nor by promise.

  2. It is, therefore, a human invention, which may be freely practiced but is not required to be believed.

  3. This freedom from the requirement to believe is what Luther means by *freedom of conscience.*

  4. One of the most crucial principles of Lutheran theology is that it is sin to teach or practice such human inventions as if they were necessary for faith or Christian life.

  5. By this principle, the Catholic sacrament of holy orders is sinful.

  6. Above all, Luther rejects as unbiblical the notion that ordination makes a fundamental interior change in the person ordained, so that he can perform the special functions of the priesthood, such as saying Mass.

D. At the beginning of the *Babylonian Captivity*, Luther counts penance as a sacrament, but by the end, he has changed his mind.

  1. He thinks of it as a sacrament because it is founded on Christ's promise ("whatever you loose/absolve on earth is loosed in heaven," Matthew 16:19).

  2. But he later rules it out because it contains no external sign other than the word of absolution itself.

3. Nonetheless, he retains it as a sacrament in a sense, because it is really (in his view) part of the sacrament of baptism.
4. In particular, Luther heartily endorses the practice of private confession and absolution as a great comfort to troubled consciences.
5. What happens in penance is that we return to baptism.
6. Penance is not a "second plank" to save you after you make a shipwreck of your baptism, but a returning to the ship, which is still sound (because it is based on God's promise, not our obedience).
7. Hence, Luther rejects the whole panoply of penitential works developed in late-medieval Catholicism: pilgrimages, works of satisfaction, special vows, indulgences.

III. The sacrament of baptism is founded on a divine promise of new life in Christ.

A. The promise attached to baptism is: "whoever believes and is baptized is saved" (Mark 16:16).

B. The sign is immersion in water, and its significance is death and rebirth, hence, new life in Christ.

C. Believers are to have faith in the promise and, therefore, to be certain that its significance (salvation, rebirth in Christ) is present in their lives.

D. Although the sign is over with quickly, the significance is enduring: For their whole lives, believers are living by the baptismal promise and growing in the new life, dying to this world and alive to Christ.

IV. The sacrament of bread and wine is a gift of Christ that Luther thinks Rome has tried to take captive in three ways.

A. Communion in both kinds (that is, both bread and wine) should not be prohibited.

1. Church law at the time forbade the laity to receive from the cup as well as the host.
2. Luther thought this was a wicked and unjustified restriction but that it did no great harm, because it concerned only the sign, not the thing signified.

B. Luther criticizes but does not abominate the Catholic doctrine of transubstantiation.

1. *Transubstantiation* means that the very substance or essence of the bread and wine is changed into the body and blood of Christ.

2. After the consecration of the Eucharistic host, there is no bread left, only the appearance ("species") of bread.

3. Although Luther always affirms the real presence of Christ's body in the sacrament, he thinks the miracle of transforming the bread into Christ's body is superfluous and has no support in Scripture.

4. In Luther's teaching, the bread remains bread, but Christ's body is in it, fulfilling his promise, "This is my body, given for you."

5. According to this *doctrine of Real Presence*, Christ's physical body is physically present in the bread, though perceptible only to faith, not the senses.

C. Luther abominates the Catholic doctrine that the Mass is a sacrifice or good work.

1. The practice he has in view here is the private, endowed masses in which priests are paid to say masses for someone's soul in purgatory or some other spiritual benefit.

2. The key Catholic claim is that the priest offers Christ himself to the father as an "unbloody sacrifice" every time Mass is said, and that this earns various spiritual benefits worth paying for.

3. The Mass is, thus, a good work that "works" *ex opera operato*, simply by "working it" right.

4. Most Protestants see this as a sort of superstitious magic; Luther sees it also as blasphemy, the claim to have power over Christ.

5. For Luther, on the contrary, the sacrament is not a human work but a divine gift.

6. Much of Luther's criticism of the medieval church can be summed up this way: These are people trying to give things to God so as to earn a reward, rather than receiving from him what he has freely promised in Christ.

Essential Reading:

Luther, *The Babylonian Captivity of the Church*, in *Luther's Works*, vol. 36; Dillenberger (under the title "Pagan Servitude"); and Lull (excerpt on the Mass).

Supplemental Reading:

The Catechism of the Roman Catholic Church, Part II (for current Roman Catholic teaching on the sacraments).

Duffy, *Stripping of the Altars*, chapters 3 and 8 (for a sympathetic description of the medieval piety of the Mass and "magical" prayers).

Questions to Consider:

1. What is your understanding of what happens at Christian baptism?

2. What is your understanding of what happens at the Christian celebration of bread and wine?

Lecture Ten—Transcript

The Captivity of the Sacraments

In this lecture, we're going to talk about a book of Luther's or a treatise entitled *The Babylonian Captivity of the Church*. Remember the Babylonian Captivity is this event in the Bible in which Israel goes into exile in Babylon, but the phrase was applied in the Middle Ages to the papacy in the 14th century, when the pope was in Avignon in France instead of in Rome, where he belonged. Luther takes the phrase and applies it to the church as a whole because of what's going on with the church and the sacraments.

He says the sacraments are being taken captive. He's writing a treatise about the institutional, and sacramental, and religious life of the church. It's a set of religious practices, especially these central practices known as *sacraments*. He's not attacking the sacramental system, as is often said; he's defending the sacraments, he's thinking, from this captivity. It's interesting; this is one of these major treatises written in 1520 before the Diet of Worms, where Luther had this breathing space to write these very influential theological treatises.

You can think of the three most important of them as dealing with the soul, the state, and the church. *The Freedom of a Christian* is about the soul, about the human being. The address *To the Christian Nobility* is about politics, the state, and the political responsibility of the state for the church. And then, *The Babylonian Captivity of the Church* is all about the central institutional life of the Christian church. So, the most important things are the soul, the state of politics, and the church. But it is not accidental that we're starting with something called freedom; *The Freedom of a Christian* is a treatise on the human being's soul, and we're ending with a treatise on captivity. We start with the freedom that God gave us in Christ, and we end up with the medieval church, and that's not freedom but captivity—so we need to do something about this slavery, this captivity, that the pope has imposed upon the sacraments that Christ gave us. That's the general drift of the treatise.

In the Roman Catholic Church to this day, there are seven sacraments, and those are the seven sacraments of the medieval church as well. That was solidified in the fourth Lateran Council of 1215. There are seven sacraments. I'll name them, and we'll talk about each one of them: baptism, confirmation, Eucharist, penance, marriage, holy orders (which is ordination), and extreme unction (which is the old name for it)—that means anointing the dying with oil. Unction is oil; *extreme* means "at the end of your life." Those are the seven sacraments. The short way to summarize Luther's book is to say he counts only baptism and Eucharist as sacraments. So instead of seven Catholic sacraments, you've got two Lutheran sacraments.

To see why he eliminates the other five, we have to get his definition of sacraments, so let's think about what a sacrament is for Luther, and then we'll launch into these seven examples of sacraments. Remember Augustine now. Augustine says a sacrament is an external sign signifying an inner grace; that's the key notion of a sacrament throughout the Middle Ages. But the medieval church adds this extra point: The sacraments are external signs that not only signify grace—they confer grace. They give grace; a sacrament has the power to confer what it signifies. That's where the institutional life of a church meets the soul or the conscience; this external institutional thing affects the state of your soul, affects the state of your conscience.

The danger this raises, of course, is that Christian piety might become ritualized or externalized, or the danger that Luther's concerned about really is that the inner gift that you get from the sacraments is something that you need for your salvation, and it's dependent on something external that can be controlled institutionally and may be withheld from you. Suppose the pope doesn't like you and excommunicates you, or the pope is fighting with your king and your land is under interdict, and nobody in your whole country gets to have the sacrament of Christ's body and blood, the Eucharist, without which you can't be saved. You need this for grace; your soul needs it, and the pope is saying the whole country can't have it. The external aspect of the sacrament can be controlled for political purposes that can be bad for your soul; that's the real captivity that Luther's concerned about.

Luther has sometimes been seen as a critic of externalism in the Catholic sacraments, but I don't think that's right because as I suggested, the very notion of the Gospel, for Luther, is an external word, an external sign that gives what it signifies—so, for Luther, the Gospel has a kind of sacramental structure. It's an external word that gives the inner gift of grace that it signifies. I think that Luther is, in fact, defending the sacraments; that's how he thinks of it clearly. What he's doing is he's bringing to the notion of sacrament his theology of justification by faith in Christ's promise, and he's thinking of the sacraments in terms of Christ's promise. That's what he adds to the medieval notion of the sacrament.

Instead of the notion of priests having a spiritual power to control these external sacraments, Luther says the sacrament has its power from the promise of Christ. It's instituted by Christ's promise, and there is always some kind of promise associated with it, or attached to it, or spoken in the sacrament, so that the power of it is Christ's alone, and we receive it by faith alone—not by good works, not by contrition, not by any of those other things. In order to understand the sacrament, for Luther, you have to discern Christ's promise; that becomes the central notion in *The Babylonian Captivity of the Church*. With that emphasis on Christ's promise and then this external sign that gives an inner gift, Luther looks at the seven Catholic sacraments.

Let's look at some easy cases first. Marriage is a sacrament according to the Catholic Church. Luther says marriage is wonderful; it's a gift of God, but it's not a sacrament of the church. It's something that the whole human race has received from God. It's a good thing, but it's not a sacrament; Christ didn't institute it; God instituted it way back in Genesis, and it's not just for the church—it's for the whole human race, so marriage is a good thing, not a sacrament.

Likewise, confirmation—that's when the priest lays hands on usually a young member of the church and confirms him or her in the Holy Spirit as a member of the church; Luther thinks this is a great practice. It goes back to the New Testament; you can read about it in the New Testament, and the Lutheran churches still practice it, but it's not a sacrament—it's not instituted by Christ. It (confirmation) doesn't have Christ's promise attached to it and, therefore, unlike the true sacraments, Luther thinks, it doesn't serve to give you Christ. That's what the sacraments are all about. Just like the Gospel, the sacraments are there to give you Christ. Confirmation is a good thing; it's a good practice, but its purpose is not to give you Christ—it's something else.

The sacrament of extreme unction, the anointing of the dying—that's another practice that is instituted in the New Testament, but not by Christ. You can read about it in the letter of James, the fifth chapter, where James writes, "Is any of you sick? He should call on the elders of the church to pray over him and anoint him with oil in the name of the Lord, and the prayer of faith will save the sick person. The Lord will raise him up. If he has sinned, he will be forgiven." This practice of anointing a sick person comes from this Biblical passage. There's even a promise attached to it. If he's sick, the Lord will raise him up, which is not actually what was intended in the sacrament of extreme unction, which was meant for the dying, but in any case, there's a promise there, but it's not Christ's promise. It's not about God giving you Jesus Christ through external means, and that's what a sacrament is about for Luther. Extreme unction is another good Biblical practice that people should do, but it's not a sacrament.

There's only one Catholic sacrament that Luther simply rejects, and even that is a qualified rejection; that's the sacrament of holy orders. Luther has no objection to a church practice or ritual of ordination, but holy orders is supposed to make the priest into a special kind of person who has the special spiritual power rooted right there in a special mark down in the depth of his soul, an indelible mark on his soul, which makes him a different kind of person who can do this magic of saying the Mass, and we'll get to the notion of the magic of saying the Mass in a minute. Luther says this is just not Biblical, there's no command or promise associated with this in the New Testament. It's not established in the New Testament, not by Christ or by anybody else.

It's an invention of the church, which makes it a human invention. It has no authority in the church, and therefore if you want to do it, that's fine. Nothing wrong with doing something that's not in the Bible; we do that all the time. We are free to do things that are not in the Bible. Even the church is free to do things that aren't in the Bible, but the church is not free to make it a requirement. The church is not free to establish new kinds of power, new kinds of spiritual power, that don't come from Christ's promise.

We are free not to believe in all this stuff about ordination, and that, of course, undermines the whole purpose. If you don't have to believe that the priest has a special character, a special spiritual power rooted in his soul, if we don't have to believe that, then the priest doesn't have it. If you're free to disbelieve this sacrament of holy orders, then it's not a sacrament at all. It's just a human invention, and the church has no business imposing human inventions on people as if they had to believe them. That's a notion that we're going to get back to later; it's a real key notion in the whole Reformation. The human doctrines have no right to invent new spiritual powers and to make people believe in them. If you want to do it, that is fine; it's OK, but don't require people to believe it as a matter of conscience.

We've got three sacraments left: baptism, Eucharist, and penance. Here comes the twist. It turns out in the beginning of *The Babylonian Captivity of the Church*, Luther says there are three sacraments: baptism, Eucharist, and penance. At the end of *The Babylonian Captivity of the Church*, he says there are really only two sacraments. He changes his mind over the course of the treatise. This is typical of Luther; he's always thinking and changing his mind. It's not so often that you actually see this happen in one treatise, from the beginning to the end, but it happens. We'll talk about why he does that and why it's not a big change of mind, but let's look at penance, and then we'll see what's going on.

At the beginning, he's thinking of penance as a sacrament because it is founded on Christ's promise. That's the really crucial thing for him in this treatise; Christ promises: "whatever you loose or absolve on earth is loosed [or absolved] in heaven." Remember, he wrote that sermon on the sacrament of penance, which I think is so important for his understanding of the structure of the Gospel—so, he really likes the sacrament of penance. He thinks it's associated with Christ's promise. It's the way that Christ gives us himself, which is what sacraments do.

But when he gets to discussing it in the treatise later on, he realizes there's no external sign associated with this sacrament. A sacrament is supposed to have not just Christ's promise, but also some kind of external sign—like water in baptism, and bread and wine in Christ's body and blood in the Eucharist—and there's no external sign associated with penance. Actually, in 1519, he said the external sign of penance is the word, but here he's saying you've got to have both word and an external sign, which is something other than a word, and penance doesn't have that—so strictly speaking, it's not a sacrament. You wonder if the word "sacrament" really matters much at this point, and what's the cash value of this notion of sacraments. All that matters, really, for Luther is where you find Christ's promise. It looks like it doesn't fit the definition of sacrament; let's not call it a sacrament.

But Luther's certainly never hostile to this practice of penance, especially the practice of private confession; he loves it. You go to your priest, or your pastor, or a good Christian friend with your conscience burdened by your sense of sin, and you confess your sins, and this Christian friend, or pastor, or whoever can say to you: "Your sins are forgiven; in Christ's name I absolve you of your sins in the name of the Father, and the Son, and the Holy Spirit." Who wouldn't want to hear that; so, of course, Luther wants to keep practicing it, and he does for the rest of his life, and most of the Lutheran churches continue some form of it—so it's a really good practice, which you don't have to practice; it's not instituted by Christ with an external sign, but, my goodness, who would want to not do it, Luther thinks.

Luther, in fact, in one sense, even at the end of the treatise, thinks of penance as a sacrament because what he does is he suggests that penance really is the sacrament of baptism. Penance is a sacrament; it's just not a different sacrament from baptism. At the end of the day, I think, that's his position. There are only two sacraments, the Eucharist and baptism/penance, because what happens in penance, Luther thinks, is that we return to our baptism. Every time we repent of our sins, what we're really doing is going back to this baptismal promise of Christ. That's why even the word of absolution, the word that is spoken at the end of the sacrament of penance, where the priest says: "I absolve you of your sins in the name of the Father, the Son, and the Holy Spirit," that is patterned after the baptismal formula: "I baptize you in the name of the Father, the Son, and the Holy Spirit," to remind you this is really about your baptism.

That's a new way of thinking about that penance, and Luther critiques the Catholic way of thinking about it, which in his day was focused on this notion of penance as a "second plank" after baptism. What that means is you're saved by baptism, you're born again by baptism, according to Catholic and Lutheran teaching (we'll talk about that; that's very different from a lot of Protestantism). You're saved by baptism, by being born again through baptismal faith. That means you get on the Gospel ship; you're on the ark with Noah; you're being saved from the world. But when you commit mortal sin, the really serious sins, then that's like a shipwreck. The ship of your baptism is wrecked—it's destroyed, it's floating off in pieces—and you get one little plank of that ship, and that's called penance. It's a second plank after the shipwreck that you make of your baptism.

Luther just hates that notion, and he says:

> Baptism is not founded on my sinlessness; baptism is founded on the promise of Christ, so the ship never sinks, there's no shipwreck. It's like you jump off the ship with your sins sometimes. The ship is fine; you've just jumped off the ship.

Every sin is mortal for Luther; there's no such thing as a menial sin or minor sin. Every sin is abandoning Christ, and every repentance is coming back to Christ—coming back to the baptism, to this baptismal pledge. There's a kind of covenant that God makes, where God promises you Christ: "I baptize you in the name of the Father, the Son, and the Holy Spirit." You belong to the holy trinity, and then in response you're supposed to live like a Christian, and you don't, and so you keep on returning in this process of penance to your own baptism.

That also means that because the baptism is still there; the crucial thing is simply to remember to believe in what God said to you in your baptism. Always, just remember that Christ said this: "I baptize you Phillip in the name of the Father, the Son, and the Holy Spirit." Believe that, for heaven's sakes; that's the fundamental thing that you're supposed to be doing rather than the practices of sacramental penance, well, not sacramental penance. Luther's problem as a monk is that he wasn't doing sacramental penance; he was doing penitential works. He was doing all that he could to confess his sin, to hate his sin—it was all inward, but the overarching context was this penitential system, as it were, and Luther wants to just get rid of that. We don't please God by doing penitential works, hating ourselves, fasting so many days of the week, or something. We please God by believing that when he baptized us, he was telling us the truth. It's the truth of Christ's promise.

That leads us very naturally to the next sacrament, the sacrament of baptism, which again really isn't a different sacrament, for Luther. Very briefly, Luther says some very nice things about baptism, you can imagine. The promise attached to baptism is: "whoever believes and is baptized is saved." Christ instituted baptism with that external sign, which is the sign of immersion in water. The significance of the baptism is death and rebirth. You drown, die with Christ, come up out of the water reborn and, thus, baptism gives you new life in Christ, makes you Christian, makes you born again. Believers should have faith in the promise and therefore be certain that its significance is present in their lives. If you ask Luther: "Are you born again?" He will say: "Yes, of course, Christ baptized me, and I don't have a right not to believe that." Luther has no doubts about whether he's a Christian, or if he does, he thinks that's a sin because he ought to be believing what Christ says in his baptism.

Christ made him a Christian by baptizing him, so you believe this. That's what you should be doing. The sign of baptism is, of course over quickly; you're dunked and you come out, or you're sprinkled, then the word is said and the baptism is over. But the significance of baptism endures. For your whole life, if you're a believer, you should be living by this baptismal covenant, this promise of God and your promise of living as a Christian in return. The baptismal ceremony usually has some sort of promise like that. And you should be growing in this new life, dying to the old self, and living through Christ, and penance is part of the way of living out that baptismal covenant, killing "the old Adam" and living the new life in Christ. Luther says baptism is one of the few things that really survived this captivity of the church. Baptism is still here, even in the Roman Church, even in the church of the pope—so that's good, we've got baptism.

On now to the central sacrament of medieval Catholic piety, the sacrament of what do we call it? The Eucharist is the traditional name for it. Luther doesn't actually use that name very often. He sometimes calls it "the sacrament of the altar," but that's an old medieval name that suggests there's a sacrifice being made at this sacrament, and Luther rejects that, so let's not call it that. Let's call it the sacrament of Christ's body and blood; that's Luther's favorite term for it in his mature works. The Catholics will also call it the Mass. Even the nomenclature for the sacrament is a matter of controversy. What goes on in the Mass, the Catholic Mass?

Let me say one thing that is fairly superficial, and then get to some deeper issues. First of all, in the Catholic Church at the time, and up until fairly recently, when someone came to take communion, they were given the bread but not the wine; actually, it wasn't bread, but it looks like bread. They were given something, given the host, the bread-like thing, but they weren't given the wine, they weren't given the cup. This is called "communion in one kind"; *kind* means "kind of thing, or one species of things," so the laity, the ordinary non-clergy, only got the host and not the cup. Luther thinks that this is a law that the church imposes on the sacrament, "a shackle" he calls it, which has absolutely no authority in Scripture.

When he blesses the cup at the first Lord's Supper, Jesus says: "Take this all of you, and drink from it," he seems to mean everybody. Of course, everybody at that time (at the table) were apostles, so maybe that's all clergy, but at any rate, Luther's thinking this is a church law that puts restrictions, puts shackles, on the practice of the sacrament that are not there in the Bible, have no authorization, and indeed seem to be quite contrary to Christ's words; so, this is a wicked and unjustifiable restriction. But it also doesn't do a great deal of harm. What matters above all is the promise, the word of Christ, so if people don't take communion of both kinds, that is, both the host and the cup, it's not going to do them much harm, but still the church has no right to do this.

Let's get into the second shackle that's put on this sacrament in *The Babylonian Captivity of the Church*. This is the doctrine of transubstantiation, and let me say a little about this. Transubstantiation is the Catholic doctrine that when the priest says the words of consecration: "This is my body, given for you" (he says it in Latin, of course, in the Middle Ages), what happens then is that the bread becomes no longer bread. It is changed into the body of Christ, and likewise the wine gets changed into the blood of Christ. It is a complete change of substance; substance in medieval thought means the essence of the thing; that is, the essence of bread is no longer there; it's no longer bread, it's now the body of Christ.

It looks like bread, it tastes like bread, it feels like bread, it smells like bread—all these accidents they're called, are still there, all the qualities of the bread are still there, but the substance of the bread is gone. The reality of the bread is gone, and it's Christ's body instead. It's interesting; Luther is very convinced that when you take the sacrament of Christ's body and blood, Christ's body is there. He agrees with the Catholics; Christ's body is there. But he thinks it's kind of silly to say that there's no bread left. Luther will say Christ's body is in the bread; there's bread there, Christ's body is in it. The Catholic doctrine is there's no bread left; it's just Christ's body and the appearance of bread. Luther is thinking it's important that Christ's body is there, but why this extra miracle of making it look like bread, when it's not?

Luther thinks that this is more miracles than you need in order to have the sacrament of Christ's body and blood, and it's not Biblical and, therefore, above all, it shouldn't be required. If you want to be a theologian and say this is what happens, Luther says, you can be some kind of silly speculative medieval theologian and say that's what happens, but don't require people to believe this. Once again, it's the issue of freedom. Luther's willing to let it be a theological opinion, but not something that you're required to believe. We'll have to wait until later, and we'll see Luther is very insistent that you are required to believe that Christ's body is present in the sacrament because he says Christ says so, "This is my body"; so, you are required to believe Christ's promise, and there's a huge fight he has with Protestants about this, but at this point there aren't any other Protestants around to fight with; he's fighting with Catholics.

The transubstantiation issue is not a huge issue. The issue of the presence of Christ's body in the sacrament will be a huge issue. Luther will be fighting with other Protestants about that; that's coming up later, and we'll get to that. In Luther's teaching, the bread remains bread, but Christ's body is in it, fulfilling his promise that "This is my body, given for you." You'll sometimes get the Lutheran phrase "The body of Christ is in, with, and under the bread," but he also will just say something like "It's in the bread," and like the Catholics, he does say you're never going to see it. You can't see it there; it's not visible to the senses; it's only visible by faith. Is there a big issue here? Luther will say it's not a big issue; the Catholics will say it's a big issue precisely because the issue is whether it's required to be believed.

Actually, this is an interesting feature about these disagreements. When you disagree with someone to the right of you, someone more restrictive, more conservative, you'll typically be saying: "It's not a big deal; we can be a little bit more relaxed about this issue." The person to the right of you, who's more restrictive, will say: "It's a big deal; you're stepping beyond the pale; you're stepping beyond the borders. I want the borders to be closed in and narrow. You're stepping beyond; it's a big deal." Luther will say "It's not a big deal if I step beyond these borders."

Then, to the left of him, come other Protestants—people like Presbyterians and such—and they're saying: "We don't believe the Christ body is literally present there in the bread, like you literally chew him with your teeth, and that's not a big deal. We both believe there's a spiritual presence of Christ and we spiritually receive Christ," and Luther will say: "It's a big deal. You can't go beyond this border." So, the more narrow your view is, you look to the people who have a less narrow view, and you'll say it's a big deal; whereas, if you have the more broad and open-minded view, maybe it's not such a big deal. That's typical about how these disagreements work; they're asymmetric in that way. You don't even agree about how big the disagreement is. Transubstantiation—Luther critiques it, but he thinks it's not a big deal.

On to the third of the shackles of the sacrament of Christ's body and blood; that is the doctrine that the Mass is a sacrifice. Luther thinks that this is an abomination; this he's really mad about—this is awful. Why? Remember, what he really has in mind here is not the Eucharistic celebration, where there's a whole congregation and people receive communion. Interestingly, for most Catholics in the Middle Ages, that happened maybe once a year. Actually there are several levels. There's once a year; most medieval Catholics would receive the Eucharist, receive the host, on Easter, once a year, because it was such an awesome thing that this was Christ's body, and who would dare receive it unless they were more or less required to. In fact, they were required to receive it at least once a year on Easter.

Then on other Sundays, they would come and hear Mass. That was the typical phrase, "you would hear Mass," but you wouldn't touch the stuff. That's Christ body; you can adore it, you worship it, you pray before it, but you don't go ahead and just gobble it up all the time. Then there's a third level of Mass, and this is what Luther's really concerned about, and that's when you walk through the church, you go through the church in Wittenberg in 1519, and all these priests were at the side altars saying Mass, and there's nobody there. There's nobody hearing the Mass. Occasionally there's some bystander. What they're doing is they're treating the Mass as a special kind of good work.

You know what Luther thinks about good works; you should do good works, but don't think that they somehow please God, or don't think they somehow justify you or have any spiritual power. Only God's Word received in faith has special power. So, here are these priests doing these good works, and the good work they're doing is a sacrifice. Luther is dead set against the sacrifice of the Mass, which is the Catholic doctrine that says when the priest lifts up that host and says: "This is my body, given for you, and all of you will know this as a gesture of elevation of the host," (Lutherans still do it, but they don't believe it has the same significance) the priest is elevating the host, offering it to God, and says: "This is my body, given for you." At that moment, the bread becomes the body. That's a sacrifice; the priest is offering Christ's body to God. The priest is offering Christ as a sacrifice to God.

The Lutheran and Protestant doctrine says: "No, Christ sacrificed his body once. It happened on Calvary way back when, and there's no such thing as a contemporary sacrifice of Christ, as in he gets sacrificed over and over again," an "unbloody sacrifice" is the Catholic doctrine, the bloody sacrifice on the cross and then this unbloody sacrifice every time a Mass is said. If you believe that, then saying the Mass is a really powerful thing, and that's why the Mass might have the power to get souls out of purgatory and so on. That's why people are paying for this—so this notion of sacrifice of the Mass not only gives a very powerful spiritual power to the clergy, it also has economic ramifications. It's how a lot of clergymen make their living; it's how a lot of money gets into the coffers of the church. Luther says, "No."

Let me say two things about the way he criticizes it. One is according to the Catholic doctrine; the sacrifice of the Mass "works" *ex opera operato*, the Latin phrase meaning something like "it works simply by working it." You just do the right thing, say the right words; you have to be a priest who's ordained, has holy orders, and if you do the right thing, say the right words, then, by magic, it's a sacrifice. You don't have to be a good man, you don't have to have faith; you just have to be ordained and say the right words, and there it is. It's a sacrifice, it's valid, and this is very important because you've got people paying for Masses. They don't want the spiritual power of the Mass to be dependent on the spiritual state of the soul of the priest. They just want it to work automatically. Protestants look at this and say: "You want it to work like magic—say the magic words and it happens." That's what *ex opera operato* means when Luther is attacking it. It's like saying magic words when it happens. That's making Christ's gift into a work.

Here's the fundamental criticism. Luther's thinking the sacrament, all sacraments really, are Christ's way of giving himself to us: "This is my body, given for you." What's really happening in a sacrament is Jesus Christ gives himself to us, and then the Roman Church says: "No, what's really happening is we're giving Christ to God. We're the ones who are giving. We're the ones who are giving God something," and Luther's criticism is: "No, you've turned God's gift into man's work, as if you're doing things to give something to God, when God wants to give something to you. Can't you be humble enough to let God give you something, indeed his own son, instead of trying to give God back to God, as if you're the one offering Christ, as if you are the one giving the gift? You've got to learn not just to give to God, but to receive." That's the criticism.

Lecture Eleven
Reformation in Wittenberg

Scope:

The Reformation that sweeps Europe in the 1520s begins in Wittenberg, Luther's hometown. This is where he learns to make the reforms work to build the life of the church rather disrupt it, with a focus on making the Gospel heard and understood by ordinary laypeople. This is also where his own life is drastically changed by the Reformation, as monks and nuns themselves become ordinary laypeople and the ex-monk Martin Luther marries an ex-nun named Katherine von Bora. They live in the old monastery; raise a large family; keep house for dozens of relatives, guests, and boarders; and set the pattern for clergy marriages ever afterward in the Protestant tradition. We know a great deal about Luther's home and marriage because his guests often wrote down his table talk at dinner, thus creating one of the most characteristic and endearing records of the Lutheran Reformation.

Outline

I. While Luther was in hiding at the Wartburg, the practical reformation of the church began in Wittenberg.

    A. The crucial figures were cautious Philip Melanchthon, a brilliant young academician but never quite sure of himself, and impatient Andreas von Karlstadt, who eventually became Luther's first important Protestant enemy.

    B. Key changes begin to be made in public worship.

        1. References to the sacrifice in the Mass are removed.

        2. The words of institution ("This is my body" and so on) are said in German, and eventually, the whole service is in the vernacular rather than in Latin.

        3. The cup as well as the bread is given to the laity.

    C. The problem arises of those with "weak consciences" who are anxious about the loss of old ways and not confident with the new.

        1. Karlstadt was willing to impose the changes by compulsion, and others used intimidation and violence.

2. When Luther returns to Wittenberg he opposes going too fast, compelling weak consciences, and violence.

D. Karlstadt condemned the use of images, which Luther thought was a matter of indifference, so long as they were not thought of as necessary works.

II. Luther rejects clerical celibacy in the name of Christian freedom.

A. While Luther is away, priests begin to marry and he approves.

  1. The reasoning here is simple: Given that God's Word does not command clerical celibacy, priests are free to marry.

  2. This also serves to erase the distinction between clergy and laity.

B. Monks are a more difficult issue, because of their solemn vows of celibacy.

  1. Karlstadt and Melanchthon wrote about the various reasons and circumstances under which monks may legitimately be released from their vows.

  2. Luther's approach is more radical: Monastic vows are not binding under any circumstances because they are contrary to the freedom of the Gospel.

C. This judgment of Luther's uncovers the key logic of Christian freedom.

  1. Things in themselves allowable (such as a vow of celibacy) become sin when they turn into a law of works that binds the conscience with obligations apart from faith in the Gospel.

  2. *Monkishness, self-chosen worship, works-righteousness*, and *the doctrines of men* are Luther's terms for any kind of spirituality that makes any obligations a matter of conscience apart from faith in the Gospel.

  3. These same practices are allowable if free, that is, not binding on conscience.

  4. Hence, they can be required as civic law demanding conformity to outward regulations.

  5. Luther rejects the position later associated with Puritanism: that Christian worship must be "pure," that is, free from any non-biblical accretions.

III. One of the consequences of this judgment against monastic vows is that Luther himself becomes a husband and father.

    A. In 1525, he marries Katherine von Bora, the last of a batch of runaway nuns who all needed husbands.

    B. They live at Luther's old monastery in Wittenberg, where they raise a family, take in numerous boarders, and become one of the most well-known families in history.

    C. His boarders, students, and many invited guests took notes of his dinner-table conversation, which give us a vivid sense of his personality and family life.

    D. Characteristics of his table talk include joviality, a lively and self-deprecating sense of humor that is often coarse, tenderness toward his children, a tendency to tease his wife, and bitterness toward the pope and other enemies of the Gospel.

Essential Reading:

Bainton, *Here I Stand*, chapters 11–12, 17.

Luther, "Eight Sermons at Wittenberg (March 1522)" (also known as the "Invocavit Sermons"), in *Luther's Works*, vol. 51, pp. 70–100, and Lull, chapter 20.

Supplemental Reading:

Luther, "Receiving Both Kinds in the Sacrament," in *Luther's Works*, vol. 36.

———, "The Judgment of Martin Luther on Monastic Vows," in *Luther's Works*, vol. 44.

———, "Table Talk," in *Luther's Works*, vol. 54 (makes wonderful browsing).

Questions to Consider:

1. Does Luther's rationale for releasing monks from their vows seem sound to you, or is it an excuse to break a binding vow?

2. Do you think you would have liked Luther if you had met him?

Lecture Eleven—Transcript

Reformation in Wittenberg

When we last left Martin Luther, he was stuck in a castle in Germany all by himself in a place called the Wartburg overlooking Eisenach. That's when the Lutheran Reformation starts in Wittenberg, back in his hometown where he would like to be, but he's not, so the Lutheran Reformation starts without Luther. The practical work of changing the life of the church, its sacramental life, its worship life, happens when Luther is off in hiding in this castle called the Wartburg.

Luther is kept apprised of events by letters from his friends, especially his friend Philip Melanchthon, his best friend, the second most important theologian of the Lutheran Reformation, a brilliant young man of 24. Luther thinks he's a much better writer, much more concise, much more precise in his thinking, all of which is actually true. Luther thinks that Philip Melanchthon's book, a systematic theology called the *Commonplaces*, is the best book of theology, after the Bible. He really admires Philip Melanchthon, but Philip Melanchthon is not a leader of the people. He's a brilliant young scholar, but he's not a leader of the people.

There's another guy on the scene, another university professor from Wittenberg (Melanchthon is the professor of Greek there). The senior theology professor at Wittenberg is a man named Andreas von Karlstadt; Karlstadt is the name to remember, it's actually German for "Charlestown." Karlstadt is a senior professor; he actually conferred the doctrine on Luther back in 1512 in Wittenberg, and he feels like he's ready to take charge. He wants to be a leader of the people. He's a bit impatient and most scholars regard him as a bit unstable. He was all over the map theologically, but we'll get back to him. He becomes a very important figure in what goes wrong in the Reformation in Luther's view.

Here we are in Wittenberg. We've got these two professors who aren't quite what's really needed, but they're there and Luther isn't, and they start making key changes in the life of the church at Wittenberg. First of all, there are changes made in public worship, and the very first thing they do is they get rid of all language about the sacrifice of the Mass, because Luther and the other Lutherans regard this as an abomination. This is good works in place of God's

Word; get rid of it. The Mass is not our work; it's God's Word. It's not a sacrifice; we don't offer anything to God in the Mass; God offers us himself. We don't give, God gives, etc. Get rid of it; it's awful. That's the first thing to go.

The next thing that happens is that the words of institution in the Mass are spoken in German. The Masses, of course, are all in Latin at this point. The first thing that gets translated into German are the words: "This is my body, given for you," so that the people of Wittenberg can hear God speak in their own language, speaking his promise, his word, his Gospel, for the first time so that it's no longer this magical ceremony done in this magical language that no one understands, that does this magical thing. It's God speaking in German. That becomes a theme of the Reformation because, of course, soon the whole Mass will be translated into German, and then the whole Bible (Luther is at work at that in the Wartburg); so, God's Word is going to be translated into German—God's going to speak German to these people.

Another change is that the cup, as well as the bread, is given to the laity. You get "communion in both kinds," as it's called—so, it's not just bread but also the wine, and ordinary people get to do both bread and wine. Associated with this, the ordinary people, the laity, get to touch the bread with their hands—which most of them, in fact, are afraid to do. One person was so scared of touching the Eucharistic bread with his hands that he dropped it on the floor, and then was really terrified.

What's freedom to some people seems like lawlessness or sacrilege to others, and that's a serious problem. This is the problem of what Luther calls "weak consciences," and he means good people born under the pope who are used to the way that things are in the papal church, who are terrified of these changes. They're not sure what's going on: "I'm supposed to touch this? Touch God? I'm supposed to take both kinds, but that's sacrilege isn't it? I'm not supposed to take a cup? I'm not allowed to. Who says I'm allowed to?" Luther says: "God says you're allowed to," but it takes a while to convince people of that. Or imagine you are one of these old-fashioned Catholics who are saying things like: "You mean I can't pay for a Mass for my dead father? But it's in my will, I promised. It's my duty as his son. Am I required to drink from the cup? Touch the bread with my hands? Is it really allowed? Is that safe?"

That's how someone with a weak conscience talks. Luther thinks you've got to be kind to these people, be gentle with them, take it slowly, and you don't force them to do stuff that they're not ready to do. You just preach to them, and you tell them, and when they're persuaded then they're OK. It's one thing to say in a treatise like the *Babylonian Captivity of the Church* that the church has no right to forbid the laity to take the cup. It's another thing to compel ordinary people to take it when they don't feel safe doing it, so be nice to these ordinary people. The problem is that Karlstadt is impatient; he wants to force things along. He wants to know quicker. He'll say that it is some mortal sin to take communion in only one kind, without taking the cup. That scares people; you've got these nice ordinary Catholics who are being told that being who they are is a mortal sin, and it's not only that Karlstadt is telling people that this sort of stuff is mortal sin. Something goes further.

There's a monk in Luther's cloister in the monastery in Wittenberg that Luther is part of (not there anymore, of course; he's in the Wartburg); this man is one of the leading monks now in the monastery in Wittenberg, and his name is Zwilling. He leads a riot, with monks going through the church, smashing the altars where the private Masses are. This notion of the sacrifice of the Masses is so offensive to them that they're going to trash the place; they're going to get rid of those altars. There are also riots led by townsmen or students carrying knives, throwing stones, pushing priests away from the altars, dragging them off, scaring them, intimidating them. Not only do these poor people with weak consciences get threatened— "It's a mortal sin if you don't take the cup"—some of them get intimidated by violence.

Luther ends up being very displeased with this, but he's not there. He stays in the Wartburg for a number of months, from May of 1521 until March of 1522. Eventually, he's got to go back. The town council of Wittenberg writes him a letter saying: "Please come back." Of course, the letters have to be sent secretly, but by March of 1522, everyone knows that Luther's still around, and they send him a letter saying: "Please come back, we need you, this is getting out of hand." Luther comes back, and he preaches a series of sermons in March of 1522, where he settles people down, and he says: "Treat these people with weak consciences gently. Just preach to them; don't force them; don't be violent with them. "It should be preached and taught by tongue and pen," he says, "that to hold Mass in such a manner [i.e., as sacrifice] is sinful, and yet no one should be dragged away from it by the hair."

"It should be left to God, and His Word should be allowed to work alone." The power that changes things, Luther thinks, is God's Word. This is the song that he's going to be singing the whole time; it's words that do everything. It's words that have the power. Stop forcing people; that's not what's going to change the hearts. God's Word will change their hearts. God's Word and His Word alone should be allowed to work without our work or interference. Why? "Because it is not in my power or hand to fashion the hearts of men as the potter molds the clay," says Luther. "I can get no farther than their ears; their hearts I cannot reach. And since I cannot pour faith into their hearts, I cannot, nor should I, force anyone to have faith. That is God's work alone…so we should preach the Word, but the results must be left solely to God's good pleasure."

Luther is a powerful preacher, and he does, in fact, get control of the situation in Wittenberg, partly by using his own personal influence. He threatens to leave if they don't start calming down. He says in one of these sermons:

> And if you do not stop this [all this stuff], neither the Emperor nor anyone else will be needed to drive me away from you [maybe back to the Wartburg]; I will go without urging; and I dare say that none of my enemies, though they have caused me much sorrow, have wounded me as you have…[He says to the Wittenbergers] I will leave you unasked, and I shall regret that I ever preached so much as one sermon in this place…

Let's stop this stuff, or I'm getting out of here. If you want me around to help you out, then cut it out. Cut the violence; stop compelling people. People want to believe; people really want Luther around. He's the hero; Melanchthon and Karlstadt are not, so they get in line.

Meanwhile, let's say one thing about the crucial logic of Luther's positions. He wants to say that there are a lot of things that you shouldn't be compelling people about. There are a lot of things that are what he calls "free" in these sermons; later Protestant tradition calls them "indifferent," or *adiaphora* in Greek. You can do them or not, like elevating the host. Luther thinks it doesn't really mean an offering or a sacrifice, and so, since it doesn't, you're free not to do, or you're free to do it. It doesn't matter; it's not commanded in Scripture; it's not forbidden in Scripture. If it's not forbidden in Scripture, you can do it. Luther in that sense is not a Puritan. The Puritans are those later in Christian history who wanted a "pure" Biblical worship, which meant if it's not in the Scripture, you don't do it. If it's not in the Scripture, if it's not forbidden, you can do it, it's free. You don't have to do just what the Bible says. You can do things that aren't in the Bible as long as you don't require them. That's the logic of Christian freedom for Luther.

He also sets himself against a very important trend in the 16th century called "iconoclasm," the word for breaking up images. There's a whole wing in the Reformation that destroys statues in churches, breaks stained glass, paints over paintings on the walls of churches. Luther says: "What's the problem here? As long as no one's worshiping these images, you can leave them alone. The images are not idols; it's OK to have them in church," so Lutheran churches can have statues, and stained glass, and so on, just like Catholic churches, as opposed to most Calvinist churches, where you have whitewashed walls and no images of any kind. Luther's not a Puritan. "You don't have to get rid of all the stuff; you don't have to break stuff up. Let's get away from this violence of breaking images, breaking glass, painting stuff over, and so on."

Another thing that happens in Wittenberg is the clergy start getting married. Luther's already been mentioning this in the appeal to the German nobility, so he has no objection whatsoever for priests to get married. He encourages it, and that, of course, also serves to erase that deep gulf between clergy and laity, which Luther thinks is illegitimate. All Christians are priests—so everyone can get married, including Christian priests. The real issue actually, the real difficult issue, is the monastic vows, the celibacy of monks, because unlike ordinary priests, monks have promised in a solemn vow to be celibate. Melanchthon and Karlstadt both try to figure what to say about this.

Could we say that if a monk really can't restrain himself, that he's allowed to marry—that you can let him off the hook and let him get married because, really, it's just inhuman to require him to try to keep his vows? What are the circumstances under which you can let a monk get out of his vows? Luther says this is too complicated; this is too much back and forth. Remember how Luther likes to simplify things. None of this back and forth for the pope; he's Antichrist, forget it. Likewise, none of this back and forth about monastic vows—when do you have to keep them, when do you not? When you make a vow, you've got to keep it. If you make a promise, you should keep it. But it has to be a legitimate promise.

Under the law, for instance, if you take out a contract on someone to murder someone, that's not a valid contract. You can promise to murder someone, but you're not obligated to keep that promise; so, invalid promises you don't have to keep, and Luther's approach is to say monastic vows are not valid promises. They're not valid; they're never ever obligatory. No one has a right to make monastic vows, just like no one has a right to make a promise to kill someone—so he gets rid of the whole thing, the process of cutting the Gordian knot. Let's not untie this thing strand by strand; less just slice through it. All monastic vows are illegitimate. Why? Because they violate the logic of Christian freedom.

They basically make something required that is not required by the Gospel. You can do stuff that's not required by the Gospel, but you can't make things required that aren't required by the Gospel. These monastic vows require someone to do something, engage in a spiritual life, this celibate life, in a way that the Gospel does not require. They're making their own requirements. This is, again, this notion of human doctrine, "self-chosen works." Those are illegitimate. If you want to be celibate, you can be celibate, people can be celibate, that's OK, but to make a vow out of it, to make it into your spiritual life, as this makes you acceptable to God because you're a better person because you've made this vow, you're a monk, you're spiritually superior, that's offensive to the Gospel.

That's offensive to the whole logic of the Gospel, where there's no justification by good works, there's no justification by our spirituality. It's all just receiving Christ's gift. Monastic vows are illegitimate; get rid of them. That is a huge book. It's a book he writes called *The Judgment of Martin Luther*, on monastic vows. It drops like a bombshell because what ends up happening is monks start leaving the monastery in droves. There are a whole lot of monks who became monks when they were kids. Their families sent them to the monastery; they didn't really have much choice about these vows, and they're really glad to get out of them. So, the monasteries start emptying, and this is a huge social change because, as I mentioned, monasteries are wealthy. There's a lot of money in monasteries, and all of a sudden they're dissolving.

Another consequence of this attack on monastic vows is that Martin Luther, the monk, gets married. Who would have thunk it? As Luther said at one point, reminiscing many years later:

> I am the son of a peasant, and grandson, and great-grandson. My father became a miner, and he wanted me to become mayor. Instead, I became a monk and got the master's and doctor's degrees. My father didn't like it. Then I got into the pope's hair and married a renegade nun. Who could have read that in the stars?

Who would've thunk it? He marries a nun who is from a convent because, of course, the attack on monastic vows affects nuns as well as monks.

It's quite a story. Nuns were escaping from convents in droves, and this was illegal. Nuns were not allowed to leave their convents; it was against the law, and to help a nun escape from the convent was legally a form of kidnapping, and that was a capital crime, so it had to be done on the sly, and Luther actually cooperated in a number of schemes to get nuns out of their convents. One group of nuns, in fact, escaped in a set of empty barrels, herring barrels, fish barrels. The fish seller came in with his barrels, with the full barrels, and later he comes out with these empty barrels, but they're not empty; they've got nuns in them, around a dozen of them.

In they come to Wittenberg, in their wagons, in their fish barrels, and one of the students in the university of Wittenberg mentions this. "A wagon load of vestal virgins has just come to town," he writes to his friend, "all more eager for marriage than for life. God grant them husbands before worse befall." After all, the worst could befall. These are women on the loose, the original meaning of "loose women." They don't belong to the convent; they don't belong to their family anymore. What's going to happen to them? You've got to marry these people off. Most of them did; they married fairly quickly, but there's one straggler, one woman that they can't figure what to do with. She's still serving as a housemaid, and she needs a husband.

Her name is Katherine von Bora; she is from a noble family, but she's getting past prime marriageable age. She's 26, which is pretty old for a woman in those days. She's looking for a husband. She seems to have been sweet on a young man who was living far away, but he breaks the engagement, so Luther tries to get her matched up with an elderly doctor. She complained: "I don't want to marry this guy, but Dr. Luther, I'd take you or your friend Amsdorf there." Luther consults with his friend, and at first he takes it as a joke, but then he consults with his father. Remember, his father never approves of Luther being a monk and wants grandchildren, so his father actually liked the idea of Luther getting married.

Luther said, "I want to get rid of these monastic vows, but I'm not going to get married. You're not getting me a wife," he'd said a couple of years earlier, but now he's talking with his father, and his father is saying: "I want you to get married. I want to have grandchildren," and so Luther looks again at Katherine von Bora, and asks her consent. They're engaged just long enough for the family to come in for the wedding—his father and mother—and before you know it, an ex-monk has married an ex-nun. That becomes a big event; everyone is commenting on that. The Catholic comment, of course, is predictable. Luther just couldn't restrain himself; he couldn't deal with his lust. He's a lustful monk who just can't keep his vows, and so he falls into this terrible sin of marrying an ex-nun.

I don't think that's actually very accurate. Luther tells us, in his reminiscences later, that he never had much trouble with lustful thoughts as a monk. You might not believe that when anyone says it, but I think it's convincing from Luther because we know about Luther's terrors, this anxious conscience, this sense of absolute terror in the face of God's judgment, and also the fasting that practically broke his health—he was thin as a rail. I think he was just too caught up with terror to be interested in sex. If you're really terrified, sex is not what's on your mind, so I don't think it was about lust. In fact, Luther's interesting because, remember, his father had disapproved of him becoming a monk and said, "God commanded you to honor your father and your mother."

Luther is one of the few major Christian theologians who felt guilty for being celibate. I don't think he felt guilty about sex; he felt guilty about celibacy, about violating his father's wishes, which meant violating the command to honor his father and mother. I think he marries in good conscience. He's doing what his father wants, and therefore what God wants, and he's also putting his money where his mouth is, as it were, practicing what he preaches. He says: "I'm anxious to be myself, an example of what I've taught," and he's spiting the devil and the pope. He says: "I'm doing it to make the angels laugh and the devils weep." He gets married, and that is one of the crucial events in the Reformation.

Let's say a little bit about his life with Katherine von Bora, "Katie" as Luther calls her. He does say, "I am not infatuated; I do cherish my wife, but I'm not infatuated." He'll actually say, "Infatuation or falling in love is like a drunkenness; the intoxication wears off, and then the real married love begins." There's clearly no evidence that he fell in love with her, and then married her. That's not how it goes; he never expected anything like that. You can't imagine Martin Luther going on a date; he just asked for her consent and they got married.

But notice how he's thinking about this. It's not about falling in love. Real married love begins after the intoxication wears off. How does that work? Luther has written about real married love way back in 1519 in a sermon on the state of marriage, back when he was a monk, and really he's thinking of marriage as an image of Christ's love for the church and the human soul's love for God, and here's what he says about it in 1519, as a monk. A bride's love for her husband [he says]

> ...glows like a fire and desires nothing but her husband. She says, "It is you I want, not what is yours; I want neither your silver nor your gold...I want only you. I want you in your entirety, or not at all." [That's what married life is like, says Luther.] It wants only to have the beloved's own self completely.

He's really talking about Christ and the church, just as the illustrations I gave you from *The Freedom of A Christian*, the prostitute who becomes a queen when the king's son marries her. That's what he's really thinking about, but he does actually take this seriously. This is how married love is supposed to be. You want this person; you want all of them. You don't want what they have; you want what they are; you want who they really are. He actually puts this into practice. Let me tell you a little bit about Martin's relationship with Katie, and we get this from his letters and from his table talk.

> Katherine, my dear rib, greets you. [He writes in a letter. He loves calling her his rib, sometimes as "my rib greets your rib," writing to a friend, "and all the little ribs," the rib being, of course, Adam's rib] Katharine, my dear rib, greets you. She is quite well, thank God; gentle, obedient, and kind in all things, far beyond my hopes. [He's writing a year after they get married.] I would not exchange my poverty with her for all the riches of Croesus without her.

They're having financial problems; they will always have financial problems, but Luther is not willing to trade in this woman. He says things like, "If I were to lose my Katie, I wouldn't take another wife, though I were offered a queen." It's not because he idealizes her, however. Here's another one of these statements, "I would not give my Katie for France and Venice together, for God has given her to me—and other women have worse faults." So she's not perfect, but she's my wife. She's the woman God gave me. He'll say the same thing in reverse. He thinks that Katie should feel the same way about him. He writes to her, "Katie, you have a husband who loves you. Let someone else be Empress." There's a theological point here, of course. A woman is a gift of God to a man. It's hard to say this in English because in German the same word means both woman and wife, so a woman/wife is God's gift to a man. This goes back, of course, to Genesis 2, the beginning of the Book of Genesis, when Adam is created, and he's created alone, and there are all these animals. He can name them all, but a partner for him has not been found until he finds Eve, his rib.

God gave him Eve because God said first of all, "It's not good for the man to be alone." The other side of this is in the Book of Proverbs in the Bible, "He who finds a wife finds a good thing." Luther's theology of marriage is based on the notion that the man ought to recognize that this woman is God's gift to him. To find a wife is to find something good, not something that's a pain in the neck. When writing against the monks, Luther said the problem with these monks, and this papacy, and all this is that they don't want all the pain, and the suffering, and the work of marriage, diapers and a woman to take care of. They don't recognize the work of God; they don't recognize where God's goodness is. It's not good for the man to be alone, and it is good when he finds a wife. Katie is God's gift to Martin Luther, and he's bound and determined that he's going to live that out, and it seems he does.

The greatest tribute to Katherine von Bora, I think, is when he describes his favorite book of the Bible. Of all the tributes, I think, this is the best. He loves Paul's letter to the Galatians. He thinks that's the best, clearest description of the Gospel of Christ in all of the Bible, and in his preface to his commentary on Paul's letter to the Galatians, he says: "This epistle of Paul's, this letter of Paul's, is my Katie von Bora." He named his favorite part of the Gospel after his wife. That's high praise for Martin Luther.

They don't just get married, of course; they have children, six of them. One of them dies as a child, one of them dies at age 13, and four of them live to adulthood. The Elector of Saxony, Frederick "the Wise," gives them the old monastery, the monastery where Luther used to live with the other monks. It's now empty, 40 rooms, 40 monastic cells that get filled up not just with Luther's children, of course, but with dozens of relatives that they take in, nieces and nephews, orphans of friends, and then, eventually, student boarders. Students from the university of Wittenberg are boarded at this monastery. Katie insists on charging them money. Luther probably wouldn't have, but the wife does. It turns out she's the practical one.

She has to do quite a bit of work. She supervises this large household, with the household staff of servants. She does cattle (herding, milking, slaughtering); she raises pigs, chickens, and geese. She has a vegetable garden outside the house, and an orchard just outside of town, and a farm about two day's journey from town in a place called Zulsdorf. Luther will write her letters when she's at Zulsdorf, kidding her. He'll call her "The rich lady of Zulsdorf, Frau Doktor Katherine Luther, who lives in the body at Wittenberg but in the spirit at Zulsdorf, *meine Herzliebe,* the love of my heart, greetings." His addresses to his wife in the beginnings of his letters are sometimes just a hoot. "Lord, my lord Katie," he calls her sometimes, because she does run his life in all practical matters; in fact, he says this: "In practical matters, domestic affairs, I defer to Katie. Otherwise I am led by the Holy Ghost."

His theology is his own, but his domestic life is all up to Katie. She runs the finances; she keeps the books; she pays off the servants; she collects the money from the boarders, which Luther wouldn't do. She makes sure that they keep track of income. One bishop once gave him a present of 20 gulden, quite a bit of money, and Luther wanted to just return it for some reason. Katie insisted no. He also wanted to give lavish presents as wedding gifts, and he wrote a letter saying: "I'm going to give this wedding gift as soon as I find out where Katie has hid it." Katie is running a whole lot of things. On the other hand, this is a patriarchal system. At the dinner table, Katie calls him "my lord," or "doctor," and she uses the formal "you," and Luther uses the informal "you."

But that's actually another interesting feature. We know a lot about the texture of Luther's life with his wife because we hear a lot of what they talk about at the dinner table. There are all these student boarders. There are also faculty friends who come in for dinner. There are guests; there are visitors; there are travelers. They're all at the dinner table, and a bunch of them are taking notes, and so we have Luther's table talk. We have several volumes of notes of things that Luther said at the table, his conversations with his wife, and so on, so we know a lot about what their family is like. It's one of the most famous families in history. We know more about what Luther is like with his shirt unbuttoned, patting his stomach after a good meal. We know what that's like because we have these notes.

Perhaps one of the most moving moments in these notes, and I'll close with this, is his talk about the death of his 13-year-old daughter, Magdalena. One of those things that the pope doesn't have to deal with is children dying. Actually, popes did have children, but they didn't have legitimate children. Luther is saying not only is the woman a good gift to man, the children are a gift of God. We should boast of God's gifts, he says. "In the last 1,000 years, God has given to no bishop such great gifts as he has given me [for one should boast of God's gifts]," and he says that as his daughter is dying. She dies in his arms; his wife is outside because she can't stand to be in the room when it happens.

The separation from her hurts him beyond description, but he says: "How strange it is to know that she is at peace in heaven, that all is well with her, and yet to be so grief-stricken, so sorrowful!" And he wouldn't trade it for the world. "The pope is not worthy of this," he says about his children. He holds his child once—another problem with children, his oldest son is cutting his teeth and is making a joyous nuisance of himself, crying and holding a temper tantrum—and says: "These are the joys of marriage, of which the pope is not worthy." It's a real affirmation of the ordinary life and its ordinary sorrows, troubles, and work, and it's very appealing to the ordinary people of Germany—not the spiritual life of the monks, but the life of the family, the life of wife, husband, and children. That is the Christian life and Christian piety as Luther teaches it and as he lives it.

Lecture Twelve

The Work of the Reformer

Scope:

Luther did more than write scholarly treatises against the pope. His work as a Reformer, aimed at bringing the Gospel into the hearts of ordinary people, left an indelible mark on German culture. First of all, he translated the whole Bible into German, so that people who were not scholars and knew no Latin could read it. That in itself is an amazing accomplishment for one man, but Luther did more. He composed catechisms for Christian instruction that are still used today. He wrote deeply sensitive letters of spiritual counsel, giving pastoral advice to all sorts of people in all sorts of difficult circumstances. And he wrote music designed to fill people's hearts with the Gospel, including such famous hymns as "A Mighty Fortress Is Our God."

Outline

I. Luther's translation of the Bible is one of his most powerful contributions to the Reformation, as well as to German culture.

    A. Luther translates directly from the original Hebrew and Greek, not from the Latin version most familiar to clergy at the time.

    B. Although not the first translation of the Bible into German, Luther's Bible was the first to make God speak good German.

    C. Luther's extraordinary gift for the German language is acquired by listening carefully to ordinary people and taking their speech as the standard of good German.

    D. What he gives them in return is God speaking to them in their own tongue, which is accordingly ennobled.

    E. Luther loves the distinctive resources of the German language, such as the word *liebe*, usually translated by the English word "dear" but actually closer to "beloved."

    F. Although wanting ordinary people to have God's Word in their own language, Luther does not advocate private interpretation of the Bible, apart from the tradition of Christian teaching in creed and catechism.

II. Luther's two catechisms are also powerful means of bringing the Reformation Gospel into the hearts of ordinary Germans.

    A. The *catechism,* when Luther uses the word, means essentially: instruction in the Lord's Prayer, the Ten Commandments, the creed, and the sacraments.

        1. In the preface to the *Small Catechism,* Luther complains about the terrible ignorance of churches he has visited where the people are not taught these things.

        2. In the preface to the *Large Catechism,* he insists that he is himself still a student of the catechism.

    B. The catechisms Luther writes are, thus, his commentary on the basic truths of the Gospel and how they should be taught to all Christians.

    C. The *Small Catechism* is intended for memorization by unlearned people.

        1. It emphasizes the goodness of God, as seen by all he has done for us.

        2. It memorably expands the Ten Commandments into an ethic for the whole of Christian life.

        3. In contrast to other Protestants churches, it retains the practice of private confession of sins to a pastor.

        4. It is characterized by a distinctive note of cheerfulness.

    D. The *Large Catechism* is far more discursive and argumentative and includes authoritative summaries of Luther's theological position.

        1. It is famous for its definition of God as "that from which the heart seeks all good things."

        2. It affirms the piety of ordinary people doing humble jobs over the spirituality of the monks.

III. Luther's letters of spiritual consolation show him at his personal best, aiming to comfort those in all kinds of trouble, anxiety, and distress.

    A. He writes for women suffering miscarriages or infants who have died without baptism, assuring them that, according to Romans 8:26–27, their sighs baptize and save the child.

B. He writes his mother as she is dying, addressing the anxieties of late-medieval people facing death and insisting that she believe the comforting words of Christ.

IV. Luther's hymns, to which he wrote both words and music, are also meant to bring the Gospel into people's hearts.

   A. Luther has astonishing things to say about the power and value of music, which is next to

   B. One well known hymn is "From Heav'n on High to Earth I Come," which rehearses the Christmas story in 15 verses.

   C. Most famous is "A Mighty Fortress Is Our God," which was originally published under the title Psalm 46.

Essential Reading:

Luther, *Small Catechism*, in Leith and in Tappert.

———, Letter to his Mother, in *Letters of Spiritual Counsel*, pp. 33–36.

———, "Comfort for Women Who Have Had a Miscarriage," in *Luther's Works*, vol. 43, pp. 247–250.

Supplemental Reading:

Luther, *The Large Catechism*, also found in Tappert.

———, *Letters of Spiritual Counsel* (makes wonderful reading).

———, "On Translating," in *Luther's Works*, vol. 35.

———, Liturgy and Hymns, in *Luther's Works*, vol. 53.

Questions to Consider:

1. How does Luther's approach to religious instruction compare with your own experience?

2. How do Luther's hymns compare with your favorite music?

Lecture Twelve—Transcript
The Work of the Reformer

In 1521, all of Europe is holding its breath. Martin Luther has confronted the Emperor there at the Diet of Worms, "Here I stand, I cannot do otherwise," and he's going back from Worms to Wittenberg, and he's kidnapped. It's a plot to actually keep him safe; it's actually a ruse. He ends up in the Wartburg, as you recall, but most people don't know that it's a friendly plot to keep him safe. They hear the rumor about him being kidnapped; they don't know what's happened. Europe holds its breath. Has Martin Luther been killed? What's going to happen next? What's going to happen to this immense Gospel movement that he got started? But it hasn't really gotten underway in any institutional way yet. The Reformation hasn't begun; we've just heard about it.

Here's the reaction of Albrecht Durer, the great German artist, when he hears of the kidnapping, but he doesn't know what's going to happen next. He writes in his journal:

> I don't know if he's alive or if they've murdered him. [He suffered for the sake of Christian truth—and because he rebuked the unchristian papacy…which strives to deprive us of the work of our blood and sweat, which is then shamefully consumed by idlers (those priests and so on)]. If we lose this man, who has written more clearly than anyone else in centuries, may God grant his spirit to someone else…O God, if Luther is dead, who will ever proclaim so clearly to us the Holy Gospel? What might he have written for us in the next 10 or 20 years?

Durer gets to find out. Luther does a lot of writing, maybe not as important as the theological treatises of the 1520s, but in another sense, they're not as theologically important, but they're terribly important for the shaping of German culture and church life, the things he writes in the 1520s. He writes dozens of hymns; he writes two catechisms and, most importantly of all, he starts translating the Bible. He starts this in the Wartburg in 1521, and he completes the whole translation of the complete Bible in 1534, but he already has the complete New Testament translated and ready to be printed in September of 1522.

The task of the Reformer, the work of the Reformer, is to bring God's Word to the people—the kind and gracious word of the Gospel—and to do that, you need to have God speaking in German. The opening wedge of the whole Reformation really is that moment when the words of institution: "This is my body, given for you," are spoken in German and not in Latin, so that the Mass doesn't seem like some kind of magic being done by this special magician called a priest. It seems much more like Jesus Christ telling you this is his body, and it's given for you. Of course, that is exactly Luther's intention. God is going to speak German, so the people can hear his word and get that word in their hearts.

His Bible—beginning with the whole New Testament, published in September of 1522—is a huge success. It's printed many times; it's revised many times, and his Catholic opponents take notice of this. They complain; here's one of his Catholic opponents writing in the 1520s:

> Even tailors and shoemakers, indeed women and other simple idiots, who had accepted this new Lutheran Gospel—though they could read only a little German—read it eagerly as if it were a foundation of all truth. Some carried it in their bosoms and learned it by heart. Thus they claimed within a few months such skill and experience that without timidity they debated not only with Catholic laymen, but also with priest and monks...

Ordinary people got to know the Bible well enough that they could debate with priests and monks.

This Catholic theologian did not like this at all. Of course, that's exactly Luther's intention; let ordinary people know enough of the Bible that they can know it better than the priests and the monks. To do that, you have to make God speak good German. To do that, of course, you have to know how to speak good German yourself. Luther has an extraordinary gift for words. His German is extraordinarily powerful, vigorous, pure, and simple. He, in fact, boasts of the fact that he teaches even his opponents how to speak German.

How does he learn to speak good German? He learns by listening. All of Luther's life is about words—speaking and hearing, and he's such a good speaker because he is a great listener. He says that if you want to know how to translate the Bible, you don't go back to the old Latin Bible, which all of the academic people of Luther's time would know. Luther says:

> We do not have to inquire of the literal Latin how we are to speak German...Rather we must ask the mother in the home, the children on the street, the common man in the marketplace. We must be guided by *their* language, the way *they* speak, and do our translating accordingly. That way they will understand it and recognize that we are speaking German to them.

He goes to the butcher to learn the parts of animals when he translates the part of the Bible where the sacrifices are made and animals are cut up. He goes to the treasury to learn about the names of the jewels. He listens to good German and, therefore, he can speak good German. He speaks good German because he speaks their German, the German of the German people, and he's heard it, and he gives it back to them as God's Word. This doesn't leave German unchanged; it's like what happens to English after Shakespeare, or Italian after Dante. A great user of the language shapes the language, and Luther certainly had a huge influence on the German language.

He convinced people that the German language could be used to express complex ideas. One of the complaints that the academic theologians had is that German is too simple; you can't express a complex idea in German. There were some German mystical writers who proved them wrong already, people like Meister Eckhart, but Luther was maybe the first great writer that used pure, simple German to express deep and complex ideas. The German language needed somebody like him, just as the Italian language needed Dante, but the Italians had Dante back in the 13th century. The Germans have to wait for Luther in the 16th century.

The other thing that Luther does linguistically is that when he translates the Bible, he goes back to the original language, not to the Latin. Even though the Latin Bible is more or less the Bible he grows up with as a student, when Luther thinks about the Bible, the first thing that comes into his mind is really the Latin Bible, but he goes back to the Hebrew and the Greek, and he translates direct from the original languages, not from Latin. Let me give you an example of how he uses the original language and gets it to German, and how he uses the unique resources of the German language to do something new and distinct. Here's a famous example of Luther's translating.

In the Gospel of Luke in the Christmas story, the angel Gabriel comes and announces to Mary that she's going to be the mother of our Lord. He says to her, the angel Gabriel says to Mary: "Hail Mary, full of grace," that's the English translation. It's pretty much a literal translation of the Latin: *Ave Maria, gratia plena*, full of grace, and it's like that in the German, older translation: *Gegruesset seistu, Maria vol gnaden* [modern: *Gegruesset seis du, Maria voll Gnaden*], full of grace. Luther comments on this: "What's a German to make of this? What does it mean to say she's full of grace? Is she like a mug full of beer, or a purse full of coins? A German is not going to understand this if you talk about Maria being full of grace, *voll Gnaden*. We've got to go back to the original language."

What does the Greek say? Not the Latin, not the *Ave Maria, gratia plena*, but the Greek, the original language of the New Testament. That's more like it, if you were to translate it literally: "Hail be-graced one," but the problem is if you translate it literally, it comes out ugly: "Hail be-graced one," you can't say that in English, and you can't say it in German either, so what are you going to do? You're going to say it in good German. Luther, in order to get to the good German, goes back even further. He goes from the Greek to the Hebrew. He figures the angel came to Mary, who was a Hebrew maiden; he probably spoke to her in Hebrew. How do angels speak to people in Hebrew when they greet them?

He goes back to the Book of Daniel, and he notices that an angel addresses the prophet Daniel and says basically: "Hail beloved one, beloved man" and Luther says: "I bet that's how the angel talked to Mary," so what he said is something like this to make the angel speak good German: *"Gott grusse dich, du liebe Maria,"* God greet you, you dear Maria, *Liebe Maria. Liebe* is the German word for dear; when we start a letter with dear so-and-so, it's *Liebe* so-and-so, but it also means "beloved," and no German can miss this. *Liebe* is the word for "love." You say, "I love you," that's usually *Ich liebe dich*—so *du liebe Maria* is "you dear Mary, you beloved Mary." You can't quite say that in English. You can't say, "you beloved Mary"; that's too much; but, if you say, "dear Mary," that seems too little. It seems too trivial and pallid, whereas this German word *liebe* is both ordinary, just as ordinary as dear Mary, but also resonates deeply with this notion of love.

Luther comments:

> Whoever knows German knows very well what a fine, heartfelt word this word *liebe* is…I do not know whether this word…can be said in Latin or in any other language with such fullness of feeling, so that it pierces and rings in the heart, and through all the senses, as it does in our language.

I think he's right; there's nothing quite like this word in any other language, so when he translates the angel's greeting in the Bible to Mary, he's using resources of German language that are unique and yet capture something deep about what's going on in the Bible. That's just one hint or example of how Luther makes God speak good German, makes God's Words speak in the language of the people instead of in the stilted translations that were there before. There were other translations in the Bible into German before Luther, but they came from the Latin; they were literalistic; they were ugly; they weren't good German.

The other thing that Luther does is he writes catechisms; that's the next thing to think about. The catechisms are important because Luther is concerned about something that lies behind that Catholic criticism, that sour Catholic note, that says: "You're letting ordinary people talk as if they know God's Word and arguing with priests and monks. They don't have a right to do that." The serious concern behind that is that if you let people read the Bible all by themselves without the guidance of the church, they become heretics. Heretics love the Bible; they get most of their ideas from it. They have to learn how to read the Bible the way the church reads it. One response to this problem is to say that no one gets to interpret the Bible except for authorized people like the priests.

But Luther's approach is just the opposite. We've got to have everybody interpreting the Bible and do it together, and ordinary people ought to be taught how to read the Bible the way Christians read the Bible. Don't withhold Christian doctrine from ordinary people and keep it safe in the hands of the priests. Give it out to everyone; let everyone learn Christian doctrine; let everyone learn God's Word; let everyone learn to understand the Bible the way the church and the Christian tradition have always understood it. That's what the catechism is for.

The "catechism," for Luther, always means five basic elements: There's the Lord's

Prayer, the Ten Commandments, the creed, and then the two sacraments of Eucharist and baptism. Often, when he says the word "catechism," he does not mean the catechisms he wrote; he means just those five items: the Lord's Prayer, the creed, the Ten Commandments, and so on. But he does write a commentary on these things, two of them, in fact, a Small Catechism that's about 10 pages long, and a Large Catechism that's about 100 pages long, a small book. Both of them are designed to teach people. The Small Catechism is designed to teach ordinary, illiterate people; they can memorize it. The Large Catechism is meant more for pastors. Both types of catechisms are meant to make sure that people get to learn how to understand the Bible.

The Small Catechism grows out of the practice of visitation conducted in 1527–28, where the German prince, acting as an emergency bishop, sends theologians around the parishes saying: "Let's visit these parishes and find out how well the teaching is going in the Christian teaching of these people," and Luther is appalled by the results. In the preface to the Small Catechism, he writes: "The common people, especially those in the countryside [that is, the peasants] have no knowledge whatever of Christian teaching, and unfortunately many priests are quite incompetent and unqualified to teach." Many of them probably were semi-literate; they had memorized the Latin Mass and that's about it. You give them a catechism so that not only can the common people be taught, but the priests can learn how to teach.

Luther is a teacher of teachers. He's a theologian who teaches pastors how to teach ordinary folks. That's what he writes the Large Catechism for. But the preface of the Large Catechism is interesting because Luther the teacher insists that he's still a student of the catechism. This is very characteristic of Luther. He writes:

> As for myself, let me say that I too am a teacher and a preacher...yet I act like a child who is being taught the catechism. Every morning, and whenever else I have time, I read and recite word for word the Lord's Prayer, the Ten

Commandments, the Creed, the Psalms, and so on. I must still read and study the Catechism daily, yet I cannot master it as I wish, but must remain a child and pupil of the Catechism, and I do it gladly.

This is like that theme from the *Treatise on Good Works*; you can spend all your life learning how to obey the Ten Commandments, but there's no outgrowing the basics of the Gospel and of God's Word, no graduating beyond hearing the same words. In fact, he complains:

Look at these bored, presumptuous saints who don't want to read and study the Catechism daily, [the people want to be more spiritual than just to believe the ordinary things of Christian faith.] They evidently consider themselves much wiser than God himself...[for] God himself is not ashamed to teach [the catechism] every day, for he knows of nothing better to teach, and he always keeps on teaching this one thing.

God doesn't get tired of preaching the Gospel to people. Why should we?

These Lutheran catechisms are still in use in the Lutheran church today; most Lutherans have memorized some of these things. Let me give you a little taste of this Lutheran instruction in how to understand God's Word. Here is from the Small Catechism, some stuff from the Ten Commandments: "Thou shalt not kill. What does this mean? Ask the catechism. The answer? We should fear and love God, and so we should not endanger our neighbor's life or cause him any harm, but help and befriend him in every necessity of life." Notice how the prohibition "Thou shalt not kill," means much more than just thou shalt not kill; it means you have to help and befriend your neighbor. Luther expands each of the commandments so that it's a positive command, not just a negative command, not just a prohibition, and this is typical of Christian readings of the Ten Commandments.

He is teaching these people to read the Ten Commandments the way the Ten Commandments have always been read in the church. You shall not commit adultery. What does this mean? We should fear and love God, and so we should lead a chaste, pure life in word and deed—each one loving and honoring his wife or her husband. It's not just a narrow prohibition. You shall not bear false witness against your neighbor. What does this mean? We should fear and love God, and so we should not tell lies about our neighbor, nor betray, slander, or defame him, but should apologize for him, speak well of him, and interpret charitably all that he does, and so on. You can see how Luther's taking the Ten Commandments and turning them into an ethic for all of Christian life, and that's typical of Christian readings of the Ten Commandments. That's how you learn to read the Bible like the church.

Another note that I don't want to miss here in the Smaller Catechism, Luther will say this note of cheerfulness in the Ten Commandments and throughout the catechism. After you say your prayers in the Ten Commandments in the morning, you should go cheerfully to your work, or here's his summary of the Ten Commandments, and he explains why you do this fear and love God thing that you've heard now. What does all this mean? God threatens to punish all who transgress his commandments; we should therefore fear his wrath and not disobey these commandments. On the other hand, he promises grace in every blessing to all who keep them. You should therefore love him, trust him, and cheerfully do all that he has commanded. Part of the Christian life, this necessary part of Christian life, is cheerfulness because God is good, and all of God's Word is good for us.

Likewise, in the Large Catechism, the Large Catechism begins its treatment of the first commandment, "Thou shalt have no gods besides me," by giving a definition of God. What is a god? A god is that to which we look for all good. You look to God for good things. What is it to pray? It is to call upon God in every need. We're always looking for God to give us stuff, and that's OK, Luther's saying. We're not supposed to be unselfish; we're supposed to want stuff from God. This is diametrically opposed, 180 degrees against what he was saying way back in 1516, in the lectures on Romans, where he was saying: "God created all these good things, but they're all evil for us because of our sin, so instead of seeking good things, we should seek evil things; we should hate ourselves." No, if you want to know God, if you want to love God, seek good things from God and be cheerful.

Let me mention one of my favorite parts of the Large Catechism is where Luther talks about the fourth commandment in his numbering, that's "Honor thy father and thy mother." Here's his comment, part of a longer comment: "Every child who knows and does this [honors his father and his mother] has...the great comfort of being able joyfully to boast in the face of all who are occupied with [self-chosen works]: 'See, this work is well pleasing to my God in heaven, this I know for certain.' " That's what the commandments do; they tell you if you're doing this, then God is happy. Not that this justifies you—faith alone justifies you—but if you want to know what to do to please God, you don't have to be like a monk and make up stuff. "O how great a price all the...monks and nuns would pay," says Luther, "if in the exercise of their religion they could bring before God a single work done in accordance with his commandment and could say with a joyful heart in God's presence, 'Now I know that this work is well pleasing to Thee.'"

The monks live in uncertainty. This is not fair to monks today; I don't think this is at all true of most Catholic monks today, but it was true of Luther's monastic experience, where he was constantly trying to please God by inventing one more form of spirituality, one more form of self-hatred, one more way to go beyond God's Word and try to be holier than God. Here's the key contrast; this is a wonderful moment a little bit later. He's expanding the commandment to honor father and mother because he thinks that honoring father and mother means obeying all authorities, all legitimate authorities, not just father and mother—so here he's expanding it to the housemaids and man servants: "What a child owes to father and mother," says Luther, "the entire household owes them likewise."

Therefore man servants and maid servants should take care not only to obey their masters and mistresses, but also to honor them as their own parents and do everything that they know is expected of them, not from compulsion and reluctantly, but gladly and cheerfully, and they should do it because it's God's commandment and is more pleasing to him than all other works. "If this truth could be impressed upon the poor people," Luther comments, "a servant girl would dance for joy, and praise and thank God." Isn't it a wonderful thing to be able to boast yourself: "If I do my daily work, my housework faithfully, that is better than all the holiness and austere life of all the monks"? How can you lead a more blessed or holy life as far as your works are concerned?

In the sight of God, it is really faith that makes a person holy; faith alone serves him, while our works serve other people. You don't have to justify yourself by your works, but if you want to know what pleases God, the commandments tell you, you don't have to be like these monks. The housemaid, the servant girl, sweeping the floor in obedience to the father of the house pleases God more than all the monks in the world with their self-chosen works. You see what's going on here; he's affirming the life of ordinary people, and their piety is better than the works of all the monks. You can see how this would be very attractive to ordinary people.

He also complains (here's another one on the theme of finding good things, all good things in God):

> We have rightly rejected the prayers of monks and priests [says Luther, commenting on the Lord's Prayer], these monks and priests who howl and growl frightfully day and night [saying all their masses and so on], not one of them thinks of asking for the least thing. They have never prayed wholeheartedly for so much as a drop of wine. They only thought of doing a good work as payment to God, not willing to receive anything from him, but only to give something. No, true Christian piety receives what God gives rather than tries to offer God our own good works.

This is great comfort for people; this is an affirmation of ordinary people; you can see why it's popular.

Two more things to mention about Luther's attempt to bring God's Word into the ordinary people's lives. Luther writes letters of spiritual consolation to people who are troubled. He writes letters to ordinary people who are suffering all kinds of trouble. Here's one to women suffering miscarriages who are anxious because their children haven't been baptized. This also covers women whose infants have died right after birth, who have not had a chance to be baptized. What about their salvation? Luther writes:

> It is to be hoped that the woman's heartfelt cry and deep longing to bring her child to be baptized will be accepted by God as an effective prayer. It is true that a Christian in deepest despair does not dare to name, wish, or hope for help [Luther knows how that feels]…[but] a Christian is not a Turk, a pagan, or an atheist. She is precious in God's sight

and her prayer is powerful and great…whatever she sincerely prays for, especially in the unexpressed yearning of her heart, becomes a great, unbearable cry in God's ears.

This goes back to the letter to the Romans, where Paul says: "The Holy Spirit helps us in our weakness. We don't know how to pray as we ought, but the spirit intercedes for us with sighs that are too deep for words." The sigh of someone who doesn't even dare hope is heard by God. The woman baptizes her dead infant by her sighs, her inability to even hope for the salvation of her child, her longing, God hears it. Imagine how comforting that must have been.

Here's another letter, written to his mother. She's dying, and he knows it. What's he going to say to her? What comfort can he give her? Remember, so much of Luther's theology is based on this moment of, you're facing God, you're facing God's judgment; it's like the hour of your death. What do you write to your mother when she's close to the hour of her death? Here's what Luther writes:

> You know dear mother, the real foundation and ground of your salvation from whom you must seek consolation in this and all other troubles, the cornerstone Jesus Christ, our savior. He says: "Be of good cheer, I have defeated the world," and if he has defeated the world, then he has certainly overcome the king of this world.

Luther has an enemies list, a Christian enemies list: the world, flesh, and the devil. Jesus Christ has defeated them all. "We must certainly not doubt that these words are really true: 'I have defeated the world,' and we're told to receive this consolation with joy and all thanksgiving." Once again, we're supposed to be cheerful, even in the face of death. "Anyone unwilling to be comforted by these words would be doing a real injustice to our dear comforter." These words are true; he has defeated the world; he has defeated the devil. Believe them, he's saying, believe these words, "so let us rejoice now, full of assurance and happiness, and if any thought of sin or death frightens us," he says to his dying mother, "we should fight it by lifting up our hearts and saying 'Look dear soul, what are you doing? Dear death, dear sin," there's that German word *liebe*, dear death, dear sin.

> How is it that you are still alive and frightening me? Don't you know you've been defeated? You, death, don't you know that you are thoroughly dead? Don't you know the one

who says about you: "I have defeated the world"? I won't listen to your frightening ideas or take any notice of them. Rather, I'll take notice of my savior's consoling words "Be of good cheer, I have defeated the world." He is the conqueror, the true champion, who with his words: "Be of good cheer" gives me his victory and makes it mine. I will stay with him and hold fast to his words and his consolation. Whether I stay here or go beyond, I will live by those words, for he does not lie to me.

Luther's putting words in his mother's mouth here. This is typical of him; he's always writing these mini-dialogs, putting words in people's mouths, always thinking in terms of speaking and hearing, and he's being a little bossy. Notice he doesn't say something like: "Dear Mother, make a decision for Christ." That's not how Lutheran evangelism works. It's more like Jesus said these comforting words; you'd better believe them. What right do you have to call him a liar? So, be comforted. You have to be comforted. Don't believe the devil; believe Jesus. And so this kind of bossiness in Lutheran evangelism is meant to comfort and to strengthen. I think this would be a great letter to receive when you're facing the terrors of death. Luther wants God's Word to comfort people, and that's why he also put God's Word to music.

That's the last bit of the work of the Reformer. I want to talk about. Luther writes hymns; he writes a lot of hymns. Luther loves music; he thinks that this is very important. There are some Reformers who do not want to have music in church, especially organ music, instrumental music. That's entirely foreign to Luther's thinking about this. He says: "Next to the Word of God, music deserves the highest praise." It is second only to the Gospel in getting down into the bottom of our heart and cheering us up. Music drives away sadness and the devil, he says, just like the Gospel, and that's why music and the Gospel go together, so he puts the Gospel to music.

He composes hymns, all sorts of hymns. He composes hymns on the catechism, the Ten Commandments, the Lord's Prayer, and the creed. He puts a lot of the Bible to music. He puts the Christmas story to music, some famous ones. Here's one that Bach particularly loved; Bach is a Lutheran composer who puts a lot of Luther's hymns to music. Bach does marvelous things with this little tune. This is a Christmas hymn:

From heaven above to earth I come
To bring good news to everyone
Glad tidings of great joy I bring
To all the world and gladly sing.

That's the angel bringing glad tidings, singing the Gospel, and then there are 14 more verses telling the whole Christmas story about the baby in the manger. But, of course, the most famous Lutheran hymn is "A Mighty Fortress is Our God." Luther probably wrote both the words and the music to this one, at least the scholars think. Every Lutheran knows this one, but I'm going to sing it in a slightly different way, closer to the 16th century. Here it goes:

A mighty fortress is our God, a bulwark never failing;
Our helper He, amid the flood of mortal ills prevailing:
For still our ancient foe doth seek to work us woe;
His craft and power are great, and, armed with cruel hate,
On earth is not his equal.

Did we in our own strength confide, our striving would be losing;
Were not the right Man on our side, the Man of God's own choosing:
Dost ask who that may be? Christ Jesus, it is He;
Lord Sabbaoth, His Name, from age to age the same,
And He must win the battle.

Once again, Jesus is the one who fights for you; he overcomes and defeats sin, death, and the devil. He is the Lord of Hosts, the Lord of Sabbaoth. What's striking is when this is published in the 16th century; it doesn't come published under the title "A Mighty Fortress is Our God." It's titled Psalm 46. It's Luther's translation of a Psalm of the Bible, which talks about the Lord of Hosts and the God of Jacob fighting for Israel. Who is the Lord of Hosts? Luther's very clear on this: Jesus Christ. That's the doctrine of the trinity for you. He reads the doctrine of the trinity into the Bible, the way any Christian would, and he teaches you to read the Psalms, the Old Testament Psalms, as hymns of victory sung for Jesus Christ to comfort all those who need to hear of someone who is powerful enough to defeat sin, death, and the devil.

Timeline

1076–1084 ....Conflict between Pope Gregory VII and Emperor Henry IV over lay investiture.

1213 ....King John of England, giving way to Pope Innocent III after excommunication and interdict, makes England a fief of the pope.

1215 ....The fourth Lateran council (a council of the Catholic church meeting at Rome) establishes the medieval sacramental system, including the obligation of private confession and the taking of communion at Easter.

1302 ....Boniface VIII publishes the bull *Unam Sanctam* declaring the superiority of the pope over all secular rulers.

1309–1377 ....The pope resides in the French city of Avignon rather than in Rome (the "Babylonian Captivity" of the papacy).

1378–1417 ....Great Schism (rival claimants to the office of pope reside in Avignon and Rome).

1414–1418 ....Council of Constance ends the Great Schism, appoints a new pope, condemns the writings of John Wyclif, and has John Hus burned at the stake as a heretic.

1453 ....Fall of Constantinople to the Turks, marking the end of the Byzantine Empire and the beginning of the Turkish threat to Western Europe.

1455 ....Johannes Gutenberg publishes the first printed Bible, inaugurating the era of the printing press.

1478 ....The Pazzi Conspiracy, in which Lorenzo and Guiliano de Medici are attacked and the latter is killed while at Mass in the cathedral in Florence; the current pope (Sixtus IV) is in on the conspiracy, while both the victims are fathers of future popes (Leo X and Clement VII, respectively) who reigned during the Reformation.

1483 .... Martin Luther is born in Eisleben, November 10, son of Hans and Margarethe ("Hanna") Luder.

1502   Luther takes Bachelor's degree from the University of Erfurt.

1503–1513 .... Reign of Pope Julius II (called the "warrior pope" and *il Terribile*, that is, "the Terrifying").

January 1505 .... Luther takes Master's degree from the University of Erfurt.

July 1505 .... Following a vow made in a thunderstorm, Luther enters an Augustinian monastery.

1506 .... Pope Julius II lays the foundation for the new St. Peter's in the Vatican, to be funded in part by indulgences sold in Germany.

1507 .... Luther says his first Mass.

1508 .... Pope Julius II commissions Michelangelo to paint the ceiling of the Sistine chapel.

Luther, at this point an unknown monk, visits Rome as the traveling companion of an older monk; he is disgusted by its worldliness and doubtful if pilgrimages to Rome do any spiritual good.

Luther is appointed professor at the University of Wittenberg.

1513–1521 .... Reign of Pope Leo X.

1514 .... Luther is appointed town preacher at Wittenberg.

1516 ....Erasmus publishes the first printed critical edition of the New Testament; Luther immediately uses it in his classes.

October 31, 1517...........Luther posts the 95 Theses on the church door at Wittenberg.

1518 ....Shortly after the imperial Diet at Augsburg, Luther submits to a formal interview with Cardinal Cajetan, who fails to obtain his recantation.

1520 ....Luther publishes the most important theological treatises of his life: the *Treatise on Good Works* (May), the appeal *To the Christian Nobility* (August), *The Babylonian Captivity of the Church* (October), and *The Freedom of a Christian* (November). The papal bull *Exsurge Domine* is published in June, condemning Luther's teachings and ordering his books to be burned; Luther responds in December by burning the bull, together with papal decretals and canon law.

1521 ....Luther testifies before the emperor at the Diet of Worms in April but is condemned as a heretic in May; he spends the rest of the year hiding at the Wartburg while practical reformation of the church begins in Wittenberg, accompanied by much tumult.

1522–1523 ....Reign of Pope Hadrian VI.

1522 ....In March, Luther returns to Wittenberg and takes charge of the reformation there; in September, he publishes his German translation of the New Testament.

1523–1534 ....Reign of Pope Clement VII.

1524–1525 ....Great Peasant War in Germany.

1525 ....Luther marries Katherine von Bora, escapee from a convent.

1527 ....Emperor Charles V invades Italy and takes the pope prisoner for six months, while his troops (mostly Germans sympathetic to Luther) sack Rome.

1529 ....Luther and Zwingli fail to reach agreement on the Lord's Supper at the Marburg Colloquy.

At the Diet of Speyer, Lutheran princes lodge a formal protestation against the enforcement of the Edict of Worms, which earns them the name "Protestants."

The Turkish advance into Europe is halted at the gates of Vienna, though "the Turk" remains a threat throughout Luther's lifetime.

1530 ....Diet of Augsburg, where the Lutheran princes submit the *Augsburg Confession* to the emperor, who does not accept it.

1531 ....Protestant princes form the Schmalkald League for defense against the likelihood of invasion by Catholic princes, including the emperor.

Death of Zwingli in the battle of Kappel in Switzerland.

1534–1549 ....Reign of Pope Paul III.

1534 ....Luther publishes a complete German Bible.

1534–1535 ....Revolutionary Anabaptists take over the Dutch city of Münster by force and try to create a utopia in expectation of the last days; they are besieged and slaughtered.

1535 ....Luther's lectures form the basis of his most extended treatment of the doctrine of justification in the "great" Galatians commentary (in contrast with the quite different "small" Galatians commentary of 1519).

1536 ....John Calvin begins work as a reformer in Geneva, shortly after publishing the first edition of his *Institutes*.

Martin Bucer works out the Wittenberg Concord with Luther and Melanchthon, an ambiguous and temporary compromise on the Lord's Supper.

1545 ....Opening session of the Council of Trent, the key Roman Catholic response to the Reformation; the council will last, with interruptions, until 1563.

1546 ....Luther dies while visiting Eisleben, his town of birth, to mediate a dispute between local aristocrats.

1547 ....Protestant princes of Germany are defeated by Emperor Charles V in the Schmalkaldic war; Electoral Saxony and the town of Wittenberg are taken by Charles's troops, and Elector John Frederick, long Luther's protector, is captured and removed from office.

1548 ....Charles V imposes the Augsburg Interim on the subjugated Lutheran principalities of Germany; it restores the Catholic church but allows married clergy and other Protestant practices to continue until the Council of Trent settles disputed issues.

1555 ....The emperor gives up all attempts to wipe out Lutheranism under the Peace of Augsburg, which establishes the peaceful coexistence of Lutheran and Catholic territories in Germany under the principle that each territory's religion is determined by its prince (*cujus regio, ejus religio*).

1580 ....The Formula of Concord (or *Concordia*) is published as the basis of Lutheran unity, resolving key doctrinal disputes within the Lutheran churches of Germany.

1643 ....The Peace of Westphalia ends the Thirty Years' War in Germany and reinstitutes the terms of the Peace of Augsburg, now extended to include the Reformed churches (but not Anabaptists).

Glossary

Many familiar terms are included in this glossary because their familiarity can be deceptive: In 16th-century discussions, they were used in a way that is subtly, but sometimes profoundly, different from today.

Absolution: A formal announcement of the forgiveness of sins, as in the Catholic sacrament of penance, where absolution is pronounced using the words "I absolve you of your sins in the name of the Father, the Son and the Holy Spirit."

Adiaphora: Greek term for "indifferent"; used by later Protestants to designate church practices that Luther calls "free" (that is, not binding on the believer's conscience). They are indifferent because they make no intrinsic difference to a person's salvation. There is serious disagreement between Puritans and other Protestants, such as Luther, about which things are _adiaphora_ (for example, images in church, which Puritans regarded as idolatrous, not _adiaphora_). (See Lecture Eleven.)

Allegory: General term for a variety of symbolic or figurative strategies for reading the Bible widely practiced by patristic and medieval theologians; not a favored mode of biblical interpretation among Protestants.

Anabaptists: Greek for "re-baptizers"; radical or left wing of the Reformation, including Mennonites, Hutterites, and Amish. Thinking of themselves as a holy community separated from the world (including the part of the world that calls itself "Christendom") and marked by adult baptism and the use of the ban of excommunication as the central form of church discipline, they were severely persecuted. Even the term used to refer to them is one they would not accept, because their point is that infant baptism is not valid (that is, not real baptism at all), so that Catholics and Lutherans joining them are not really re-baptized, but, rather, truly baptized for the first time, when they receive baptism as adults. (See Lecture Fifteen.)

Anfechtung: German for "assault," the word Luther uses to translate the Latin _tentatio_ ("temptation"). Luther's notion is that temptation is an assault on the soul by the devil, whose aim is to undermine faith in Christ. (See Lecture Twenty-Two.)

Annates: A portion of the first year's income from a benefice, claimed by the pope as a kind of tax. (See Lecture Two.)

Antichrist: A biblical term for an apocalyptic figure or figures opposed to Christ (see, for example, 1 John 2:18). When Luther uses this term, he does not mean simply one historical individual (as in the apocalypticism popular with many contemporary American evangelical Protestants) but, rather, an institutional principle: For Luther, it is the papacy rather than any particular pope that is Antichrist —a judgment that was crucial to his decision to break with Rome. (See Lectures Eight and Nine.)

Apocalyptic: Having to do with events at the end of time, especially as depicted in the Apocalypse of St. John (the last book of the Bible, also known as the Book of Revelation), including its vision of a violent supernatural transformation of society in the last days, which was often an inspiration for revolutionary violence in the 16th century. (See Lecture Thirteen.)

Arminianism: A theological reaction against Calvinism in Holland, characterized by an emphasis on God's desire to save all people (versus the Calvinist-Augustinian doctrine of election) and the capacity of human free will to resist grace, which makes human choices the ultimate determinant of who is saved. Much of the American evangelical heritage is Arminian because of the influence of John Wesley, the founder of Methodism, who embraced Arminian theology. (See Lecture Twenty.)

Augsburg: Southern German city, frequent site of imperial diets, including (1) in 1518, when Luther (near the beginning of the indulgence controversy) had a private hearing with Cardinal Cajetan, the papal legate; (2) in 1530, when the Lutheran princes presented the *Augsburg Confession* to the emperor; (3) in 1548, when the Augsburg Interim is imposed on the Lutheran princes; and (4) in 1555, when the Peace of Augsburg in effect ratified the status quo, according to which some areas of Germany remained Lutheran and others, Catholic.

Augsburg Confession: The founding document of the Lutheran church, composed by Philip Melanchthon and presented by the Lutheran princes to the emperor Charles V at the Diet of Augsburg in 1530.

Augsburg Interim: Temporary religious settlement imposed on the Lutheran princes in Germany, who were defeated by Emperor Charles V in 1548; the Catholic church was restored, but Protestant practices, such as married clergy, were to be tolerated for the time being until the Council of Trent decided disputed issues.

Augustinian: Stemming from the theology of Augustine (see Biographical Notes). Catholic, Lutheran, and Calvinist theologies are all Augustinian, and even their disagreements can be understood only in terms of the Augustinian framework they have in common. (See Lecture Three.)

Avignon: French city in which the pope resided from 1309 to 1377, a period known as the Babylonian Captivity of the papacy.

Babylonian Captivity: Referring literally to the exile of ancient Israel in Babylon described in the Bible, this phrase was also used symbolically to refer to the years when the pope resided not in Rome but in Avignon (1309–1377). Luther picked up the phrase and used it in the title of one of his most important treatises (*The Babylonian Captivity of the Church*) to describe the continuing spiritual captivity of the church under the papacy. (See Lecture Ten.)

Baptism: A ceremonial washing accompanied by the words "I baptize you in the name of the Father, of the Son and of the Holy Spirit." For Luther, as for Catholicism, this is the sacrament of regeneration, or new life in Christ, which is properly given to infant children of believers (the practice of infant baptism). In contrast to many other forms of Protestantism, for Lutherans, the Christian life begins when one is born again in baptism.

Benefice: An ecclesiastical office (such as a bishopric) to which is attached a source of income, such as land, tithes, or endowments. In essence, this is an ecclesiastical fief, the fundamental way of funding priests and bishops in feudal society. (See Lecture Two.)

Bishop: Holder of the fundamental ecclesiastical office, exercising authority over priests and laity in a diocese, a designated geographical area in which is located the bishop's see, or seat, also called his bishopric.

Bishopric: See **Bishop**.

Bottom of the Soul: Translation of a term used by German mystics, *Grund der Seele*, which designates the deepest and most inward part of the self; Luther identifies this with the conscience, which is our sense of how we stand before God's judgment.

Bull: An official document publishing the judgment of the pope on some issue; for example, in the bull *Exsurge Domine*, Pope Leo X condemned the teachings of Martin Luther. (From the Latin *bulla*, "bubble" or "boss," for the distinctive way the document is embossed and sealed.)

Canon law: The written legislation of the Roman Catholic Church. By Luther's time, an elaborate code of canon law had been developed, which Luther and the Reformation rejected *in toto*.

Canossa: Castle in the mountains of Italy, outside of which Emperor Henry IV walked barefoot in the snow in penance for defying Pope Gregory VII in 1077; thus, the name *Canossa* marks one of the highpoints of papal power.

Catholic: From the Greek word for "universal," a description of the church used by both the Reformation and its Roman opponents. For clarity's sake, it is often helpful to use the term "Roman Catholic" for the latter.

Clergy: In the medieval church, this includes bishops, priests, monks, and friars. All bishops are priests, and all priests are ordained through the sacrament of holy orders, which gives them a special inward spiritual character or mark on their souls, allowing them to perform the Mass and, thereby, change bread and wine into Christ's body and blood. Monks and friars are not all priests, but all have taken vows to live under the written rule of a particular religious order (such as Benedictine monks or Franciscan friars). For Luther, members of the clergy do not have a spiritual status different from the laity, because all believers are spiritually priests. Hence, members of the Lutheran clergy are not called priests or fathers but ministers of the word and pastors of the faithful. (*Minister* literally means "servant"; *pastor* literally means "shepherd.")

Communicatio idiomatum: Latin for "sharing of properties," the doctrine that the properties of Christ's divine nature are shared with (or "communicated to") his human nature. Though widely affirmed by orthodox Christians, this doctrine is emphasized in a particularly realist way by Lutheran theology with its doctrine of ubiquity, according to which the divine omnipresence is a property really communicated to Christ's human body, so that the man Jesus is present everywhere.

Compatibilism: The philosophical theory that free will and determinism are compatible. The Augustinian doctrine of predestination includes the compatibilist thesis that God can determine all the events and choices that take place in the world without taking away human free will. (See Lecture Nineteen.)

Conciliarism: The view, held in some sectors of the late-medieval church, that the pope is subject to the authority of a general council of the church. Some theologians held conciliarist views out of practical necessity, because a general council was the only way to end the Great Schism; others held these views out of theological principle as a democratic reform needed by the church. Luther's appeal to a general council, as a court of final appeal that could reverse the pope's judgment that he was a heretic, was based on conciliarist theology.

Concord: The Formula of Concord (1580), or *Concordia*, a document that settled doctrinal disputes within the Lutheran church and became the basis of orthodox Lutheran teaching thereafter (which is why a number of Lutheran colleges and seminaries are named Concordia).

Confessor: In the sacrament of penance, this is the term for the priest to whom confession is made; the person making the confession is called the penitent.

Confirmation: Literally, "strengthening," a Christian ceremony of laying hands on (usually) young adult believers to bless, receive, and strengthen them, normally after a period of instruction in the faith; in Roman Catholicism, this ceremony is regarded as a sacrament.

Conscience: For Luther, this means the inner awareness of sin and the anxiety about displeasing God that such awareness provokes. A free conscience is one that is certain of pleasing God (by faith alone); a bound conscience is one that feels required to perform works that are supposed to please God but are not certain to do so; and a terrified conscience is conscious of sin and, therefore, of displeasing God.

Constance: Swiss city where, over the course of four years (1414–1418), an end was finally brought to the Great Schism; the council deposed two supposed popes, received the abdication of a third (Gregory XII, later regarded as the true pope of that time), and appointed a new pope (Martin V). The council also condemned the writings of reformers John Wyclif of England and John Hus of Bohemia and burned the latter as a heretic.

Contrition: True hatred of one's own sins (sometimes called "inner penance"), a requirement in the Catholic sacrament of penance, which Luther comes to think should not be required, because it only causes uncertainty about whether one's soul is in a state of true contrition.

Creed: A Christian confession of faith (from the Latin word *credo*, "I believe," with which it begins) recited every Sunday by Roman Catholics, Eastern Orthodox, Lutherans, Anglicans, and many but not all Protestants. It includes belief in God as Father, Son, and Holy Spirit (the three articles of the creed, as Luther calls them), and the second article includes a basic narrative of Christ's redemptive work: "He was crucified, died and was buried….on the third day he rose from the dead…" and so on. When Luther gives the content of the Gospel, he typically repeats a portion of this second article of the creed. (See Lecture One.)

Cujus regio, ejus religio: Latin for "his region, his religion"; motto expressing the basis for the Peace of Augsburg (1555), under which each of the German princes established his own religion (Lutheran or Catholic) in his territory but tolerated the other. (See Lecture Twenty-One.)

Curia: The papal bureaucracy, which stood at the center of the system of papal power in the Renaissance church.

Deus absconditus: Latin for "the hidden God," Luther's famous description of God deciding to predestine some people to be saved and others to be damned, in contrast to "the revealed God," who speaks in the Gospel and wants all to be saved. (See Lectures Eighteen and Nineteen.)

Diet: Official but irregularly scheduled parliament of the emperor and his princes held to decide on imperial legislation. During the Reformation, important diets were held at Augsburg (1518, 1530,

154,8 and 1555), Worms (1521), and Speyer (1526 and 1529), among other places.

Disputation: Originally an academic exercise sponsored by a medieval university, this practice came to include formal public debate of theological issues, such as those sponsored by town councils in the Swiss Reformation. Both kinds of disputation became important focal points of the Reformation, as for example, the Heidelberg Disputation (1518) and the Leipzig Debate (1519), in which Luther was involved.

Donation of Constantine: A document purported to be by the emperor Constantine (280–337), donating all the lands of the West to the pope; exposed as a fraud by the humanist scholar Lorenzo Valla in 1440.

Ecumenical: Having to do with the whole Church. In the past century, this means specifically the discussions among Catholic, Protestant, and Orthodox churches about how the Church might again be one.

Edict of Worms: Judgment rendered against Luther at the conclusion of the Diet of Worms (1521), condemning him to death as a heretic and putting him under the imperial ban; support of Luther was thenceforth a criminal act.

Elect: From the Latin verb for "to choose." Theologically, this term designates those chosen by God: In the Old Testment, Israel is the elect people of God; in the Augustinian theologies of Luther and Calvin, the elect are those predestined by God for salvation (see Lecture Nineteen); and in apocalyptic revolutionary theologies, such as Thomas Müntzer's or those of the Münster rebels, the elect are those who bring in the kingdom of God through sacred violence. (See Lecture Thirteen.)

Elector: One of seven German princes (including three archbishops) who had a vote in the election of the Holy Roman Emperor. One of these was the elector of Saxony, Luther's prince, who ruled Electoral Saxony, which was different from Ducal Saxony, whose ruler (the duke of Saxony) was not an elector.

Emperor: In these lectures, this term always refers to the ruler of the Holy Roman Empire, the distant successor of Charlemagne, who in the 16th century is the feudal lord over Germany. For most of Luther's career, this was Charles V of the house of Hapsburg.

Eucharist: Ancient term for the central Christian practice that Luther more often calls the sacrament of Christ's body and blood, Roman Catholics typically call the Mass, and the Reformed prefer to call the Lord's Supper.

Evangelical: From the Greek term for Gospel (*evangelion*); in the 16th century, this was the most widely used term for "Protestant" (as it still is in Germany today), in contrast to the current situation in America and England, where "evangelical" designates only one wing of Protestantism.

Excommunication: A judgment of the church excluding an unworthy Christian from sharing (taking communion) in the Eucharist; in the Middle Ages, a prerogative of the pope.

Ex opera operato: Latin for "from the work worked," which means roughly, "just by doing it correctly"; a phrase used to describe the Roman Catholic view of the Mass as a sacrifice that is valid and effective simply by virtue of being properly performed, by a priest who is properly ordained. Sometimes, the same idea is phrased *opus operatum*. (See Lecture Ten.)

Extra Calvinisticum: Latin for "the Calvinist 'outside,'" this is the Lutheran label for the Calvinist doctrine that Christ's divinity exists *outside* his human flesh. Contrast ***ubiquity***. (See Lecture Fourteen.)

Extreme unction: The Roman Catholic sacrament of anointing those who are on the point of dying. (See Lecture Ten.)

Faith: Luther always uses this word to mean belief in Christ, not just belief that God exists or "having faith" that things will work out in the end. Faith for Luther is not an answer to the question of whether God exists, but a solution to the problem of how I can be rightly related to him as a good and beloved child of God, rather than as a wicked and damned sinner. Also, it is useful to know that Luther made no distinction between faith and belief, because German and Latin, like most European languages, have only one word for both. Hence, whether a translation uses the word *belief* or *faith*, Luther is talking about the same thing.

Fanatic: Translation of Luther's term for theological opponents, such as Müntzer, Karlstadt, and Zwingli, who claimed to base their theology on the inspiration of the Holy Spirit. The German term is *Schwärmer*, which means something like a raving visionary and suggests that the spirit who speaks through them is diabolical rather than holy.

Fides historica: Latin for "historical faith"; Luther's term for believing that the Gospel story about Christ is true but not realizing that the things Christ did in this story are done for me. (See *pro me*.)

Forensic: Describes a doctrine of justification centered on God's declaring sinners righteous by imputing to them the merits of Christ. Such a doctrine is called *forensic*, because it understands justification not as a change taking place in sinners' hearts but as a verdict rendered in a divine courtroom (Latin *forum*, from which comes "forensic"). Lecture Sixteen argues that Luther's doctrine of justification, unlike the Reformed doctrine, is not fundamentally forensic.

Freedom of a Christian: Probably the most important treatise Luther ever wrote, this is the first classic elaboration of the Protestant doctrine of justification by faith alone, union with Christ by faith, and the relation of faith and works.

Grace: A biblical term that, in Augustinian theologies such as Luther's, means an inner gift of God causing the soul to love God and neighbor freely and gladly and, thus, fulfill the Law of God. How grace is related to free will becomes an issue, because grace is by definition unmerited, given to undeserving sinners, and hence, not in the power of our free will to attain.

Great Schism: Period during which Europe was divided in loyalty to two, sometimes three, different men claiming to be the rightful pope (1378–1417). Ended by the Council of Constance.

Guilt: When Luther uses this term he always means the fact rather than the feeling of guilt (for example, being actually guilty of a crime rather than feeling bad about it). The feeling that goes with guilt, for Luther, is terror. (See Lecture One.)

Holy orders: The Roman Catholic sacrament of ordaining a priest. (See Lecture Ten.)

Humanist: A Renaissance movement to recover a more historically accurate knowledge of ancient languages and literature, including not only the pagan classics (particularly appreciated in Italy) but also the Bible and the works of the church fathers (more emphasized in the Northern Renaissance by such scholars as Erasmus and Melanchthon).

Impute: To count or reckon, a key concept in the forensic doctrine of justification, according to which we are counted or reckoned righteous when the merits of Christ are imputed to us.

Indulgences: A formal promise by the church (in Luther's day, typically in a written document that could be purchased) that someone meeting certain criteria (such as participating in a crusade, going on a specified pilgrimage, purchasing a written indulgence) will receive a reduction in the amount of time spent suffering in purgatory. In Luther's day, this reduction could be applied to oneself or to others, like a kind of credit.

Interdict: Papal prohibition of sacramental life throughout a whole country (no priest may perform Eucharist, baptism, Christian burial, and so on), a severe sanction used in the course of medieval politics between popes and kings.

Justification: Literally, "becoming just." The doctrine about how sinners become just or righteous in God's sight (see also **forensic**). Disagreement between Catholics and Protestants about this doctrine was a central issue in the Reformation.

Laity: Or "lay people" (from a Greek word meaning simply "the people"). The ordinary people of the church, as distinct from the clergy. Catholicism makes a much sharper distinction between clergy and laity than Protestantism.

Law: When Luther contrasts this term with the Gospel, he means specifically the commandments of God in the Bible, which tell us how we ought to live but do not give us the power to do as they say (especially not to do so with a free, willing, and loving heart, as we are commanded). The Law of God, therefore, functions to accuse, terrify, and humble us, driving us to the Gospel to find the grace of Christ and forgiveness of sins. This is the evangelical use (literally, the "Gospel use") of the Law. There is also a civil use, when biblical commandments are used for the external order of society. Later Lutheran theology adds a "third use" of the Law as instruction in Christian life.

Lay investiture: The practice of kings "investing" (literally, "clothing") a new bishop with ring and staff as a symbol of the bishop's receiving his spiritual power from the king; a practice strongly condemned by Pope Gregory VII and defended by his nemesis, Emperor Henry V.

Love: Also called charity (in medieval theology, this terms means much more than just giving to the poor). In these lectures, *love* is a technical theological term referring to love for God and neighbor that stems from faith and obeys the command of Christ. All good works are works of love; thus, for Luther, love plays no role in our justification before God, which is by faith alone apart from works.

Magisterial reformation: Reformation of the church established or supported by state power (the civil magistrate); the term covers the Lutheran, Reformed, and Anglican reformations, but not the Anabaptist or radical reformation.

Marburg Colloquy: Discussion in 1529 between Wittenberg reformers led by Luther and Swiss reformers led by Zwingli, which tried and failed to reach a common understanding of the Lord's Supper.

Mass: The Roman Catholic understanding and practice of the Eucharist, distinguished by the doctrines of transubstantiation and *ex opere operato*, whereby the Mass is a work of grace that can be applied, for instance, to the souls of the dead in purgatory.

Merit: A person's status as deserving of reward. *Condign merit* (a notion developed from Augustine) means that works of love done by God's grace are promised the reward of eternal life. *Congruent merit* (a notion developed in the late Middle Ages) means that prayers and works of penance may, by gracious divine agreement, earn the gift of first grace. Protestants reject both concepts, insisting that even after people receive grace, none of their works is meritorious. (See Lecture Four.)

Mortal sin: The Roman Catholic doctrine that some sins are severe enough to result in the loss of the new life in Christ that is conferred by baptism. Anyone who dies in a state of mortal sin goes to hell. (See Lecture Three.)

Münster: Dutch city where, in 1534–1535, violent Anabaptists took over and tried to create a revolutionary utopia in expectation of the end of the world. (See Lecture Thirteen.)

Opus operatum: See *ex opera operatum*.

Original sin: In Augustinian theology, the guilt that every human being except Christ inherits from Adam, causing all humanity to be sinful from birth. (See Lecture Three.)

Papist: Pejorative term for "papal"; a term the Reformers frequently used for the Roman Catholic church and its theology.

Peace of Augsburg: Treaty in 1555 between the emperor and the German princes, under which the emperor gave up for good trying to suppress the Lutheran Reformation, acknowledging the existence of Lutheran churches under the principle that each prince determines the religion of his own territory (*cujus regio, ejus religio*) but tolerates the other religion (Lutheran or Catholic). (See Lecture Twenty-One.)

Peace of Westphalia: Treaty in 1648 ending the Thirty Years' War in Germany, which reaffirmed the Peace of Augsburg and set up an extended version of the *cujus regio, ejus religio* principle, in which minority religions (now including the Reformed but not the Anabaptists) are not only tolerated but granted equal rights. (See Lecture Twenty-One.)

Pelagianism: The heresy in opposition to which Augustine developed his doctrine of grace; the Pelagians taught that our free will is sufficient to obey God, do good works, and be saved, without the inward help of God's grace assisting us. Protestants often (usually unfairly) accuse Catholics of being Pelagian at heart. (See Lecture Three.)

Penance: The Catholic sacrament in which penitents confess their sins to a priest (that is, a confessor) to receive absolution. The inward state of penance (in the soul of the penitent) is called contrition. (See Lecture Seven.)

Pluralism: In the Middle Ages, this meant the practice of clergy holding more than one benefice for the sake of acquiring wealth and power. Before becoming pope, for instance, Julius II was bishop of almost a dozen cities at the same time. (See Lecture Two.)

Pope: The bishop of Rome, understood in Roman Catholic doctrine to be holder of the Apostolic See as successor of Peter (the first bishop of Rome), head of the church on earth in his role as Vicar of Christ, and focal point of the unity of the church.

Predestination: The Augustinian doctrine, shared by Aquinas, Luther, and Calvin, that God chooses before the foundation of the world whom he shall save by the grace of Christ. (See Lectures Eighteen and Nineteen.)

Prince: In the 16th century, this did not mean only the son of a king. It referred, for example, to any of the rulers of larger areas in Germany (for example, the duke of Prussia, the landgrave of Hesse, and the elector of Saxony), all of whom were princes to whom local lords and barons owed feudal allegiance and who, in turn, owed allegiance to the emperor.

Pro me: Latin for "for me," a phrase Luther uses to mark an essential feature of true Christian faith—the belief that Christ not only died, but he died for me (contrast ***fides historica***). For Luther, the Christian faith is most aptly defined using the first-person pronoun, because faith is not only about Christ but relates the believer personally to Christ.

Protestants: The name given to the Reformation churches after Lutheran and Reformed princes submitted a formal protest against a decision to renew imperial suppression of the Reformation at the Diet of Speyer in 1529. (The term does not refer to protest against the church.)

Purgatory: According to Roman Catholic doctrine, this is a place of purification for Christian souls who died in a state of grace but are not yet cleansed of the moral stain of their sins. Depicted in Dante, Catherine of Genoa, and modern Catholic teaching as a place of ardent love and hope, but in popular late-medieval writings, known to Luther as a place of hellish torture and agony.

Puritanism: Originally a 17th-century Protestant movement for biblically "pure" worship in opposition to the Church of England's "middle way," which made use of ceremonies and liturgy still redolent of Catholicism; this has given its name to the principle, already known and repudiated by Luther, that only things taught in Scripture may be allowed in Christian worship.

Rabies theologorum: Latin for "the rabid fury of the theologians"; found on a scrap of paper written by Philip Melanchthon just before his death, listing reasons why one should not be afraid to die: Death means escaping finally not only from sin and anxiety but also from the rabid fury of the theologians. (See Lecture Twenty-Two.)

Reformation: A 16th-century movement for church reform beginning with Luther in Germany and Zwingli in Switzerland, which eventually produced Lutheran, Reformed, and Anabaptist churches, separated from the Roman Catholic Church and from each other. In the 16th-century context, the term covers the same ground as *Protestant* and *evangelical*.

Reformed: This term refers to only part of the Reformation, not including the Lutherans and Anabaptists. Beginning in Switzerland, the Reformed tradition includes the legacy of Zwingli and Calvin; in America, Presbyterians and Congregationalists were originally Reformed churches. (See Lecture Fourteen.)

Reformers: In these lectures, this term refers specifically to theologians who promote the Reformation, for instance, Luther, Zwingli, and Calvin.

Regeneration: From the Latin word for "born again," referring to John 3:3 ("unless you are born again, you cannot see the kingdom of God"). Lutherans, like Roman Catholics, Eastern Orthodox, and Anglicans, teach that people are born again when they are baptized (the doctrine of baptismal regeneration). Most Protestants (Reformed, Baptist, and Anabaptists) disagree.

Righteousness: An old translation of the Latin word for justice (*justitia*) and its Greek equivalent (*dikaiosune*). It is important to realize that, for Luther, righteousness and justice were exactly the same thing—they were even the same word (*Gerechtigkeit* in German). It is only later that the English word, "righteousness," came to mean something more like self-righteousness, which for Luther, is the exact opposite of true righteousness. True righteousness in God's sight is a gift of God in Jesus Christ, received by faith alone. (See also **justification**.)

Sacrament: An external sign that is a means by which the grace of God is given to Christian believers. For Catholics, there are seven different sacraments: baptism, Eucharist, penance, confirmation, matrimony, holy orders (that is, ordination to the priesthood), and extreme unction (anointing of the dying). Luther came to regard only the first two as distinct sacraments (he regarded penance as a part of baptism).

Sanctification: Literally, "becoming holy" (from the Latin *sanctus*, "holy," which is also the root of the word *saint*). For most Protestant theology, this designates the process of moral improvement (including good works) that follows justification, which is by faith alone, apart from works.

Satisfaction: Part of the sacrament of penance in which the penitent is assigned to do certain works in order to satisfy ("make up for") sins that are already forgiven (as a thief might be expected to return what he stole even after his theft is forgiven). The punishments in purgatory are works of satisfaction.

Saxony: Name of two different but neighboring principalities in northern Germany, Ducal Saxony and Electoral Saxony, the one ruled for much of Luther's life by Duke George, an opponent of the Reformation, and the other by his cousin the Elector Frederick ("the Wise"), followed by Frederick's son John ("the Steadfast") and John's son John Frederick ("the Magnanimous"). Luther lived in Wittenberg in Electoral Saxony and was, thus, a Saxon.

Scholastic: In these lectures, this is a technical designation for the dominant form of theology in the late Middle Ages, produced by teachers in the universities, such as Thomas Aquinas, in contrast to teachers in the monasteries, who were more prominent in the early Middle Ages, such as Bernard of Clairvaux. Scholastic theology was logical and argumentative, less devotional and meditative than that of the monastic teachers. Although Luther despised the scholastic theologians and routinely called them sophists, he admired some of the monastic writers (especially Bernard), as well as the older theological writers called *church fathers* (especially Augustine), who lived before the foundation of the medieval universities and were bishops rather than professors.

Schwärmer: See **fanatic**.

Scripture: The Bible. See *sola scriptura*.

See: Latin for "seat," meaning the location to which a bishop's office and authority is attached. The Apostolic See is the bishopric of Rome, that is, the papacy.

Semper reformanda: Latin for the principle that the church is "always being reformed."

Simony: The sin of buying a benefice; widely practiced in the Middle Ages and forcefully resisted by reform-minded popes, such as Gregory VII. (See Lecture Two.)

Simul justus et peccator: Sometimes labeled simply, "the *simul*," this phrase is Latin for "at the same time righteous and a sinner." This important and distinctive doctrine in Luther's theology insists that all believers remain sinners their whole lives, even while they are justified by faith and, therefore, righteous. This paradoxical Lutheran doctrine is one of the hardest for Catholics to make sense of. (See Lecture Five.)

Sin: Disobedience to God's Law, particularly the command to love God and neighbor. See **mortal sin**, **original sin**.

Sola fide: Latin for "by faith alone," catchword for Luther's doctrine of justification, according to which we become righteous simply by believing the Gospel, quite apart from any good works. (See Lecture Five.)

Sola gratia: Latin for "by grace alone," catchword for Luther's doctrine that we are saved simply by God's grace, without any contribution of our own merit or even our free will. (See Lecture Eighteen.)

Sola scriptura: Latin for "Scripture alone," catchword for Luther's doctrine that no teaching is binding on the conscience as necessary for salvation except what is taught (explicitly or by clear implication) in Scripture. (See Lecture Seventeen.)

Supercessionism: The doctrine, almost universal among Christians of Luther's time but now increasingly rejected, that Christians have superceded the Jews, so that the latter are no longer God's people. (See Lecture Nineteen.)

Temporal power: In medieval theology, the political power of princes and other rulers, in contrast to the spiritual power of clergy; it is called "temporal" because it is concerned not with eternal life but with our transitory mortal life on earth (the word *temporal* refers to time and contrasts with eternity). Often called the "temporal sword" and contrasted with the "spiritual sword" (as in **Unam Sanctam**, below). (See Lecture Two.)

Tithe: A mandatory church tax (enforced not just by the church but by the state) that supports priests, bishops, or pastors holding a benefice. (See Lecture Two.)

Tradition: From the Latin term *traditio*, which means a "handing down" from generation to generation; in Christian theology, this means the lore of Christian practice, teaching, and biblical interpretation handed down in the church over the centuries. In keeping with the *sola scriptura* principle, Protestants deny that tradition has authority independent of Scripture, but in practice, they do not treat it as a merely human invention that can be dispensed with.

Transubstantiation: Roman Catholic doctrine that at the Eucharist, the substance (reality) of bread and wine is changed into the substance (reality) of Christ's body and blood. (See Lecture Ten.)

Ubiquity: From the Latin term for "everywhere," this is the label for the distinctively Lutheran doctrine that Christ's human body is present everywhere in the world (not to be confused with the standard Christian doctrine that God is omnipresent, which of course, Lutherans affirm, along with the rest of the Christian tradition). (See Lecture Fourteen. See also ***communicatio idiomatum*** and ***extra Calvinisticum***.)

Unam Sanctam: Title of a bull by Boniface VIII (1302) that declared in the most uncompromising terms the superiority of the pope over all powers on earth. (See Lecture Two.)

Uncreated grace: God Himself (specifically the Holy Spirit) in his gracious action or union with a believer. "Uncreated" refers to what exists but has never been created and, hence, applies only to God, not to anything created by God, including the soul. Thus, uncreated grace contrasts with created grace, which is the Roman Catholic concept of grace as a quality or habit of the soul; Protestants rejected this concept. (See Lecture Sixteen.)

Wartburg: Site of a castle near the German city of Eisenach where Luther went into hiding for nearly a year (May 1521–March 1522) after the Diet of Worms, while the practical work of reformation got underway in Wittenberg. (See Lecture Eleven.)

Wittenberg: Northern German town, site of the university where Luther taught from 1511 to his death, center of the Lutheran Reformation.

Wittenberg Concord: Compromise agreement on the Lord's Supper worked out in 1536 between Martin Bucer (on behalf of the Reformed) and Lutheran theologians (including Luther himself), which did not last because of crucial ambiguity on the point of *manducatio indignorum*.

Worms: German city, site of the imperial diet at which Luther was tried before the emperor as a heretic and refused to recant; after this point, Luther was an outlaw under the Edict of Worms. (See Lecture Nine.)

Zwickau prophets: Luther's term for three men from Zwickau, a town not far from Wittenberg, who came to Wittenberg late in 1521 preaching an apocalyptic Gospel of the Spirit.

Biographical Notes

Albert (or Albrecht) of Brandenburg (1490–1545): Margrave of Brandenburg, bishop of Halberstadt, and archbishop of Madgeburg, a member of the house of Hohenzollern. In the interest of family ambition, he also succeeded in acquiring the archbishopric of Mainz, which he financed by a sale of indulgences that precipitated Luther's 95 Theses.

Alexander VI (1431–1503): Pope from 1492–1503; one of the most famous Renaissance popes, father (among numerous other children by his various mistresses) of Lucrezia and Cesare Borgia.

Aquinas, Thomas (1225–1274): Dominican friar and theologian, central figure of medieval scholasticism (called, in Luther's day, the *via antiqua*, or "old way") and of later Roman Catholic theology.

Aristotle (384–322): Athenian philosopher, student of Plato, key inspiration for scholastic theologians, such as Aquinas.

Augustine (354–430): The most influential theologian of the Western world and the most important authority for medieval Christian teaching outside the Bible; his doctrine of grace was immensely influential for both Catholics and Protestants. Luther's theology, like Catholic and Calvinist theology, is a development out of Augustinian theology.

Barth, Karl (1886–1968): Swiss Reformed theologian who proposed a profound revision of the doctrine of predestination by re-focusing it on Christ.

Bernard of Clairvaux (1090–1153): Leading figure of 12th-century monasticism, whose writings were highly admired by both Luther and Calvin.

Boniface VIII (c. 1235–1303): Pope from 1294–1303; author of the bull *Unam Sanctam*, which declared in the most uncompromising terms the superiority of the pope over all Christian rulers.

Bora, Katherine von (1499–1552): Former nun, married to Martin Luther in 1525, mother of six children.

Bucer, Martin (1491–1551): Strasbourg reformer who tried to work out a compromise between Reformed and Lutheran theology on the

Lord's Supper and temporarily succeeded with the Wittenberg Concord of 1536.

Cajetan, Thomas de Vio (1469–1534): Dominican friar, philosopher, and theologian (one of the most important commentators on Thomas Aquinas), also cardinal and papal legate to the Diet of Augsburg in 1518, where he conducted three days of interviews with Luther concerning indulgences and the authority of the pope.

Calvin, John (1509–1564): French theologian and reformer who lived most of his life in Geneva, where he led the reformation of the church and wrote the most influential text of Protestantism, his *Institutes of the Christian Religion.*

Carlstadt: See **Karlstadt**.

Charles V (1500–1558): Emperor of the Holy Roman Empire (1519–1556), as well as king of Spain (1516–1556); member of the Hapsburg dynasty. He presided over the Diet of Worms (1521), where Luther was tried for heresy.

Clement VII (1479–1534): Pope from 1523–1534, while the Reformation gathered steam; born Guilio de Medici, nephew of Lorenzo the Magnificent and, thus, cousin of Pope Leo X. His father, Guiliano, was murdered in the Pazzi conspiracy in 1478, with the knowledge of Pope Sixtus IV.

Constantine (c. 280–337): Roman emperor from 306–337, converted to Christianity and, thereby, became the first Christian emperor.

Dante Alighieri (1265–1321): Italian poet and author of the *Divine Comedy,* an epic poem in which Dante journeys through hell, purgatory, and heaven; important source for a humane view of purgatory and for a medieval Catholic judgment on various popes, at least one of whom is found in each of the three places in the poem.

Erasmus, Desiderius (1469–1536): Leading northern humanist scholar; published the first printed Greek New Testament (1516) and editions of church fathers; an advocate of reform within Catholicism and a critic of clerical abuses. His early sympathy with Luther dissipated both because he did not want to break with the Roman Catholic church and because of his disagreement with Luther over the issue of free will and predestination.

Frederick III, "the Wise" (1463–1525): Elector of Saxony (1486–1525); Luther's prince, who in the early years of the Reformation protected him from trial and execution by a deliberate policy of delay and inaction.

Fuggers: The family owning the big banking house in northern Europe that financed most of the major ecclesiastical deals of the 16th century, such as Albert of Brandenburg's purchase of the archbisophric of Mainz.

Gregory VII (c. 1020–1085): Pope from 1073–1085; fought with Emperor Henry IV over lay investiture.

Henry IV (1050–1106); Holy Roman Emperor who fought with Pope Gregory VII over lay investiture.

Hus (or Huss), John (or Jan) (1374–1415): Bohemian (Czech) theologian and reformer; condemned by the Council of Constance and burned at the stake.

Innocent III (c.1160–1216): Pope from 1198–1216; perhaps the most powerful pope in history; excommunicated King John of England and put the whole country under interdict, with the result that John gave in, made England a fief of the pope, and promised payments of 1,000 marks a year, in return for which Innocent declared the Magna Carta null and void.

John (c. 1167–1216): King of England from 1199–1216; excommunicated by Pope Innocent III, he made England a papal fief, in return for which Innocent nullified the Magna Carta, which John had signed under duress from his barons.

John Frederick: Elector of Saxony (1532–1547), son of John the Steadfast.

John the Steadfast (1468–1532): Elector of Saxony (1525–1532), brother of Frederick the Wise.

Julius II (1443–1513): Pope from 1503–1513, member of the della Rovere family. Known as the "warrior pope" because of his success as a military commander in Italy and as *Il Terribile* ("the Terrifying") because his fierce temper was so intimidating. Commissioned the rebuilding of St. Peter's church in Rome, as well as Michelangelo's painting of the Sistine chapel (named after his uncle, Pope Sixtus IV).

Karlstadt (or Carlstadt), Andreas Bodenstein von (1486–1541): Colleague of Luther's at the University of Wittenberg; later, his theological opponent and precursor of the Radical Reformation.

Leo X (1475–1521): Pope from 1513–1521, born Giovanni de Medici, son of Lorenzo the Magnificent; a classic Renaissance pope, patron of the arts, nepotist, and big spender, he was the pope who excommunicated Luther and officially condemned his teachings.

Luther (or Luder), Hans (? –1530): Martin Luther's father, son of a peasant who became, with hard work and thrift, a successful small businessman operating copper mines in Mansfeld and Eisleben.

Luther, Katherine. See **Bora, Katherine von**.

Luther (or Luder), Margaret (or Hanna) (? –1531): *Née* Lindemann, mother of Martin Luther and at least eight other children.

Luther, Martin (1483–1546): German theologian, ex-monk, founding figure of Protestantism, Professor of Bible at the University of Wittenberg.

Melanchthon, Philip (1497–1560): Theologian, humanist, and reformer; Professor of Greek at the University of Wittenberg; Luther's colleague and best friend; and author of the *Augsburg Confession*. Less combative than Luther, he often acted as a mediator, peacemaker, and friend of other Reformers, such as Calvin, for which he later came under suspicion by some "pure" Lutherans.

Müntzer (or Münzer), Thomas (c. 1490–1525): Former student of Luther's who becomes pastor at Zwickau, claiming authority from the Spirit to preach the violent overthrow of the wicked in the end times; accordingly, he leads one wing of the peasant rebellion of 1525 until his defeat, capture, and execution.

Ockham (or Occam), William of (1285?–1349): Franciscan philosopher and theologian, leading figure in late-medieval scholasticism (the *via moderna*, or "modern way").

Paul, St. (?–64?): Early Christian missionary, author of many of the letters in the New Testament, and a central influence on Luther's theology.

Paul III (1468–1549): Pope from 1534–1549; called the Council of Trent.

Prierias, Sylvester (1456–1523): Dominican, "master of the sacred palace" (that is, chief theologian of the papal curia), who in 1518 writes the first official condemnation of Luther's 95 Theses, arguing on the basis of a radical doctrine of papal infallibility that horrifies Luther.

Simons, Menno (1496–1561): Anabaptist leader from Frisia, founding figure of the Mennonites, decisive for the Radical Reformation's turn to nonviolence.

Sixtus IV (1414–1484): Pope from 1471–1484 and uncle of Pope Julius II; a classic Renaissance pope, he built the Sistine (or Sixtine) Chapel. He was also heavily involved in Italian family politics, including the Pazzi conspiracy to kill Lorenzo and Guiliano de Medici in 1478.

Tetzel, Johann (c. 1465–1519): Dominican indulgence salesman, whose activities just across the border from Electoral Saxony prompted Luther to post the 95 Theses.

Wyclif (or Wycliffe), John (1320?–1384): English theologian whose writings, condemned by both king and pope, inspired later movements for church reform, especially that of John Hus.

Zwingli, Ulrich (or Huldreich) (1484–1531): Swiss reformer based in Zurich, took a "low" view of the Eucharist, which made him one of Luther's most important Protestant opponents.

Bibliography

Essential Reading:

Althaus, Paul. *The Theology of Martin Luther.* Philadelphia: Fortress Press, 1966. Still the best one-volume summary of Luther's theology and still in print.

Bainton, Roland. *Here I Stand: A Life of Martin Luther.* New York: Penguin, 1995. Originally published in 1950 but still a favorite, this biography is immensely readable and a great introduction to Luther.

Lindberg, Carter. *The European Reformations.* Oxford: Blackwell, 1996. Well-written narrative history covering not only the Lutheran reformation but also the Reformed and Radical movements, the English reformation, and the Catholic Counter-reformation.

Lull, Timothy, ed. *Martin Luther's Basic Theological Writings.* Minneapolis: Fortress Press, 1989. The most extensive one-volume anthology of Luther's writings in English, using the same translations as the standard American edition of *Luther's Works*, below.

Luther, Martin. *The Large Catechism.* Philadelphia: Fortress Press, 1981. A large catechism but a short book, this contains the best one-volume summary of Luther's theology by Luther himself.

————. *Letters of Spiritual Counsel.* Vancouver, BC: Regent College Publishing, 2003 (reprint edition). Perhaps the best introduction to Luther the man: letters of deep humanity written to people sick or dying, in doubt or anxiety, in grief or trouble or despair.

————. *Luther's Works.* Edited by J. Pelikan. St. Louis: Concordia Publishing (vols. 1–30) and Philadelphia: Fortress Press (vols. 31–55), 1955–1976. The standard American edition of Luther's writings (you can recognize it by its red covers), comprising 54 volumes plus an index volume. Though far from a complete collection of Luther's vast literary output, these well-done and helpfully annotated volumes do include most of what is of lasting importance. The set should be found in any good college or seminary library.

Supplementary Reading:

Anselm. *Proslogion.* Indianapolis: Hackett Publishing, 2001. One of the most characteristic pieces of medieval theology, beginning with a prayer that beautifully illustrates the Augustinian paradigm of spirituality.

Augustine. *Answer to the Pelagians IV: To the monks of Hadrumentum and Provence*, in *The Works of St. Augustine: A Translation for the 21st Century*, Part I, vol. 26. New York: New City Press, 1999. Contains treatises written late in Augustine's life dealing with the topics of grace and predestination, including *Grace and Free Choice* and *Rebuke and Grace*, which are the most illuminating of Augustine's writings on the topic of predestination and free will.

―――. *Later Works*. Philadelphia: Westminster Press, 1955. Contains a translation of Augustine's treatise *On the Spirit and the Letter*, which was extremely important for Luther's thinking on grace.

Bainton, Roland. *Women of the Reformation*. Boston: Beacon Press, 1974. Includes a chapter devoted to Katherine von Bora, Martin Luther's wife.

Barth, Karl. *Church Dogmatics*, vol. 1, part 1. Barth revives Luther's theology of the hearing of the word of God, in contrast to Protestant liberalism and all attempts to make Christian faith be fundamentally about human experience. Barth's Germanic style is heavy going for beginners, but once you get the hang of it, it can be a thrilling read.

―――. *Church Dogmatics*, vol. 2, part 2. Contains Barth's epochal reworking of the Augustinian doctrine of predestination and election, re-centering it on the good news of Jesus Christ.

Bernard of Clairvaux. *Selected Works*. Mahwah NJ: Paulist Press, 1987. Contains the exquisite little treatise *On Loving God*, which was very important for Luther's early theology.

Bettenson, Henry, and Chris Maunder, eds. *Documents of the Christian Church*. 3rd ed. New York: Oxford University Press, 1999. A selection of important documents in the history and theology of the Christian Church from the beginning to the 20th century, including many of those used in Lecture Two.

Braaten, Carl E., and Robert W. Jenson, eds. *The Catholicity of the Reformation*. Grand Rapids: Eerdmans, 1996. A group of mostly Lutheran theologians reflects on how catholic the Lutheran reformation was and is.

————. *Union with Christ: The New Finnish Interpretation of Luther*. Grand Rapids: Eerdmans, 1998. An introduction to the most important alternative to forensic interpretations of Luther's doctrine of justification. According to these Finnish scholars, justification for Luther does not mean simply that God imputes Christ's righteousness to us but that he gives us Christ so that we are united with him in heart and made partakers in his divine attributes, such as righteousness.

Calvin, John. *Institutes of the Christian Religion*. 2 vols. Edited by John T. McNeill. Philadelphia: Westminster, 1960. Calvin's major work, the most influential systematic theology text in the history of Protestantism, in a contemporary translation with excellent annotations and extensive indexes.

Cary, Phillip. "Believing the Word: A Proposal about Knowing Other Persons," in *Faith and Philosophy* 13/1 (Jan. 1996): 78–90. For anyone interested in my philosophical reasons for valuing Luther's notion that we come to know God by believing his word. The article argues that to know other persons, we have to believe their word. Luther is not explicitly mentioned, but his theology of the Word is an essential part of the background.

Catherine of Genoa, St. *Purgation and Purgatory, The Spiritual Dialogues*. Mahwah, NJ: Paulist Press, 1979. The first of the two writings in this volume, usually known by the title *Treatise on Purgatory*, gives a humane and deeply spiritual account of souls in purgatory motivated by love for God to embrace their sufferings because of their desire to be purified and their joy in God's will. Written probably while Luther was a child but not published until after his death, Catherine's treatise, which received papal approval in 1683, is much closer to the current Catholic view than the kind of scare-tactics found in popular treatments of purgatory in the late Middle Ages, which portrayed souls suffering hellish tortures.

Cohen, Jeremy, ed. *Essential Papers on Judaism and Christianity in Conflict*. New York: NYU Press, 1991. Informative scholarly papers on key topics in the history of Christian anti-Judaism and Jewish responses to it from the ancient world to the Reformation, including a chapter devoted to Luther.

Dante Alighieri. *The Divine Comedy, Vol. II: Purgatory*. Translated by Mark Musa. New York: Penguin, 1985. The second of Dante's great three-part Christian epic, in which he journeys through hell, purgatory, and heaven; particularly important for showing the medieval understanding of purgatory at its best, both poetically vivid and theologically deep.

Dillenberger, John, ed. *Martin Luther: Selections from His Writings.* Garden City, NY: Anchor, 1961. A handy one-volume selection of Luther's most important writings, though not as extensive as Lull's anthology.

Duffy, Eamon. *Saints and Sinners: A History of the Popes.* New Haven: Yale University Press, 1997. Lavish illustrations and lively writing by an excellent historian, who is appreciative of the institution but not uncritical of its occupants, make this the best popular history of the papacy.

———. *The Stripping of the Altars: Traditional Religion in England, 1400–1580.* New Haven: Yale University Press, 1992. A fascinating, sympathetic account of what medieval Catholic piety meant for the laity and how this was undone by the Reformation. Though set in England rather than Germany, this book affords a richer sense than any other known to me of the fundamental religious practices at stake for ordinary people in this period.

Edwards, Mark U., Jr. *Luther and the False Brethren.* Stanford, CA: Stanford University Press, 1975. A study of Luther's attitude toward his Protestant theological opponents, this book goes far toward explaining Luther's attitude toward his other enemies, as well.

———. *Luther's Last Battles.* Ithaca: Cornell University Press, 1983. More on Luther and his enemies, focusing particularly on the polemical writings of his later years.

Eire, Carlos. *War against the Idols: The Reformation of Worship from Erasmus to Calvin.* Cambridge: Cambridge University Press, 1986. Fine study of the origins and development of the iconoclastic Reformed strand of Protestantism, which contrasts with Luther's more catholic Reformation.

Erasmus, Desiderius. *The Essential Erasmus.* Edited by John P. Dolan. New York: New American Library, 1964. A fine selection of Erasmus's writings, including representative religious treatises and his satiric masterpiece, *The Praise of Folly*.

———. *On the Freedom of the Will.* See Rupp and Watson, below

Gerrish, Brian. *Grace and Reason.* Oxford: Oxford University Press, 1962. A convincing argument that although Luther is a critic of reason, he does not simply reject it.

———. *The Old Protestantism and the New.* Chicago: University of Chicago Press, 1982. Contains some of the best essays in English comparing Luther and Calvin.

Greenblatt, Stephen. *Hamlet in Purgatory.* Princeton, NJ: Princeton University Press, 2001. Presents a vivid history of how the idea of purgatory was imagined in the late Middle Ages and debated in the English Reformation, as well as how it led to the portrayal of the ghost in Shakespeare's *Hamlet.*

Hillerbrand, Hans, J. *The Reformation: A Narrative History Related by Contemporary Observers and Participants.* Grand Rapids: Baker, 1978. A collection of 16th-century documents and pictures that helps you see what the Reformation was like for the participants.

Karlstadt, Andreas Bodenstein von. *The Essential Carlstadt.* Waterloo, Ont.: Herald Press, 1995. Treatises in opposition to Luther, in favor of more radical reformation and urging a mystic spirituality of "yieldedness," or *Gelassenheit*, as the key to becoming one with God.

Kelly, J. N. D. *The Oxford Dictionary of Popes.* Oxford: Oxford University Press, 1986. Brief digests of the life and doings of each individual pope and anti-pope. Precise scholarship, a valuable reference tool, and even a good read.

Kempe, Margery. *The Book of Margery Kempe: The Autobiography of the Mad Woman of God.* Translated by Tony D. Triggs. Ligouri, MO: Triumph Books, 1995. An extravagant example of the lay piety of the late Middle Ages in a readable modern translation.

King, Ross. *Michelangelo and the Pope's Ceiling.* New York: Walker & Co., 2003. A vivid account of the glories and the malfeasance of the Renaissance papacy and especially of the "warrior pope" Julius II, who in addition to leading armies in battle, commissioned Michelangelo to paint the Sistine chapel.

Leith, John. *Creeds of the Churches.* Rev. ed. Atlanta: John Knox Press, 1973. Contains not only the ancient Christian creeds but also confessional documents of the Reformation, such as the *Augsburg Confession* and Luther's *Small Catechism.*

Lewis, C. S. *Studies in Words*. 2nd ed. Cambridge: Cambridge University Press, 1974. The chapter on "Conscience" is extremely helpful for understanding how the Reformers use the word.

Luther, Martin. *On the Bondage of the Will*. See Rupp and Watson, below.

———. *Sermons*. 8 vols., edited by J. N. Lenker. Grand Rapids, MI: Baker Books, 1988 (reprint edition). Sermons for every Sunday of the church year and then some. The very first sermon in the set (for the first Sunday of Advent) is one of the finest expressions of Luther's faith.

Lutheran World Federation. *Joint Declaration on the Doctrine of Justification*. Grand Rapids: Eerdmans, 2000. Official statement by both the Roman Catholic and the Lutheran churches on the surprising extent of their agreement on the doctrine of justification after decades of careful ecumenical discussion.

McGrath, Alister. *Justitia Dei: A History of the Christian Doctrine of Justification, the Beginnings to the Reformation*. Cambridge: Cambridge University Press, 1986. A scholarly history of the doctrine of justification leading up to Luther.

McKim, Donald, ed. *The Cambridge Companion to Martin Luther*. Cambridge: Cambridge University Press, 2003. A useful set of essays introducing key topics in Luther scholarship.

Newbigin, Lesslie. *The Gospel in a Pluralist Society*. Grand Rapids, MI: Eerdmans, 1989. The best one-volume theological introduction to what I call "right-wing" postmodernism.

Ozment, Steven. *The Age of Reform, 1250–1550: An Intellectual and Religious History of Late Medieval and Reformation Europe*. New Haven and London: Yale University Press, 1980. An excellent general introduction to Luther's historical context, with expert sensitivity to the religious issues of the time.

———. *The Reformation in the Cities: The Appeal of Protestantism to Sixteenth-Century Germany and Switzerland*. New Haven and London: Yale University Press, 1975. Fascinating study by a theologically informed social historian about why the Reformation message found such a ready reception in the cities of northern Europe.

Pelikan, Jaroslav. *Reformation of Church and Dogma (1300–1700)*. Chicago: University of Chicago Press, 1984. This is the fourth volume of Pelikan's magisterial five-volume study of the history of Christian doctrine, *The Christian Tradition: A History of the Development of Doctrine*. It contains an extremely rich and well-documented survey of the theological doctrines discussed in these lectures, not only in the Lutheran but also in the Reformed and Catholic traditions.

Rupp, Gordon. *The Righteousness of God*. New York: Philosophical Library, 1953. Still perhaps the best single study in English of Luther's teaching and experience of justification.

———, and Philip Watson. *Luther and Erasmus: Free Will and Salvation*. Philadelphia: Westminster, 1969. Contains both Erasmus's *On the Freedom of the Will* and Luther's reply, *On the Bondage of the Will*, the latter in the same translation as in *Luther's Works*, vol. 33 (see above).

Sanders, E. P. *Paul, the Law and the Jewish People*. Minneapolis: Fortress Press, 1983. A fundamental challenge to the Augustinian, anti-Jewish reading of Paul on which Luther's theology rests.

Sasse, Herman. *This Is My Body: Luther's Contention for the Real Presence in the Sacrament*. Minneapolis: Augsburg, 1959. Still the standard treatment in English for this topic.

Sider, Ronald, ed. *Karlstadt's Battle with Luther*. Philadelphia: Fortress Press, 1978. A collection of documents from the debate between Luther and Karlstadt.

Soulen, Kendall. *The God of Israel and Christian Theology*. Minneapolis: Fortress Press, 1996. Argues against the doctrine of supercessionism (see Lecture Nineteen) and for Christian affirmation of the Jews as the chosen people on the grounds that Jews and Gentiles are to receive the blessing of God from one another.

Stendahl, Krister. *Paul among Jews and Gentiles*. Philadelphia: Fortress Press, 1976. Contains the landmark essay, "The Apostle Paul and the Introspective Conscience of the West," which challenges the Augustinian reading of Paul that was fundamental for Luther's theology.

Tappert, Theodore G., ed. *The Book of Concord*. Philadelphia: Fortress Press, 1959. The standard edition of Lutheran confessional documents in English, including the *Augsburg Confession* (1530) and the "Apology [that is, Defense] of the *Augsburg Confession*" (1531), Luther's *Large Catechism* and *Small Catechism* (1529), the

Smalcald Articles (1537), and the Formula of Concord (1580). These are the defining documents of Lutheranism.

United States Catholic Conference. *Catechism of the Catholic Church*. Libreria Editrice Vaticana, 1994. A translation of the official catechism authorized by the Vatican under Pope John Paul II, this is the first place to go to find out what the Roman Catholic church currently teaches about issues in dispute during the Reformation.

Williams, George Huntston. *The Radical Reformation*. 3rd ed. Kirksville, MO: Sixteenth-Century Journal Publishers, 1992. A big, informative book, including not only a history of the Anabaptist movement but also a lucid account of the social unrest of 16th-century Europe.

Wright, N. T. *What Saint Paul Really Said*. Grand Rapids: Eerdmans, 1997. Despite the regrettable title (as if any commentator could magically give us the meaning of an important writer with no further need for us to keep reading the text!), this is a worthwhile book by a serious scholar offering a guide for Protestants reading Paul in the aftermath of the "Sanders revolution" (see Lecture Seventeen).

Zwingli, Ulrich. *On the Lord's Supper*, in *Zwingli and Bullinger*, edited by G. W. Bromily, pp.176–238. Philadelphia: Westminster Press, 1953. This volume, part of the Library of Christian Classics series, also contains treatises by Zwingli on Scripture, education, and baptism, as well as a brief summary of his theology called *An Exposition of the Faith*.

Internet Resources

The Reformation Guide, www.educ.msu.edu/homepages/laurence/reformation/index.htm. Provides access to a wealth of information about Luther and other reformers, including many of their writings.

Project Wittenberg,

www.iclnet.org/pub/resources/text/wittenberg/wittenberg-home.html. A site that focuses on Lutheran theology, with extensive resources about Luther and many of his writings.

Notes